CRAFTING CONSTITUTIONS IN FLORIDA, 1810–1968

Government and Politics in the South

UNIVERSITY PRESS OF FLORIDA

Florida A&M University, Tallahassee
Florida Atlantic University, Boca Raton
Florida Gulf Coast University, Ft. Myers
Florida International University, Miami
Florida State University, Tallahassee
New College of Florida, Sarasota
University of Central Florida, Orlando
University of Florida, Gainesville
University of North Florida, Jacksonville
University of South Florida, Tampa
University of West Florida, Pensacola

CRAFTING CONSTITUTIONS IN FLORIDA, 1810–1968

Edited by Robert Cassanello

Sharon D. Wright Austin and Angela K. Lewis-Maddox,
Series Editors

UNIVERSITY PRESS OF FLORIDA

Gainesville/Tallahassee/Tampa/Boca Raton
Pensacola/Orlando/Miami/Jacksonville/Ft. Myers/Sarasota

Cover: Florida, Division of Tourism. *Ceremonial signing of the 1968 Constitution at the Governor's Mansion, Tallahassee, Florida*. 1968. State Archives of Florida, Florida Memory. https://www.floridamemory.com/items/show/126499

Copyright 2025 by Robert Cassanello
All rights reserved
Published in the United States of America

30 29 28 27 26 25   6 5 4 3 2 1

DOI: https://doi.org/10.5744/9780813079370

Library of Congress Cataloging-in-Publication Data
Names: Cassanello, Robert, editor.
Title: Crafting constitutions in Florida, 1810–1968 / edited by Robert Cassanello.
Description: Gainesville : University Press of Florida, 2025. | Series: Government and politics in the south | Includes bibliographical references and index. | Summary: "This comprehensive volume traces over 200 years of constitutional traditional in Florida, examining constitutions drafted in the state from the territorial era to the most recent version from 1968"—Provided by publisher.
Identifiers: LCCN 2024056876 (print) | LCCN 2024056877 (ebook) | ISBN 9780813079370 (hardback) | ISBN 9780813073804 (epub) | ISBN 9780813074054 (pdf)
Subjects: LCSH: Constitutional history—Florida. | Constitutions—Florida. | Constitutional law—Florida. | Florida—Politics and government—History. | BISAC: POLITICAL SCIENCE / Constitutions | LAW / Constitutional
Classification: LCC KFF401.5 .C73 2025 (print) | LCC KFF401.5 (ebook) | DDC 342.75902/9—dc23/eng/20241205
LC record available at https://lccn.loc.gov/2024056876
LC ebook record available at https://lccn.loc.gov/2024056877

The University Press of Florida is the scholarly publishing agency for the State University System of Florida, comprising Florida A&M University, Florida Atlantic University, Florida Gulf Coast University, Florida International University, Florida State University, New College of Florida, University of Central Florida, University of Florida, University of North Florida, University of South Florida, and University of West Florida.

University Press of Florida
2046 NE Waldo Road
Suite 2100
Gainesville, FL 32609
http://upress.ufl.edu

GPSR EU Authorized Representative: Mare Nostrum Group B.V., Mauritskade 21D, 1091 GC Amsterdam, The Netherlands, gpsr@mare-nostrum.co.uk

CONTENTS

List of Tables   vii

Acknowledgments   ix

Introduction   1
  Robert Cassanello

1. A Florida Constitution in the State of Louisiana: The 1810 Constitution of the State of Florida   16
   Samuel C. Hyde

2. The Patriot Constitution and International Constitution-Making   33
   M.C. Mirow

3. Florida's First State Constitutional Convention in 1838   60
   James M. Denham

4. The Constitution of 1861: Florida's Confederate Constitution   86
   R. Boyd Murphree

5. The 1865 Convention and Constitution   112
   Robert Cassanello

6. In Pursuit of a More Perfect Union: The Drafting and Crafting of the 1868 Florida Constitution   134
   Andrea L. Oliver

7. The 1885 Constitution   157
   Christopher Day

8. Florida's Indigenous Constitutions: Being and Becoming Seminoles and Miccosukee in the Mid-Twentieth Century   174
   Andrew K. Frank

9. Crafting Florida's 1968 Constitution   189
   Mary Adkins

Conclusion: The Twenty-First Century and a New State
   Constitution   203
   Robert Cassanello

Selected Bibliography   209
List of Contributors   215
Index   217

TABLES

2.1. The Patriot (1812) and Georgia (1789 and 1798) Constitutions   43

6.1. Apportionment Plan before the Convention Disruption—Proposal for the Florida House   149

6.2. Apportionment Plan before the Convention Disruption—Proposal for the Florida Senate   150

6.3. Apportionment Plan after the Convention Disruption—Proposal for the Florida House   151

6.4. Apportionment Plan after the Convention Disruption—Proposal for the Florida Senate   152

ACKNOWLEDGMENTS

I dedicate this collection to Andrew D. Smith. Andy and I were friends since we were ten years old. On our first career day at school Andy declared he wanted to be a lawyer. Going to law school, being a lawyer and possibly later a politician was the only career outlook he ever spoke about. The last nine years of his life he suffered and later succumbed to a stage 4 brain tumor. During those nine years he finished his bachelor's degree in political science and then completed law school. Since we were kids Andy and I talked often, even when we were far apart from each other. I can't help but think the material from this collection would have been the basis of hundreds of conversations we were meant to have.

In an anthology collection like this I want to thank the contributors to this book without whom this project would not have happened. They are Mary Adkins, Christopher Day, James M. Denham, Andrew K. Frank, Samuel C. Hyde, M.C. Mirow, R. Boyd Murphree, and Andrea Oliver. I would also like to thank Sian Hunter, senior acquisitions editor at the University Press of Florida. She worked with me over the years as we produced this project, her patience in waiting on us through pandemics and other holdups is appreciated above all else. I would also like to thank the fine staff at the University Press of Florida as well as Director Romi Gutierrez and the board who approved to publish this book. I would also like to thank the thoughtful and valuable suggestions provided by our peer reviewers. They were anonymous and were tremendously helpful.

I would like to recognize my colleagues at the University of Central Florida who spoke with me about the various constitutions over the years and this project in particular. They include Daniel S. Murphree, Barbara Gannon who helped me locate Reconstruction Era sources, and Vladimir Solonari who inquired about the project from time to time. From the UCF Library I would like to mention Rich Gause and Richard H. Harrison II who helped me locate sources. I would like to give a special mention to Joanie Reynolds, Kristine Shrauger, and the staff who work in our Document Delivery & Resource Sharing Department. They provided me with books, articles, and documents loaned from other repositories.

It would be careless of me if I did not thank the people in my life for their continued support during the production of this book. My mother and my mother-in-law, Romona Cobb, both of whom periodically would inquire when this book was coming out. My wife Susan who supported me through the highs and lows of completing this project, not to mention our feline four-legged children that brought us all kinds of joy over the years.

The inspiration for this project began at the 2018 Florida Conference of Historians. Julian C. Chambliss and I coordinated a roundtable discussion to open the conference when it was held that year in Tallahassee. Most of the contributors to this collection appeared at that event, which was a discussion of the fiftieth anniversary of the 1968 Florida Constitution. Panelists spoke about each of the state constitutions. The event was recorded and released as a podcast in 2018 titled *The Florida Constitutions Podcast* through H-Net's network H-Podcast. After the event we agreed to produce this collection. This book expands on that original roundtable. As such I would like to thank the people involved with the 2018 Florida Conference of Historians, especially the audience who listened and provided feedback to our panelists and future contributors. I would like to thank David Proctor who was president of the Florida Conference of Historians in 2018 and helped us secure the space in the old Capitol Senate Room in Tallahassee. Jesse Hingson who organized the conference and coordinated the panel with Julian and me. Most of all I would like to thank Julian C. Chambliss who encouraged me and then collaborated with me to assemble and record this panel to commemorate Florida's Constitutional tradition, warts and all.

I would also like to use these acknowledgments to recognize and memorialize the people who died in the mass shooting at Marjory Stoneman Douglas High School. The murders took place on February 14, 2018. That evening Julian and I sat in the hotel lobby to watch in horror as the details unfolded from that day. This was the evening before our roundtable at the conference. I asked those assembled for the roundtable to take a moment of silence to remember the lives lost at Parkland. Similar to my words to those in attendance on February 15, 2018, I ask readers of this collection to commit themselves to support solutions to mass gun violence.

Introduction

Robert Cassanello

In November 1930 the editor of the *Miami Herald* reflected on all the Florida state constitutions until that time. The state had been governed under the 1885 Constitution for a little over fifty years, yet the editor came to the conclusion that the 1885 Constitution was by then an "antiquated instrument." It would be thirty-eight years before the state would create a new constitution. In some way the editor of the *Miami Herald* depicted each new Florida constitution propelling the state into greater and greater "progress." For this writer the 1885 Constitution catered to a frontier state and population. He argued,

> We need a new vision of state policies. We need a sweeping away of many of the old encumbering statutes which limit our progress. There is a growing belief that the time has arrived when a new constitutional convention should be called to place Florida alongside of the more modern and progressive states of our country.[1]

In 1930 the *Miami Herald*'s owner was Frank B. Shutts who came to Florida with Henry Flagler. He purchased the newspaper as Florida was enthralled in what would be unprecedented economic growth and excess, so this editorial was in that vein. In 1930 the idea of a new state constitution was not so outrageous because the legislative race in Tampa that summer featured a candidate, Joseph R. Mickler, who made a new state constitution a key platform in that local election. The late nineteenth century was in the rearview mirror in 1930. Readers then probably did not realize that replacing a state constitution would be much harder to achieve than before. Between 1901 to 1997 only twelve states revised their constitutions and five created their first constitution. G. Alan Tarr characterized this period of state constitutional revision as one of long stretches of inactivity broken up by the US Supreme Court decision over apportionment that led to seven states adopting new constitutions from 1965 through 1974.[2]

Scholars of constitutionalism do note that constitutions, specifically state constitutions, reflect the time in which they were each drafted. This volume expands the idea of constitutions under Florida more broadly to not only include those that created state governments but those that created experiments in constitutionalism that fostered, albeit briefly, breakaway republics, also Indigenous constitutionalism that lasted much longer for both Seminoles and Miccosukees. For the constitutions that made up the government of Florida, delegates debated and revised language based on the pressing issues and political experiences of their time. As this political context changed so did the need for the constitution to change beyond what the legislature could enact into law to address the pressing needs at the times of those constitutional conventions.[3]

What does a state constitutional tradition tell us about the history of constitutional conventions in Florida? The answer to this question is what this volume is trying to achieve. Any constitutional tradition specific to Florida will be slight, as state constitutional scholars have observed over the years that state constitutions not only borrow from the US Constitution but also from other state constitutions. Additionally, if we include constitutions outside the ones that create the state governments of Florida, this gives us a broader canvas of traditions to incorporate into interpreting any tradition that might be present in the history of Florida's constitutions.

The only survey of the history of Florida constitutions and their conventions that exists is in the "Introduction" to Talbot "Sandy" D'Alemberte's *The Florida State Constitution: A Reference Guide* originally published in 1991. It is a brief seventeen-page historical overview of the history of Florida's constitutional conventions. D'Alemberte was a lawyer, former politician, and law school dean at Florida State University. Charlton W. Tebeau's *A History of Florida* was D'Alemberte's guide for his brief and synthetic history of the state. In his overview of the territorial period, D'Alemberte tells us, "The absence of civilization was the very reason that the United States put pressure on Spain to cede the area." D'Alemberte meant that US officials did not recognize a "civilization" in the Spanish colonies or especially lands occupied by the Indigenous people of Florida. The notion that a legal and political tradition with the Native people of Florida such as the Seminoles, Miccosukees, or Creeks existed before or simultaneously with the founding of the United States would not have been a widely held view in 1991. Writers who examined Indigenous legal and political traditions in Florida did not emerge until later through the works of scholars such as Harry A. Kersey Jr., Brent Weisman, Patsy West, and Mikaëla M. Adams.[4]

During the first half of the nineteenth century, constitution creation in Florida existed under a national movement toward expansion. In the case of Florida, it was an expansion south, but no different than expansion westward. Although the Republic of West Florida Constitution (1810) and the Patriot Constitution (1812) were very different documents, the context in which they were created was similar. These two constitutions, although not actual State of Florida constitutions, did resemble eighteenth-century constitutionalism more than early nineteenth-century constitutionalism. Both really represent a transition where some elements of what would become Jacksonian Democracy in the 1830s in the form of universal white male suffrage were proposed. But in both cases only landholders could hold office. There was no option for the direct election of officials, but respectively each legislative body would appoint the people who served in any executive or judicial capacity. And both constitutions were drafted as part of a hostile revolt and occupation of the Spanish Florida colonies: In East Florida the attempt to join the United States and in West Florida to create an autonomous republic.[5]

William J. Chriss in his book *Six Constitutions Over Texas: Texas' Political Identity, 1830–1900* noticed common efforts in Texas during the nineteenth century from the various state constitutions. Chriss noted that

> Law is an important marker of social control and political identity. Thus, properly understood legal history is also intellectual, cultural, and political history. It seems logical that nations and states tend to write new constitutions only at important crossroads in their sociopolitical development. Thus, not only are the "whats" of these constitutions indicative of the ideological identities that produced them, but their "whens" mark the movements when conflicts over culture and politics were most acute and meaningful.[6]

Florida lawmakers were no different than those in Texas or other states. In creating the Florida constitutions of the nineteenth century and comparatively less so with the 1968 Constitution, constitutional delegates used those moments to exert a political identity as much as social control over those people on the margins and disfranchised from the political center of Southern and state politics.

Indigenous constitutions share some common characteristics around the world. Scholars of Indigenous legal and constitutional traditions agree that Native peoples enjoyed political and legal practices before encounters with European colonizers. Often when it came time for many of these Indigenous societies to translate their political and legal practices formally, it was an effort to establish the boundaries of recognized sovereignty within a state or nation, whether in the United States, Canada, within various Latin American nations, or even Australia. What is common to Indigenous constitutionalism is the recognition of sovereignty, land, and political autonomy. Legal scholar Robert J. Miller believes there is a long tradition of not only Indigenous legal and constitutional practices but that the American and Native legal traditions influence each other. So much that Miller has documented what he terms American Indian influence on the US Constitution. Indigenous influences on Florida constitutions, including those in the 1810s, are not manifest in the same way that Miller documents with the US Constitution. There is minimal mention of Native peoples in these constitutions before 1868. When mentioned, Native peoples are treated either as a neighboring hostile force by the language used in the constitutions or, as with the case of the Republic of West Florida Constitution (1810), as subjects in the discussion of establishing the right of commerce between Indigenous people and the government of West Florida. The 1868 Florida Constitution during Reconstruction mentioned Seminoles by name and included an article whereby a Native representative, a non-white representative, could sit in the legislature on their behalf if elected by the Seminoles. The price for this inclusion into the Florida polity depended on cultural and economic assimilation to American society on the part of the Indigenous people. This provision was never enforced and there is no evidence that the Native peoples of Florida pursued it. Finally, the only mention of Indigenous people in the 1968 Constitution is to address the Indian gaming industry in Florida and point to federal law. The Indian Gaming Regulatory Act (1988) recognized the gaming industry on Native lands, a source of controversy and continued litigation since. The Seminole and Miccosukee Constitutions follow Indigenous constitutional tradition in establishing membership in their societies governed by the documents as well as defining the right to land and the nature of the relationship between the Seminole Tribe of Florida and the Miccosukees with both the federal government and the State of Florida.[7]

Over time Florida state constitutions evolved in ways that other state constitutions did around the rest of the country. John Dinan and G. Alan Tarr mention that state constitutions modernize over time. This is a byproduct of repeated and periodic substantive revisions throughout the nineteenth and twentieth centuries. The executive, legislative, and judicial branches of government grew and became more structured with each revision. The meaning of citizenship and the rights granted in those cases changed as well. In the 1838 Florida Constitution citizenship was recognized as those rights enshrined by the federal government. Within that same document specific rights such as property ownership, suffrage, and the right to serve in the state government were all defined specific to state experience. D'Alemberte pointed out that the 1838 Florida Constitution was the only constitution throughout the entire country that provided for the economic regulation of banks, a rarity for drafting a constitution. With subsequent constitutions the delegates would define citizenship of the United States and the State of Florida separately and where and how rights are conferred to any resident in either case. Although Florida is overlooked in many studies of state constitutionalism, the character and evolution of a state constitutional tradition is as present in Florida as in other states.[8]

John J. Dinan in *The American State Constitutional Tradition* argues that state constitutions are better examples of the American Constitutional tradition than the US Constitution. He states that since state constitutions are so flexible, frequently replaced, and easily amended relative to the US Constitution, they capture a more representative constitutional tradition over time. According to Dinan the reason for this was because state lawmakers and the architects of state governments feared that citizens might take extra constitutional or revolutionary means to change the aspects of state government that were not working. The founders of state constitutional traditions wanted citizens to have access to authorized channels of reform such as processes to amend and even efforts to create new state constitutions and government themselves.[9]

The difference between amending and revising federal versus state constitutions can be found in this need to appeal to the popular will of the citizens or constituents. With the revising and amending of state governments through the constitutional convention process we see over time states expanding rights and often addressing rights ignored or defeated during revision attempts on the national level. This dynamic between federal and state constitutional traditions has brought recent attention not only to the difference between national and state constitutions but an examination of state constitutionalism in and of itself.[10]

There are important differences between the US Constitution and the numerous state constitutions that have emerged over the years. One interesting characteristic mentioned by Mila Versteeg and Emily Zackin is that "like most of the world's constitutions, state constitutions are rather long and elaborate documents that set out government policies in painstaking detail." Both Versteeg and Zackin argue that the tradition of constitutionalism in the United States, either the federal or state example, is not unique or exceptional. There have been 149 state constitutions over the years, and they bear a resemblance to constitutions around the world.[11]

Constitutions as documents or texts represent a unique window of opportunity to understand the economic, social, and political context of a state at the moment the constitution was debated, drafted, and ratified. J. Alton Burdine says:

> A state constitution, framed or revised by an elected constitutional convention, inevitably reflects the environment which exists at the time the convention meets. The political history of the particular state, current political thinking, and experiences of other states are significant factors in shaping this environment. The tendency of constitutional conventions to enshrine the present through long, detailed constitutions has made frequent amendment or revision necessary. The large number of changes resulting creates difficulty for those who attempt to keep abreast of these developments.[12]

Legal theories and philosophical discourses are usually not embedded in the published records of the various state constitutional conventions; instead, debates about the relationship between people and their system of state government seem to be central to delegates. Since all states have rewritten their state constitutions at least once, we see what epitomizes the trends and great concerns of those moments. Entire American eras are encapsulated in the documents that make up the convention records, not to mention the constitutions themselves.

G. Alan Tarr, in *Understanding State Constitutions,* tells us that state constitutions are important documents for analysis. He states:

> State constitutions are as significant for what they reveal as for what they prescribe. They comprise a crucial scholarly resource for historians and political scientists, because political disputes in the states have often had a constitutional dimension, and the texts of state constitutions record those conflicts and their outcomes.[13]

The fight over apportionment, representation, and suffrage that seems to be common in all state constitutional debates. Included in debates are what processes and limitations delegates believe should be designed into their governing document. Finally, the relationship between the state and economic interests frequently spills into convention debates.[14] These seem to be the common dilemmas that delegates grapple with during the convention process.

Many scholars divide periods of state constitutional revision into definitive eras where the impetus to change state government was shared among several states resulting in similar types of revisions. Many of these eras overlap with the periodization historians have tended to use to define the political trends of the time. John J. Dinan points to the Jacksonian Era as the first period of revised state governments because of the attempt by states to respond to the expansion of white male suffrage and their political participation in forms of more direct democracy as well as new states coming into the union for the first time. Dinan then looks to the Civil War and later Progressive Era as similar yet two separate and distinct periods of state constitutional revision because of the expansion of social and political rights bookended by the Fifteenth and Nineteenth Amendments to the US Constitution. Finally, Dinan suggests there was not as much state revision again until the 1960s due to the US Supreme Court ruling in *Baker v. Carr* when the Court ruled that states needed to address legislative malapportionment. This led many states to address the apportionment between rural and urban political districts, which historically skewed to favor rural populations. Dinan finds that since the 1960s there have been few state revisions; instead revisions were primarily handled through the amendment process. Other state constitutional scholars may conceive of these constitutional convention trends in different ways, but there seems to be consensus on the broader context impacting the eras of revision.[15]

Over time state governments became more representative and adopted the characteristics of direct democracy. The one feature of state government that has been almost unanimous is the bicameral legislature, reflecting the tradition of the US government. Nebraska is the only state to create a unicameral legislature. It did so in 1935 as a cost-saving measure and in the belief that it might disincentivize political partisanship. Other parts of state government parallel the US Constitution, such as establishing the judicial and executive branches and eventually developing an executive cabinet system and state agencies to oversee growing state government bureaucracies. The advent of these civil systems would not operate exactly as their counterparts in the federal government; they do represent an indication that constitutional delegates adopted ideas from above and shaped them for the state governments that would emerge. According to Dinan, states were slower to adopt the separation of powers contained in the US Constitution as both the governor veto and judicial review were not added until the late nineteenth century. In Florida throughout the nineteenth century constitutional delegates designed a more responsive and tiered executive bureaucracy.[16]

The idea that a constitution can shape the character of citizenship is something that Dinan claims is unique to state constitutionalism and wholly missing in federal constitutionalism. Although the US Constitution in its amended form does define a citizen and spells out the rights of citizenship, many state constitution delegates believed that the constitution and state government should incentivize the behaviors of the states' residents. This specific process Dinan refers to as "citizen character." For this reason, we see state constitutions address public education, religious institutions, prohibition of alcohol, and banning gambling and lotteries. The framers of the US Constitution were not interested in regulating or nurturing citizens' character, while state delegates took that responsibility on themselves. Since the Civil War, Florida's constitutional delegates maintained a public education system, prohibited lotteries, and repudiated sexual licentiousness, as well as encouraged religious participation.[17]

The construction and protection of rights varies differently between the federal constitution and state constitutions. Mila Versteeg and Emily Zackin point to "positive rights" as rights that over time appear in state constitutions, which have been missing in the federal constitution. They claim that constitutional and legal developments around the world have influenced state constitutions. Versteeg and Zackin write, "Like the world's constitutions, state constitutions contain positive rights relating to, for example, education, labor, social welfare, and the environment. Thus, at the state level, Americans have written their constitutions much like everyone else." Positive rights also encompass rights related to how government is organized, state obligations to the public, and private autonomy. Another feature of positive rights is that they typically lend themselves to advocacy and activism by various special interest groups. Environment rights emerged from the Stockholm Declaration on the Human Environment (1972), which addressed the intersection of human rights with the natural environment. These rights absent from the US Constitution include collective rights such as workplace rights, the right to labor organizing, social and economic rights, and the right to a free public education—even enhanced rights for the individual that might conflict with some of these collective rights such as the right to work and property rights.

Most recently we have seen state constitutions introduce environmental rights into their governing documents. In 1968 Florida's constitutional delegates wrote language enshrining positive rights for public sector unions and environmental preservation.[18]

Finally, a characteristic of state constitutions is their amendable nature. Versteeg and Zackin remind us that not all state constitutions have been revised:

> To be sure, not all states are prolific constitution writers; 17 states are still operating under their original constitutions. Other states, however, have replaced their constitutions with remarkable frequency. Louisiana has had 11 constitutions, Georgia has had 9, Virginia and South Carolina have each had 7, and Florida and Alabama have each had 6. Combined, the states have produced a total of 149 documents to date.[19]

Amendable constitutions do have their limits. In three court cases, *Miller v. Johnson* (18 S.W. 522. 92 Ky. 589) (1892), *Taylor v. Commonwealth* (101 Va. 829, 831, 44 S.E. 754, 755) (1903), and *Staples v. Gilmer* (183 Va. 613, 33 S. E. 2d 49) (1945), the courts have decided that a constitution amended by various means was constitutional and did not need to be approved by popular vote.[20]

There is a deep but niche literature on the crafting of state constitutions and the evolution of state constitutionalism. In John J. Dinan's book *The American State Constitutional Tradition*, he surveys and synthesizes the characteristics and trends of state constitutionalism through what appears to be an exhaustive examination of the records of state constitutional conventions. Florida's many state constitutional conventions are not explored in the depth of other states because Dinan claims the convention records are wholly missing. Yet, this is not the case. This assumption could have come from J. Alton Burdine, a state constitutional scholar from the 1950s who created detailed charts of state constitutions over time and originally claimed that Florida's state government left no records of their debates and discussion. This is not entirely true, while for some constitutional conventions detailed records of debates might be missing, there are records and minutes preserved that can provide the historian the ability to reconstruct debates and give clues to how the delegates crafted the language of the various constitutions. What this book aims to do is examine Florida's constitutions that led to the various state governments over time but also include constitutions drafted in Florida such as the Patriot and West Florida Constitutions. This volume will also include the drafting of the Seminole and Miccosukee Constitutions not as state constitutions, but constitutions created in Florida.[21]

There are some constitutional experiments missing in this volume intentionally. Under British colonial rule the government in Florida organized legislative assemblies in both East and West Florida, which met periodically between 1766 and 1783. But there was nothing approaching a constitution or convention, and in these cases colonial governors authorized the assemblies. After the Florida colonies returned to Spain with the end of the American Revolution, the Spanish colonial government drafted what became known as the 1812 Cádiz Constitution. The Cádiz Constitution applied to the Spanish colonies in the Americas and Spanish subjects in St. Augustine who lived under its legal authority for a brief period in 1812. The 1812 Cádiz Constitution was not drafted in Florida and applied to numerous jurisdictions through the Spanish empire.[22]

The first two chapters of this collection examine constitutions developed during attempts to create independent republics in both East and West Spanish Florida during the 1810s. In chapter 1, Samuel C. Hyde examines the political and diplomatic conditions that created the West Florida Constitution of 1810. During a time when East and West Florida were colonies of the Spanish Empire, a group of settlers in West Florida drove out the Spanish military in St. Francisville and declared an independent republic. Hyde analyzes how the military and diplomatic conditions helped to shape the short-lived constitution and government of the Republic of West Florida. These events were repeated with people from Georgia who invaded East Florida at Fernandina two years later in 1812. In chapter 2, M.C. Mirow interprets the 1812 Patriot Constitution and this second effort to form an independent republic from Spanish Florida's other colony. Like the Republic of West Florida, the "Patriot Revolt" was an attempt, albeit short, to form an independent nation or republic. As such, the international, diplomatic, and political milieu surrounding this military expedition helped to shape what eventually became the Patriot Constitution of 1812. Although these constitutions are not State of Florida constitutions, they do represent attempts at constitution- and government-making in Florida that share characteristics with what scholars refer to as state constitution-making during the Revolutionary period.

In chapter 3, James M. Denham, chronicles the first state constitution, the 1838 St. Joseph's Constitution. This constitution was drafted while Florida was still a territory of the United States and the delegates to the convention had to draft a document and government that would prepare the territory for eventual statehood, which was achieved in 1845. Unlike the attempts we witnessed in the 1810s, these delegates and lawmakers drafted a territorial government within the political and economic turmoil of the time, Jacksonian America. The political and economic foundations delegates fashioned in the 1830s would get revised throughout the rest of the nineteenth century, especially the economic concerns this constitution seemed to unleash.

Probably the most unusual conditions for drafting a constitution are examined by R. Boyd Murphree in chapter 4. Murphree interprets the constitution and government created with the emergence of the Confederate government of Florida during the US Civil War. In 1861, lawmakers continued the tradition of crafting a constitution and governing documents during wartime: the revolts in East and West Florida in the 1810s between settlers and the Spanish Colonial government and the 1838 Constitution at a time during the Second Seminole War, and the 1861 Constitution during the US Civil War. Murphree chronicles the fight to create a constitution during secession and wartime as well analyzing the dysfunction of the newly created Florida Confederate government. In this chapter Murphree compares and interprets the evolution and legal wrangling of secession for Florida lawmakers.

Chapter 5 discusses the Florida Constitution of 1865, which is the Presidential Reconstruction Constitution. It is also the first state constitution, oddly enough, to take a step closer to government modernization. Not in the form of civil rights, nor citizenship rights for African Americans, but in the forms and systems of government, making the state government more similar in function to the US Constitution and government. Lasting little more than a year, it would be the shortest state government in operation; even the Reconstruction government formed from the 1868 Constitution as well as subsequent governments formed in 1885 and 1968 would carry some structures and functions of state government first conceived with the 1865 Constitution—some for the better and some for the worse.

In chapter 6, Andrea L. Oliver examines the second Reconstruction Constitution in Florida. The Constitution of 1868 would be conceived and drafted after Presidential Reconstruction during the period known as Congressional Reconstruction. African Americans were enfranchised during Congressional Reconstruction, thus Black men in Florida could not only vote on the new constitution but serve as delegates themselves. The constitution and government was more conservative Republican than radical Republican, and it became the most liberal governing document produced by a state government in Florida up to that point in time.

Christopher Day tackles the 1885 Florida Constitution in chapter 7. The 1885 Constitution replaced the constitution and government of the Reconstruction Constitution of 1868 and was intended to be a reform constitution coinciding with the rise of the Independents, Populists, and Progressives in Florida and around the rest of the country. Day points to the legal questions and court cases that laid the groundwork for the 1885 Constitution. Although delegates expressed an interest in creating a document and government more responsive to the people, its legacy was the government that would institutionalize de jure racial segregation, disfranchisement, and other structures of civic life meant to create different classes of citizenship and constitutional rights.

Andrew K. Frank in chapter 8 turns his attention to government formation and the drafting of Indigenous constitutions in Florida. Although these are not state constitutions, they are constitutions and sovereign governments forged and crafted in Florida by the Seminoles and Miccosukees. Frank takes us through the long history of civic relations formed by the Native people of Florida from the 1950s through 1970s when the Indigenous people of Florida demanded the US government recognize their societies as sovereign people. This chapter highlights the struggle the founders of these Native governments had externally with the federal government and internally with other Native peoples in the state.

Mary Adkins, in chapter 9, ends this collection with an examination of the 1968 Constitution, the constitution that forms the current government of Florida. Unlike previous attempts at forming a new government and constitution in Florida, in 1968 Adkins reminds us that Florida like many other states since 1950 took their state governments to the drawing board to address issues such as apportionment and the drive to create a state government more responsive to the people. It is a constitution that can be more easily amended and revised without the need to call for future constitutional conventions.

Although much of this introduction and later collection of chapters will touch on state constitutionalism, this is not all that this collection documents. Florida is a state, but it is also a geography. The intent of this collection is to give us a window into forms of constitutionalism grounded in not only state but other experiments and traditions in constitutionalism. Authors such as G. Alan Tarr and John J. Dinan demonstrate the unique tradition and importance of state constitutionalism within US constitutional history. Tarr, Dinan, and others have also mapped out the specific traditions, institutions, and government processes state constitutions borrowed from the federal government and those that evolved independently from the US Constitutions and its numerous amendments. Most state constitution studies ignore Florida and a handful of other states because of claims that comprehensive documents from the various constitutional conventions do not exist or are preserved for contemporary use. Thus, Florida and any constitutional tradition is more ignored than understood. This collection looks to place Florida's state constitutional tradition within the context and literature of those specific debates surrounding state constitutional traditions. Additionally, there is a secondary thesis to this collection, by including the West Florida, Patriot, and Indigenous Constitutions we can broaden our examination of constitution formation and constitutionalism in Florida. The authors of those sections in this collection make connections to when and how federal and state entities as well as international actors have impacted the short-lived governments in East and West Florida in the nineteenth century and the Indigenous constitutions of the Seminoles and Miccosukees. This collection gives us the opportunity to think and understand constitutionalism within a state in a much more dynamic and comprehensive way.

Notes

1 *Miami Hearld,* November 16, 1930.
2 *Tampa Tribune,* June 20, 1930; G. Alan Tarr, *Understanding State Constitutions* (Princeton, NJ: Princeton University Press, 2000), 136.
3 Tarr, 56–57.
4 Talbot D'Alemberte, *The Florida State Constitution: A Reference Guide* (New York: Greenwood Press, 1991), 1–17; on the Florida Indigenous legal and political traditions consult: Harry A. Kersey Jr., *An Assumption of Sovereignty: Social and Political Transformation among the Florida Seminoles, 1953–1979* (Lincoln: University of Nebraska Press); Harry A. Kersey, "The Havana Connection: Buffalo Tiger, Fidel Castro, and the Origin of Miccosukee Tribal Sovereignty, 1959–1962," *American Indian Quarterly* 25, no. 4 (2001): 491–507; Brent Richards Weisman, *Unconquered People: Florida's Seminole and Miccosukee Indians* (Gainesville: University Press of Florida, 1999); Patsy West, *The Enduring Seminoles from Alligator Wrestling to Ecotourism* (Gainesville: University Press of Florida, 1998); Mikaëla M. Adams, *Who Belongs? Race, Resources, and Tribal Citizenship in the Native South* (New York: Oxford University Press, 2016).

5 M.C. Mirow, "The Age of Constitutions in the Americas," *Law and History Review* 32, no. 2 (2014): 229–35; "Constitution of West Florida" (1810) Article 1§15 in Horst Dippel, ed., *Constitutional Documents of the United States of America 1776–1860, Part VII: Vermont-Wisconsin Addendum et Corrigendum*, Germany: K. G. Saur Verlag: 2009, 143–53.

6 William J. Chriss, *Six Constitutions over Texas: Texas' Political Identity, 1830–1900* (College Station: Texas A&M University Press, 2024), xv.

7 John Borrows, *Canada's Indigenous Constitution* (Toronto, Canada: University of Toronto Press, 2010) 1–10; Robert J. Miller, "American Indian Constitutions and Their Influence on the United States Constitution," *Proceedings of the American Philosophical Society* 159, no. 1 (2015): 32–56; see also, Robert J. Miller, "American Indian Influence on the United States Constitution and Its Framers," *American Indian Law Review* 18 No. 1 (1993), 73–132; "Constitution of West Florida" (1810) in Horst Dippel, ed., *Constitutional Documents of the United States of America 1776–1860, Part VII: Vermont-Wisconsin Addendum et Corrigendum* (Germany: K. G. Saur Verlag: 2009), 145; M.C. Mirow, "The Patriot Constitution and International Constitution Making," *Texas Review of Law & Politics* 21, no. 3 (September 20, 2017): 516; Fla. Const. of 1868, art. XVI, § 7; Robert Cassanello, "The Right to Vote and the Long Nineteenth Century in Florida," *The Florida Historical Quarterly* 95, no. 2 (2016): 213, Fla. Const. of 1968, Article X § 30; US Department of the Interior, "Constitution and Bylaws of the Seminole Tribe of Florida," Bureau of Indian Affairs, 21 August 1957, 1–11; Glenn Welker, "Constitution of the Miccosukee Nation," *Indigenous Peoples' Literature* website, accessed July 8, 2023. There was a second Patriot Revolt in 1817 that occupied Fernandina similar to 1812. This revolt was more international in scope, trying to connect to the revolutionary independence movements in Latin America. The leaders of the revolt planned to draft a constitution, organizing delegates and setting a date for the meeting, but before it could happen the Spanish colonial government in East Florida defeated them and they abandoned these efforts. See David Head, *Privateers of the Americas: Spanish American Privateering from the United States in the Early Republic* (Athens, GA: University of Georgia Press, 2015).

8 Tarr, *Understanding State Constitutions*, 23–25; John J. Dinan, *The American State Constitutional Tradition* (Lawrence: University Press of Kansas, 2006), 5; D'Alemberte, *The Florida State Constitution*, 4.

9 John J. Dinan, *The American State Constitutional Tradition* (Lawrence: University Press of Kansas, 2006), 5, 272.

10 Janice C. May, "Constitutional Amendment and Revision Revisited," *Publius* 17, no. 1 (1987): 153; John Kincaid, "State Constitutions in the Federal System," *The Annals of the American Academy of Political and Social Science* 496 (1988): 12.

11 Mila Versteeg and Emily Zackin, "American Constitutional Exceptionalism Revisited," *The University of Chicago Law Review* 81, no. 4 (2014): 1641.

12 J. Alton Burdine, "Basic Materials for the Study of State Constitutions and State Constitutional Development," *The American Political Science Review* 48, no. 4 (1954): 1142.

13 Tarr, *Understanding State Constitutions*, 3.
14 Tarr, *Understanding State Constitutions*, 4–5.
15 Dinan, *The American State Constitutional Tradition*, 9–10; see also Albert L. Sturm, "The Development of American State Constitutions," *Publius* 12, no. 1 (1982): 61.
16 Dinan, *The American State Constitutional Tradition*, 95–96, 275, 135–36; Roger V. Shumate, "The Nebraska Unicameral Legislature," *The Western Political Quarterly*, 5, no. 3 (1952): 504–5.
17 Dinan, *The American State Constitutional Tradition*, 274–75.
18 Versteeg and Zackin, "American Constitutional Exceptionalism Revisited," 1641, 1688, 1692, 1697; Dinan, *The American State Constitutional Tradition*, 213–14; Helen Hershkoff, "Positive Rights and State Constitutions: The Limits of Federal Rationality Review," *Harvard Law Review* 112, no. 6 (1999): 1196.
19 Versteeg and Zackin, "American Constitutional Exceptionalism Revisited," 1672.
20 Thomas Raeburn White, "Amendment and Revision of State Constitutions." *University of Pennsylvania Law Review* 100, no. 8 (1952): 1132–152.
21 Dinan, *The American State Constitutional Tradition*, 28; Burdine, "Basic Materials for the Study of State Constitutions," 1147–152.
22 J. Leitch Wright Jr. *Florida in the American Revolution* (Gainesville: University Presses of Florida, 1975), 18–19; J. Barton Starr, *Tories, Dons, and Rebels: The American Revolution in British West Florida* (Gainesville: University Presses of Florida, 1976), 10–12; M.C. Mirow, "The Constitution of Cádiz in Florida," *Florida Journal of International Law* 24, no. 2 (08/ 2012): 271–330.

1

A Florida Constitution in the State of Louisiana

The 1810 Constitution of the State of Florida

Samuel C. Hyde

In the summer of 1810, a group of prominent men gathered nervously in a home near the small town of St. Francisville to clandestinely foment a revolution. Situated along the Mississippi River north of the provincial capital at Baton Rouge, St. Francisville was located in a region that arguably endured the most convoluted pattern of governance found anywhere in North America. At the time of the covert meeting, the region comprised the westernmost territory of Spanish West Florida. It had changed hands many times. With the advent of European intrusion, French adventurers initially explored and later claimed the territory for France. In 1763, Britain assumed governance as part of the treaty concluding the French and Indian War before Spain forcibly wrested the territory from the British during the American Revolution.

The men meeting at St. Francisville that summer were about to add two more layers to the complicated identity of the region. The ambiguity concerning ownership of the territory, the conflicting methods of governance, and the uncertainties regarding the responsibilities of citizenship in the territory contributed to a state of chronic instability. Even worse, diverging, and often overlapping, land claims issued by the various governing powers along with the conflicting loyalties of the residents rendered the region a volatile melting pot. The St. Francisville meeting would advance the crisis of confidence in governance. And the organic law ultimately enacted by regional residents would reflect deeply ingrained concerns about property rights and the limits of liberty.

Further exacerbating conditions conducive to instability was the nature of the people who called the region home. Unlike the comparative homogeneity of the Atlantic seaboard states, or even, to a lesser degree, the Spanish-controlled territory to the west, the province of West Florida included a curious mélange of people that made the region ripe for unrest. In addition to a scattering of French settlers, Canary Islanders, and Scotch Irish "Caintucks," the territory hosted significant numbers of British loyalists who had migrated there specifically to avoid American control and the expectations of citizenship, such as voting and jury service, which life under American authority entailed. These people enjoyed the generous land grants, lax tax policies, and most importantly, the limited intrusion of government into their lives the Spanish offered.[1]

Under such circumstances, the region, perhaps not surprisingly, became a magnet for desperate characters who proved even more determined to resist the advent of effective governance than their Tory neighbors. The Spanish kept a garrison of two to three dozen men at Fort San Carlos in Baton Rouge, along with a handful farther upriver at St. Francisville. Other than an occasional small detachment posted farther east at the river port community of Springfield, along the Natalbany River, the Spanish maintained few tools to enforce their authority or maintain order in the territory. Accordingly, scores of army deserters and other desperadoes flocked to the region to exploit the absence of authority, avoid prosecution, and waylay travelers and herds of livestock traversing the multiple market trails that crossed the region en route to the port communities adjoining lakes Maurepas and Pontchartrain that serviced commerce to and from New Orleans.[2]

The framers of the 1810 Constitution of the State of Florida understood the challenges that confronted the territory. The problems of conflicting land claims, competing loyalties, and diverse cultural and legal traditions placed the fragile territory at risk. Even worse, chronic instability and pervasive political intrigue threatened to plunge the region into anarchy. The 1810 Constitution reflected the need for stability and the desire to attract internal support from widely diverse groups. And it was constructed with the haste necessary to both stabilize and appease amid the chaotic conditions that threatened to consume the territory.

In 1804, the region endured an uprising led by some disgruntled American settlers, many from the neighboring Mississippi Territory, who believed they had been treated unfairly by the Spanish legal system. The so-called Kemper Rebellion was not only promptly suppressed, but it witnessed an outpouring of support for maintaining the status quo among regional residents.[3]

In the aftermath of the Kemper rising, three distinct factions emerged in the territory. The jockeying for power among these three groups would contribute significantly to the shaping of the organic law for the soon-to-be-formed republic. The first party consisted of Americans and American sympathizers. This group included residents who were disappointed the region had not been included in the Louisiana Purchase of 1803, along with others whose Protestant sensibilities were offended by the nominal requirement that all residents must embrace Catholicism. The American faction was concentrated primarily in the westernmost portion of the territory, constituting a majority of residents in the Feliciana District and St. Helena.[4]

The second party may best be called the Independents. Residents eager to see the region independent of both the Spanish and Americans dominated this faction. Men aligned with this group were largely driven by personal ambition. They hoped that by creating an independent nation in West Florida they would be able to form a government, void existing land claims, and reap the riches of property and power manifest in an independent republic, not to mention the future potential of a new nation controlling much of the Gulf Coast and lower Mississippi River delta. They almost succeeded. This group found scattered support across the western and central portions of the territory including significant support in Baton Rouge.[5]

The final, and likely largest, faction consisted of Spanish loyalists. The residents affiliated with this group appreciated Spanish governance and the benefits it offered. The Spanish provided generous land grants to settlers, typically about 640 acres. In an effort to attract additional settlers, they did not levy taxes on private property. Perhaps most important, the Spanish adopted a "live and let live" attitude with the settlers of West Florida. With only a handful of troops in the region and no police force as we understand such services today, residents were free to live as they chose absent the requirements of citizenship found in American-controlled territory. The Loyalists feared that any change in the status quo may threaten their land claims and compromise their independent way of life.[6]

In September 1810, the swirling cauldron of intrigue that characterized West Florida boiled over when a rising broke out plunging the region into war. After driving out the handful of troops and scattering of Spanish loyalists from St. Francisville, a small army assaulted the fort at Baton Rouge and in a sharp, yet brief, firefight forced the capitulation of the Spanish government. The rebels unfurled the flag of the original Lone Star Republic over the fort, and at St. Francisville, before dispatching troops to subdue regions to the east that remained loyal to Spain and to capture Mobile.[7]

As the "army" of the Republic of West Florida sought to expand the newly independent nation's authority eastward, back in St. Francisville the revolutionaries began the process of creating a government. In the months preceding the outbreak of the West Florida Revolt, disaffected planters and merchants had organized as a "convention," with the stated purpose of assisting Spain during her time of turmoil occasioned by French pressure on the Spanish Crown. The minutes of the convention for July 27, 1810, included a list of grievances ranging from the current government's failure to punish those guilty of assault and battery, or seemingly worse in the eyes of the conventioneers, "the wicked slander," noting that "each of those crimes pass unnoticed and they well deserve the attention of this council." Instead, the convention was actually maneuvering to eventually replace the Spanish colonial government, arguing, "It becomes the duty of this province to lessen as much as possible the burden of the mother country, engaged as she is at present in a dubious contest for her own preservation." For several months, Governor Carlos de Hault Delassus feigned agreement with the convention's purpose. But when a messenger carrying a desperate plea for aid from Delassus to the Spanish governor at Pensacola, Vincente Folch, was captured by a rebel patrol, the convention morphed into a revolutionary assembly. With John Rhea acting as president, the convention authorized the attack on the fort at Baton Rouge and began to function as the newly established government of the independent State of West Florida.[8]

As the convention's army, under the direction of General Philemon Thomas, consolidated its hold on the territory by intimidating and dispersing Spanish loyalists and Independents, the assembly began the more challenging tasks of creating an organic law and forming a government. The delegates quickly forwarded a letter to Governor David Holmes in the neighboring Mississippi Territory explaining that they had been forced to act due to the perfidy of the Spanish. Writing for the convention, John Rhea pleaded for a show of support from the Americans to discourage the Spanish who were assumed to be rushing reinforcements to Baton Rouge. Pushing their advantage, three days after the capture of the fort at Baton Rouge, the convention issued a declaration of independence proclaiming, "This Territory of West Florida to be a free and independent state." The convention further claimed for themselves the "right to institute such form of government as they may think conducive to their safety and happiness."[9]

Challenging the might of Spain and declaring the right to determine the form of government for the entire province were bold claims by a few hundred men who only six years earlier had seen a similar effort at revolution founder due to ambiguity surrounding their purpose. Aware that significant factions remained hostile to their actions and virtually everyone feared a condition of anarchy, the convention issued some initial directives for governance specifically designed to assuage the fears of the other factions. On September 26, 1810, the convention asserted its right to create a government casting it as necessary "in order to secure to our constituents and our country the blessings of liberty and equal rights." To reassure those fearful of anarchy or continuing civil war within the province, the declaration stated further, "In the meantime, the laws heretofore observed in the administration of justice, and determining the right of property remain in full force." Though the convention had complained of Spanish laxity in the issuance and enforcement of the law, they now seized on that ambiguity as a means to placate those uncertain of the convention's ultimate intent, especially concerning the respect of French, British, and even Spanish land grants.[10]

Within days of the seizure of the fort at Baton Rouge, the convention had declared West Florida independent, asserted its right to govern, and even dispatched an army to suppress its opponents. On October 8, 1810, with only one dissenting vote, the convention approved the creation of a constitution to provide a legal basis for its actions. John Rhea, John H. Johnson, and John W. Leonard, all gentlemen of property and standing as well as leading figures in the revolt, were selected to serve on the committee tasked with writing the constitution. Three weeks later following three days of readings and amendments, the "Constitution or Form of Government of the State of Florida" secured unanimous approval.[11]

Suspicion and doubt about the West Florida rebels' actual purpose has long circulated among scholars. Though some casual observers have claimed that the entire West Florida Revolt was nothing more than a filibustering expedition, funded and directed by the United States, little viable evidence, if any, exists to support such a claim. Instead, scholars have debated whether the Americans belatedly got involved in events already occurring in West Florida in order to prevent the intrusion of another power, specifically England or France, or if President James Madison truly believed the Louisiana Purchase had authorized American control of the entire lower Mississippi Valley. In short, the question centered on whether the Americans were sincere in Madison's October 27, 1810, proclamation that the United States had always considered West Florida east to the Perdido River as part of the Louisiana Purchase. Or if fear of British meddling had provoked a reluctant Madison administration to act. As one East Coast editor fumed when the declaration of independence became public, "The idea of an independent state in West Florida is preposterous."[12]

The Constitution of West Florida seems at odds with the editor's consternation. The preamble to the document serves as a forthright assertion of the residents' intention to create an independent nation providing for justice, common defense, and the blessings of liberty as mandated in the Declaration of Independence dated September 26, 1810. Organized into seven articles, which are subdivided into "sections," the initial portions of the constitution describe the format or organization of the government. The bicameral legislature would include a Senate and House of Representatives with the date for election of delegates to each body identified in the document.[13]

Eligible voters included "free white men of the age of twenty-one years and upward" who resided at least six months in what the constitution defined as the five districts completing the territory of the state. Included were the districts of Baton Rouge, New Feliciana, St. Helena, St. Ferdinand, and, interestingly, Mobile. The stipulations concerning eligible voters and the included districts further the bold assumptions of the crafters of the new government. Including St. Ferdinand, a hotbed of Spanish support, revealed the framers' confidence that their rapid, and brutal, suppression of Spanish loyalists in that region was complete, just as including Mobile suggests their belief, or some wishful thinking, that the army dispatched toward Mobile Bay would indeed be successful in seizing that territory for the new state.[14]

Those owning property within the new nation who were twenty-two years old and older, and who had resided in West Florida for a minimum of twelve months were eligible to be candidates for the House of Representatives. The constitution mandated no specific minimum amount of property required of office seekers, merely directing that candidates must have a "freehold" within the state. Section fifteen defined a freehold as "any real property of the value of two hundred dollars," suggesting a more inclusive vision of property than that found in many antebellum constitutions in the South.[15]

The first representatives to the House were to be elected to serve a one-year term on November 10, 1810. Each of the five districts could elect three representatives with the exception of New Feliciana, which was allotted four, suggesting the level of influence exercised by residents of that district on the entire revolutionary process. Section four of the constitution further directed that an enumeration of residents in each district be conducted each year and the number of representatives in each succeeding legislature would be apportioned according to population. Only free-born inhabitants were to be included in the apportionment of representation.

The final point provides insight into the reasoning guiding the framers of the constitution. Unlike some later versions of the organic law in Louisiana, such as the Constitution of 1852, which counted slaves in the apportionment of representation to further the power of the plantation districts, the framers of the West Florida Constitution opted for a more egalitarian interpretation regarding white inhabitants. The framers undoubtedly sought to advance the appeal of their movement by offering greater power to the average freeholder.[16]

Each district would elect one senator at the same time as the election of members to the House. Those elected to the Senate would serve three-year terms, with one third of the members standing for election each year on a rotating basis. Eligible candidates included freeholders at least twenty-five years old who had resided in the state at least one year.[17]

Section 16 of article 1 offers insight into the condition, and concerns, of many of the more marginal inhabitants of West Florida. With the exception of treason or felony breach of peace, all electors were to be "privileged from arrest" at the polling sites in their respective districts "and in going to and returning from the same." Section 22 extended the same privilege to members of the legislature during sessions of the House and Senate as well as during travel to and from the sessions. In addition to the numerous army deserters and other desperadoes who exploited Spanish laxity, many among the region's significant population of Tories feared prosecution by their new masters. Having silenced prominent former British loyalists such as Michael Jones and William Cooper, through these sections of the constitution, the framers sought to mitigate societal divisions and galvanize support for the new state.

Section 25 of article 1 of the constitution enumerated the powers vested in the new government. In addition to claiming the expected rights to raise funds, pay debts, declare war, and establish standard weights and measures, this section reveals some particular interests embraced by the framers. Subsection 8 mandates the promotion of science and "useful arts" by securing for authors and inventors the exclusive right to their respective writings and discoveries. This section was clearly designed to cultivate and facilitate the growing artistic community emerging most notably in the Feliciana District, a group that would soon include the likes of John James Audubon among others. Subsection 12 reveals some lingering traditionalism among the framers, manifest in reservations about maintaining a standing army. The subsection authorizes the government to raise an army, but reminiscent of Old World concerns about the danger of a standing army, limits the duration of any appropriation to fund the army to no more than one year.[18]

Section 25 accordingly suggests both vision and caution. The nod to patrons of the arts and sciences suggests the framers saw themselves as progressives leading the people of West Florida from the dark confines of Spanish colonialism into a modern new world of liberty and creativity. Affording protection to the labors of this group would not only encourage their growth and development in the new state, it would also provide a system of order for developing and implementing new ideas and creative thought. At the same time, section 25 suggests that the framers remained grounded in reality. None among them had any interest in trading one authoritarian regime sustained by a standing army for another. Subsection 14 made clear that the government was to rely on the militia to suppress insurrections or repel invasions. Farmers acting temporarily as militia proved more consistent with the vision of the West Florida Republic embraced by the framers.

Article 2 of the constitution declared that the "supreme executive power shall be vested in a governor of this State who shall hold his office for a term of two years." Both houses of the legislature would vote to select a governor of no less than thirty years of age possessing a freehold of at least $5,000 within the territory. To the governor was assigned the ultimate authority over the militia, the right to declare martial law, and in an apparent later penciled-in afterthought, command of the state's army and navy. No provision for a lieutenant governor was included. Instead the president of the Senate was designated to assume the executive position should the governor be removed or die while in office. The governor was directed to appoint a secretary of state who would essentially serve as his legislative assistant, maintaining all state papers and a register of official acts.[19]

Article three established and outlined the mechanics of the new state's judiciary allowing for a Supreme Court and those "inferior courts" deemed necessary by the General Assembly. Sections 3 and 4 of article 3 reveal the framers' propensity for selectively choosing aspects of differing legal systems. In a break with the tradition of their Spanish colonial masters, section 3 declared, "The citizens of this state shall enjoy the benefit of the writ of Habeas Corpus as defined by the Common Law of England," as well as the right to trial by jury. Section four goes beyond the common law in authorizing the appointment of a "public accuser attorney or prosecuter." Public prosecution did not arrive in England until 1879, and public prosecutors proved rare in the English colonies. Instead, qualities originating from the French *procureur publique* as well as the Dutch *schout*, combined with conditions unique to the North American colonies, resulted in the office of public prosecutor. These conditions included the absence of a landed aristocracy, vast geography, cultural diversity of the people, and the uniquely American vision that the law should be used to protect the rights and property of all free men. By including this office, the framers demonstrated a creative ability to embrace anything that advanced the latent republican vision of the new government most effectively regardless of its origin or source.[20]

The potential Achilles' heel of the State of West Florida emerges in article 4 of the constitution. Few regions of the Western world could claim governance by each of the major colonial powers of the era, but West Florida remained a notable example. French settlement in the territory was minimal, and though British scheming led to some grand planning, settlement during their rule rarely extended much beyond the major waterways on the margins of the westernmost portion of the territory. In their eagerness to retain ownership of the region, both nations nonetheless issued abundant land grants, most of which, almost of necessity, proved vague. A 1776 British grant along the Amite River highlights the imprecision: "Elihu Bay receives all that tract of land situated on the east side of the River Amit [sic] about four miles back from said river upon a creek called the Three Creeks butting and bounding southwesterly unto land surveyed out to Joseph Blackwell and on all other sides by vacant land."[21]

Determined to retain the territory as a critical buffer to their holdings to the west, and to keep a toehold in the lower Mississippi Valley, the Spanish offered lucrative land grants, frequently totaling hundreds of acres, that likewise remained vague and often overlapped existing British and French grants. Illustrating the recipe for confusion, an 1804 Spanish grant declared "Luke Collins claims four hundred superficial arpents nine leagues up the east bank of the Tickfaw River, bounded on one side by William George and by public land on the other two." The Spanish happily lavished land grants on former British loyalists and other migrants to the region who had reason to resist American annexation of the territory. Substantive land grants made instant Spanish loyalists of many migrants to the territory. Their newfound loyalties, and the basis for their land ownership, seemed jeopardized by the West Florida Revolt.[22]

Tension accordingly remained extremely high in West Florida, with concern over the new government's perspective on landholdings foremost in the eyes of most regional residents. Article 4 of the constitution reveals that the delegates well understood that any misstep, at this critical moment, could have profound implications for their fledgling nation-building efforts. As a result, they reached a solution designed to satisfy the majority of landowners while also further mollifying some of their staunchest opponents. The initial sections of article 4 explicitly state that any landowner currently inhabiting and/or improving lands under grants previously respected by the Spanish government would continue as owners of said lands. Language suggesting that French or British titles to land previously endorsed by the Spanish could remain intact covered the holdings of French- and British-era residents who had cast their lot with the Spanish. Section three stated unequivocally, "All French and British patents for lands within this Commonwealth, which lands have been covered by Spanish patents, and all French and British patents for lands within this Commonwealth which have not been recognized and established by the Spanish government shall be void."[23]

With the government's position on landownership indisputably asserted, at least on paper, the framers joined in one of the great ironies of antebellum North America. Article five of the constitution reveals that all the statements appealing to republican ideals and the common good extended to white men only. Moreover, the explicit endorsement of slavery in section 1 of article 5 extends to a declaration on the limits of governmental interference with private property and the primacy of the rights of property owners. The constitution forbade the General Assembly from passing any laws "for the emancipation of slaves without the consent of the owner." The General Assembly was similarly forbidden to pass laws preventing migrants from bringing with them "such persons as are deemed slaves by the laws of this state." These measures insured that the slave system would flourish in West Florida, rendering it consistent with neighboring American-held territories.

With a harsh endorsement of slavery embedded in the document, the framers revealed a more benign vision of the slave system in West Florida. In contrast to later constitutions of Louisiana, such as the Constitution of 1852, which required legislative approval for an owner to liberate his slaves, the General Assembly was granted the right to pass laws allowing slave owners to emancipate their charges as long as creditors were protected and the freedmen did not become a charge of the Commonwealth. The Assembly could also pass laws preventing slaves from being brought into the state as saleable merchandise from any foreign nation, though this restriction could be revisited from year to year. Section 1 concludes by granting the Assembly full power to pass laws necessary to "oblige owners of slaves to treat them with humanity, to provide for them necessary clothing and provisions, to abstain from all injuries to them, extending to life, limb, or mutilation, and in case of their neglect or refusal to comply with the directions of such laws, to have such slave or slaves sold for the benefit of their owners."[24]

After validating human bondage in the first section of article 5, later sections of the same article demonstrate the influence of American liberal thought. Section 5 mandates a free toleration of religion, directing that no preference should be given by law to any one sect or form of religion above another. While this stipulation remains consistent with liberal thought in the United States, it represents a sharp departure from the required allegiance to Catholicism expected by the Spanish, just as it was certain to offend many Protestant Americans due to its welcoming attitude toward Catholics. As such, it stands as another wise straddling the middle of controversy enacted by the framers of the West Florida Constitution.

The seventh and final article of the constitution may be the most curious. It serves as a reiteration, and enhancement, of all the rights and liberties granted to residents of West Florida by the constitution. In essence, the twenty-one sections of article 7, including the final section that was clearly penciled in as an afterthought, function as a bill of rights for the inhabitants. In grandiose form article 7 proclaims "that the general great and essential principles of liberty and free government may be recognized and established we declare," before enumerating the previously identified rights. The list includes visionary proclamations of equality, "all free men when they form a social contract are equal," liberty, "all power is derived from the people," and religious toleration, "all men have a natural and indefeasible right to worship almighty God according to the dictates of their own consciences." Section 19 specifically forbade the legislature from granting any title of nobility or creating any hereditary office or distinction. The proclamations of article 7 envision a nation of political liberty, economic equality, and religious freedom for all free men. Rather than creating a document that catered to the specific interests of the framers, who were overwhelmingly plantation owners, the constitution offered a broadly worded, appealing document designed to attract the support of all classes of free men.[25]

The final portion of the constitution, simply titled "Schedule," outlines when and where elections should be held in each district. In most cases, large regional plantations were designated as polling sites, and in all cases prominent gentlemen, and supporters of the revolt, were selected as overseers. St. Francisville was chosen as the capital of the new republic, and the General Assembly was directed to select a governor on the second day after a quorum was attained. The final section of the "Schedule" directed that upon achieving a quorum of both houses of the legislature, the powers of the convention would cease. The document was signed on October 27, 1810, and the thirteen signers of the Constitution for the State of Florida read like a who's who among the rich and powerful of the territory.[26]

Analysis of the constitution of the brief, yet bold, State of West Florida reveals numerous notable peculiarities. To begin with, the very appellations assigned the new nation in its constitution are many. The designations *Florida*, *West Florida*, *State of Florida*, *Republic*, and *Commonwealth* are all employed at various points throughout the document. The variety of names utilized may have simply been an effort to avoid redundancy in the narrative. More likely, it revealed uncertainty, and caution, among the crafters of the constitution. Finding themselves in uncharted waters, and hailing from diverse nationalities and cultures, the imprecision they relied on during the course of the West Florida Revolt may have continued to serve them well as they sought to assign a title to the new nation. Suddenly free from its previous status as a colony of an autocratic nation, visions of the meaning of terms like "republic" and "commonwealth," as well as clarity in understanding where they existed in the context of Florida itself, remained vague. Moreover, considering the threats they faced, both internal and external, consigning a precise name to their new creation undoubtedly remained secondary to instituting a basis for the establishment of law and order. An appropriate name for the new nation could come later.

The Constitution of the State of Florida also reveals rapid determined action on the part of the revolutionaries. The omnipresent fear of a Spanish invasion was augmented by the capricious intrigues of French and British agents both within and without the territory. At best, no more than half the population of West Florida supported the revolt, rendering immediate and decisive action absolutely necessary. It took the new government barely a month, from the date of the declaration of independence, to craft and approve a constitution that though imprecise in certain ways, sent a clear message to the neighboring Americans that the new nation viewed governance through the same lens as did the United States.[27]

Despite the obvious and intentional consistencies with the Constitution of the United States, the 1810 Constitution of the State of Florida remained distinct. Crafted primarily as a document designed to attract internal support for the nascent nation, the 1810 Constitution reflected the diverse cultural mélange that was West Florida. Especially in terms of property rights and the mechanics of the legal system, the framers cut and pasted from a variety of legal traditions with the intent of creating a government best suited to the peculiar identity of the territory. In the process, they borrowed aspects of differing customs and institutions to create a society that provided definable mechanisms of security, and necessary services to its citizens, in a manner perceived as fair and just by most free inhabitants.

Finally, the Constitution of the State of Florida charted a course for the new nation that would be consistent with the status incumbent on both Florida and Louisiana as each transitioned into vital components of the antebellum South. The forthright endorsement of slaveholding served as a primary determinant guiding the course of economic and political development. Much like the entire history of that portion of modern Louisiana that was once a part of Florida, the 1810 Constitution, the first such document created within the confines of Louisiana, has largely been overlooked and never acknowledged as such.[28]

Barely seventy-four days after securing independence, and much to the horror of most of the officials of the new nation, in December 1810, American infantry supported by a powerful naval flotilla descended on West Florida. As the main body of the West Florida "army" continued the campaign to secure Mobile, American troops forced the capitulation of the garrison at St. Francisville as well as the fort at Baton Rouge. Captain John Shaw, in command of the gunboat flotilla that supported the American infantry as they surrounded the fort reported, "At 1:30 PM the gunboats dropped down and anchored under the Battery. At 3:00 PM the governor, escorted by a body of cavalry and accompanied by 300 troops marched into the fort and hoisted our standard, so ended the Florida Republic." Faced with overwhelming might, and eager to avoid a massacre, the garrison within the fort requested only that the Lone Star flag of the republic be respected as it was lowered.[29]

Thus ended the ambitious enterprise that in little more than two months had created a government guided by a constitution that reflected the curious status of the residents and their cause. Bitterness at the abrupt derailment of their project nonetheless remained. Territorial Governor William C. C. Claiborne advised US Secretary of State Robert Smith, "There is a dissatisfied party, and one also that is disaffected to the American government. The late change in affairs gave no satisfaction to some individuals. There are others who are hand and heart devoted to British interests, and whenever the occasion favors it, by their acts, evince their dislike of American institutions." Convention delegate Frederick Kimball summarized the anger with which many residents viewed the supplanting of their own constitution with that of the United States by insisting that most residents preferred the territory be returned to Spain if it could not remain independent. In an angry letter to an out-of-state relative, Kimball seethed, "I wish I had command of the fort when Claiborne arrived and that I had known as much as I do now, I certainly would have blown him out of the river."[30]

Analysis of the 1810 Constitution of the fledgling State of Florida reminds us that unlike the comparatively homogenous Atlantic Seaboard states, the Gulf South territories remained a chaotic cauldron of cultural and political diversity that impacted legal development. The 1810 Constitution reflected that diversity, just as it manifested the need to be appealing to all free inhabitants and to rapidly establish a respected system of law and order. Its eventual replacement, the Louisiana Constitution of 1812, proved far less diverse in historical antecedents, less inclusive in efforts to attract broad support, and an outright failure in its ability to offer peace and stability to the residents. Successive Louisiana constitutions in 1845, 1852, and into the postbellum era likewise failed to embrace the lessons of the 1810 Constitution as the unparalleled violence and social instability of the late nineteenth century in the Florida parishes of Louisiana abundantly demonstrate.

Notes

1 Stanley Arthur, *The Story of the West Florida Rebellion* (Baton Rouge, LA: Claitors Publishing, 1975), 89–108; Isaac Cox, *The West Florida Controversy: A Study in American Diplomacy* (Baltimore: Johns Hopkins Press, 1918), 493–500; Cody Scallions, "The Rise and Fall of the Original Lone Star State: Infant American Imperialism Ascendant in West Florida," *Florida Historical Quarterly* 90, no. 2 (Fall, 2011): 194–197; Samuel C. Hyde, *Pistols and Politics: Feuds, Factions, and the Struggle for Order in Louisiana's Florida Parishes, 1810–1935* (Baton Rouge: Louisiana State University Press, 2018) 18–21.

2 William C. C. Claiborne to Robert Smith, December 7, 1810, in Dunbar Rowland, ed., *Official Letter Books of W. C. C. Claiborne, 1801–1816*, 6 vols. (Jackson, MS, 1917), 5: 46–50, hereafter cited as *Official Letter Books*; David Holmes to Robert Smith, January 1, 1811, in Clarence E. Carter, ed., *The Territorial Papers of the Unit-*

ed States, 28 vols. (Washington, DC, 1934–1962), 9: 909–14, hereafter cited as *The Territorial Papers;* Hyde, *Pistols and Politics, 18–21.*

3 Cox, *The West Florida Controversy,* 152–68; Arthur, *The Story of the West Florida Rebellion,* 25–29; Andrew McMichael, "The Kemper Rebellion: Filibustering and Resident Anglo-American Loyalty in Spanish West Florida," *Louisiana History* 43, no. 2 (2002): 147–65.

4 *New England Palladium,* September 18, 1804; Cox, *The West Florida Controversy,* 152–67; Sidney J. Aucoin, "The Political Career of Isaac Johnson, Governor of Louisiana 1846–1850," *Louisiana Historical Quarterly* 28 (1945): 941–44; Samuel C. Hyde, "Setting a Precedent for Regional Revolution: The West Florida Revolt Considered," *The Florida Historical Quarterly* 90 (Fall: 2011): 123–24.

5 David Holmes to Robert Smith, January 1, 1811; Carter, *The Territorial Papers,* 9: 909–14; Frederick Kimball to Dear Nephew, August 15, 1806, and Kimball to Dear Friends, March 5, 1811, in Frederick Kimball Letters, Louisiana and Lower Mississippi Valley Collection, Louisiana State University, Baton Rouge, LA, hereafter cited as LLMVC.

6 Cox, *The West Florida Controversy,* 412; Hyde, *Pistols and Politics,* 12–13, 18–22.

7 The Convention of the State of West Florida to His Excellency the Governor of the Territory of Orleans, Baton Rouge, LA., September 29, 1810, copy maintained in Center for Southeast Louisiana Studies, Southeastern Louisiana University, Hammond, LA., hereafter referenced as CSLS; *Virginia Argus,* November 27, 1810; John Ballinger to Harry Toulmin, November 3, 1810, James Madison Papers, Library of Congress, hereafter referenced as LOC; William C. Davis, *The Rogue Republic: How Would-Be Patriots Waged the Shortest Revolution in American History* (New York, 2011), 180–87. Not only did the Lone Star flag of West Florida wave over Louisiana's Florida parishes twenty-six years prior to the raising of the Zavala Lone Star flag over Texas, many of the men responsible for the West Florida Revolt later migrated to Texas and influenced the rising there; see Colin Mathison, "A Tale of Two Republics, West Florida, Texas, and the American Quest for Continental Dominance," unpublished M.A. thesis, Southeastern Louisiana University, 2021, copy available CSLS.

8 *Virginia Argus,* November 27, 1810; James A. Padgett, ed., "The West Florida Rebellion of 1810, as Told in the Letters of John Rhea, Fulwar Skipwith, Reuben Kemper, and Others," *Louisiana Historical Quarterly* 21 (1938): 76–202; *Journal of the Convention and Legislature of the State of West Florida,* 2 vols., 1810, The West Florida Collection (hereafter referred to as *Journal of the Convention*), LOC.

9 John Rhea to David Holmes, September 24, 1810, and entry dated September 26, 1810, both in *Journal of the Convention,* LOC; Boston, *Independent Chronicle,* November 1, 1810.

10 *Journal of the Convention,* September 26, 1810, LOC.

11 *Journal of the Convention,* October 8 and 27, 1810, LOC; *Fourth Census of the United States, Manuscript, 1820, Population Schedules,* Feliciana and St. Helena Parishes, Film No. 163.

12 Washington, DC, *National Intelligencer,* December 27, 1810; William Claiborne to Robert Smith, December 1, 1810, *Official Letter Books;* Davis, *The Rogue Republic,* 221–23, 235, 241; Arthur, *The Story of the West Florida Rebellion,* 134–35; *Journal of the Convention,* September 27, 1810, LOC; William S. Belko, "The Origins of the Monroe Doctrine Revisited: The Madison Administration, the West Florida Revolt, and the Origins of the No Transfer Policy," *Florida Historical Quarterly* 90 (2011): 175–80.

13 Constitution or Form of Government of the State of Florida, Preamble and Sections 1–3, copy maintained in CSLS.

14 Constitution or Form of Government of the State of Florida, Preamble and Sections 1–3, copy maintained in CSLS.

15 Constitution or Form of Government of the State of Florida, Sections 3 and 15; Horst Dippel, ed., *Constitutional Documents of the United States of America, 1776–1860* (Berlin: Walter deGruyter, 2006).

16 For discussion of the antebellum constitutions of Louisiana see Hyde, *Pistols and Politics,* 46–47, 58–60.

17 Constitution or Form of Government of the State of Florida, Article I, Sections 7–10.

18 Constitution or Form of Government of the State of Florida, Article I, Section 25. As with other sections of the 1810 Constitution, the emphasis on arts and sciences remained consistent with other constitutions emerging in the same era. For example, see Article IV, Section 13, 1798 State of Georgia Constitution.

19 Constitution or Form of Government of the State of Florida, Article II, Sections 1–5.

20 Constitution or Form of Government of the State of Florida, Article III, Sections 3–4; Joan E. Jacoby, *The American Prosecutor: A Search for Identity* (New York: D. C. Heath, 1980).

21 Constitution or Form of Government of the State of Florida, Article IV; Henry Dart, ed., "Documents Covering Royal Land Grants and Other Transactions on the Mississippi and Amite Rivers During the English Rule," *Louisiana Historical Quarterly* XII (1929): 638.

22 John H. Napier, *Lower Pearl River's Piney Woods: Its Land and People* (Oxford, MS: Center for Southern Culture/University Press of Mississippi, 1985), 31; James Peacock, "Historical and Statistical Sketches of Louisiana," *DeBow's Review* XI (1851): 264–65; Thomas D. Clark, "The Piney Woods and the Cutting Edge of the Lingering Southern Frontier," in Noel Polk, ed., *Mississippi's Piney Woods: A Human Perspective* (Jackson: University of Mississippi Press, 1985), 64.

23 Constitution or Form of Government of the State of Florida, Article IV, Sections 1–3.

24 The concluding language in Section 1 of Article V again reveals the document's consistency with other constitutions in states of the slaveholding South such as the Kentucky Constitution of 1799 and the Alabama Constitution of 1819.

25 Constitution of Form of Government of the State of Florida, Article VII; *Fourth Census of the United States, Manuscript, 1820, Population Schedules,* Feliciana, St. Helena, East Baton Rouge, Film no. 163.

26 Constitution or Form of Government of the State of Florida, Schedule; Fourth Census of the United States, Manuscript, 1820, Population Schedules, Feliciana, St. Helena, East Baton Rouge, St. Tammany, and Washington, Film No. 163; Virginia Argus, November 27, 1810.
27 Harry Toulmin to James Madison, November 28 and December 6, 1810, "Petition of Joseph Kennedy for Writ of Habeas Corpus," December 1, 1810, all in Carter, ed., *The Territorial Papers* 4: 140–43; Sterling Dupree to Reuben Kemper and John Gray to Kemper, both November 18, 1810, in James A. Padgett, ed., "The West Florida Rebellion of 1810, as Told in the Letters of John Rhea, Fulwar Skipwith, Reuben Kemper, and Others," *Louisiana Historical Quarterly* 21, (1938): 76–202; *Journal of the Convention*, LOC.
28 Alden Powell, *A History of Louisiana Constitutions* (Baton Rouge: Louisiana State University Press, 1954); Cecil Morgan, ed., *The First Constitution of Louisiana*, reprint (Baton Rouge: Louisiana State University Press, 1975).
29 John Shaw to Honorable T. Hamilton, January 3, 1811, and Shaw to Lt. George Merrill, December 30, 1810, in John Shaw Letter book, CSLS; William C. C. Claiborne to Robert Smith, December 12, 1810, Rowland, *Official Letter Books,* 5: 53–56; David Holmes to Robert Smith, January 1, 1811, Carter, *The Territorial Papers*, 9: 913.
30 William C. C. Claiborne to Robert Smith, December 17, 1810, Rowland, *Official Letter Books,* 5: 56–58; Frederick Kimball to Dear Andrew, May 11, 1811, in Frederick Kimball Letters, LLMVC; John Shaw to Thomas Cunningham, March 19, 1811, in John Shaw Letter book, CSLS; Josiah Lawton to My Dear and Honored Sir, March 10, 1811, Josiah Lawton Letters, LLMVC.

2

The Patriot Constitution and International Constitution-Making

M.C. Mirow

Constitutions have been essential documents in the structure and function of the United States since independence.[1] Throughout the country's history, groups have successfully and unsuccessfully turned to constitutions to define their political vision and community.[2] While structuring government and establishing rights were and are central constitutional functions, scholars have increasingly noted the international dimension of constitutions and related documents.[3] Constitutions speak internationally. This function is the central aspect of a newly found constitutional text in the history of American constitutionalism, the Patriot Constitution.

In 1812, the "Patriots," military adventurers from Georgia, with a few residents of East Florida, then part of Spain, invaded East Florida with the hope of annexing it to the United States.[4] Because the province was part of the Spanish empire and because Spain and the United States were at peace, direct occupation by a military force or by populating the area with settlers from the United States could not accomplish the annexation.[5] A pretextual revolution of the Spanish population, subsequently recognized by the United States, would be necessary.[6] General George Mathews and John Houston McIntosh led the Patriots in the revolutionary process, which included the promulgation of a Patriot Constitution on July 17, 1812, to advance their aim of annexing East Florida to the United States.[7] The Patriot Constitution of 1812 was a product of this desire to shift territory from Spain to the United States during a complex period of imperial interaction along the southern border of the United States.

This chapter explores three aspects of the Patriot Constitution through the concepts of pretext, text, and context. Part I of this chapter discusses the pretext and actions needed for the United States to obtain East Florida and sets the background for drafting and promulgating the constitution. Part II analyzes the text of the Patriot Constitution. Part III contextualizes the Patriot Constitution in light of its intended transitional nature and the underlying international forces behind early nineteenth-century constitutions.

Between 1810 and 1814, under President James Madison, the United States asserted claims for the annexation of the Spanish province of East Florida.[8] In the United States, this project was supported by popular sentiment and by several intertwined economic, political, and military considerations.[9] One claim the United States asserted against Spain stemmed from its assistance to French privateers as they brought US ships into neutral Spanish ports during the 1790s.[10] With a peace concluded with France, the United States maintained this spoliation claim, valued between $5 million and $15 million, against Spain and specifically against East Florida.[11] Spain reticently admitted this claim, and the United States asserted that it held some sort of security interest in East Florida for this unpaid amount, which was to be satisfied before Spain transferred the region to any other country.[12] An additional claim arose from direct seizures of US ships by Spain.[13] There was also a US grievance against Spain from Spain's suspension of US rights of deposit at New Orleans in 1802, shortly after Spain secretly retroceded Louisiana to France in 1800.[14] This Spanish action damaged US commercial interests.[15] Secretary of State James Monroe held a lien against East Florida for these damages and asserted that they exceeded the value of the entire region.[16] On January 15, 1811, the US Congress passed a "No Transfer Resolution" asserting that the United States would not acquiesce in an attempt by Spain to transfer its American territory to other European powers.[17]

Under existing international law, such implied liens against East Florida may have served as justification for seizing East Florida under the "doctrine of attachment and reprisal."[18] Despite the availability of this remedy and although he was keenly aware of the constraints of international law, President Madison chose to use the outstanding claims against Spain differently.[19] Security and military considerations were added to these economic claims.[20] From the US perspective, Spain had manipulated Creek and Seminole people to attack and raid Georgians, and the United States sought to remove Spaniards and Indians in a concerted effort to secure its southern border.[21] The example of Spain, in which regiments of black militias were common, threatened the power structure that maintained slavery in the US South.[22]

Direct, purposeful occupation of the region was hindered by the Treaty of San Lorenzo (the "Pinckney Treaty") between Spain and the United States, signed in 1795, and later by the military pressures on the United States during the War of 1812.[23] Even before the War of 1812, President Madison sought congressional approval to annex East Florida.[24] In 1811, a secret act of Congress approved the US occupation of Florida east of the Perdido River under one of two circumstances: (1) when local authorities turned the region over to the United States, or (2) when the United States had to take the region to ensure it was not seized by a foreign power.[25] The Patriots latched on to the first justification and attempted to establish a duly constituted local authority that would almost simultaneously rebel against Spain and cede the region to the United States.[26] Direct action by the Patriots, with or without the clear sanction of the United States, was needed to obtain East Florida for the United States after "a decade of overtures, negotiations, and threats to Spain."[27]

Indeed, breaking off a portion of Spain and annexing it to the United States was not without recent precedent. Events in West Florida just two years earlier might have served as a model for President Madison and General George Mathews.[28] Stagg writes that although this process may have been in Mathews's mind as he interpreted his instructions, "Madison, in the summer of 1810, devised a separate policy for East Florida, . . . which the State Department, through the agency of Senator William Harris Crawford of Georgia, entrusted to Mathews."[29] This was a period of significant political movement and change on the southern border of the United States, and the contemporary political, military, and international events in and around West Florida would have been widely known and must have served as models for action in the southern region.[30]

Patriot leaders General George Mathews—who had gathered support from President Madison—and John Houston McIntosh recruited men and planned the expedition.[31] Before leading the Patriots, Mathews had served in the Georgia Assembly and as governor of Georgia.[32] John Houston McIntosh was the owner of a large plantation near St. Marys, Georgia, on the border of Georgia and East Florida, and held nearly 250 enslaved humans.[33] McIntosh was an educated, well-respected plantation owner with estates in Georgia and Florida who lived in East Florida under the Spanish crown.[34] His interests aligned with those of General Mathews, and McIntosh sought to have the Patriots recognized as a "constituted local authority" capable of ceding control of the region to the United States.[35] It turned out to be difficult to recruit leading citizens of Spanish East Florida for the enterprise. Many potential recruits had strong economic, religious, or social ties to established Spanish structures and rule.[36] Georgians proved to be more willing to take the risks presented for the promised rewards of land and government positions.[37] By March 1812, there were about 125 Patriots, recruited mostly from Georgia.[38]

Every rebellion or revolution deserves a declaration. The Patriots drafted theirs at Rose's Bluff on the southern bank—the Spanish side—of the St. Marys River on March 13, 1812.[39] The content of the Patriot Manifesto, or the Patriot Declaration of Independence, as it has come to be known, can only be established through reports in letters.[40] On March 14, 1812, the Patriot Manifesto was read to the Patriots.[41] It criticized Spanish rule and promised lands to its adherents.[42] Because the Patriot Manifesto and the Patriot Articles of Cession were drafted within days of each other,[43] it is likely that their contents were similar, if not identical. By March 21, 1812, Mathews sent a complete draft of the Patriot Articles of Cession and an accompanying letter of explanation to US Secretary of State James Monroe.[44] The letter sought Monroe's approval of the Articles of Cession drafted by Mathews and requested US military assistance to hold the Patriots' gains.[45] Mathews attempted to explain several provisions of the Articles of Cession to Monroe, especially those articles related to maintaining East Florida ports open to free trade until May 1813 and to ousting Spain from Pensacola and Mobile.[46]

On March 17, 1812, under the protection of US Navy gunboats, the Patriots, now a group of gun-toting settlers, crossed the international border of the St. Marys River from Georgia, United States, into East Florida, Spain.[47] Under the threat of Commodore Campbell's US gunboats and outnumbered nearly five to one, Lieutenant Justo Lopez surrendered Fernandina to Lodowick Ashley, and the Patriot flag was raised.[48] The following day, just as planned, McIntosh offered to cede coastal Amelia Island and the Spanish town of Fernandina to General Mathews, who accepted it for the United States.[49] The Patriot standard was immediately replaced with the US flag.[50]

After occupying Fernandina and Amelia Island, General Mathews pressed south toward St. Augustine, the jewel of East Florida.[51] Families and plantation owners between Fernandina and St. Augustine had little choice but to support the Patriots, and slightly more than a hundred residents of Spanish East Florida joined the Patriot cause.[52] On March 26, 1812, Mathews gave Governor Estrada of St. Augustine a similar ultimatum to that provision proffered at Fernandina.[53] A summary of the Patriot Articles of Cession was incorporated in the formal demand for surrender of St. Augustine, the Spanish capital of East Florida.[54]

Before Mathews could take action against St. Augustine, however, Governor Estrada learned that the United States no longer supported Mathews.[55] On April 4, General Mathews was rebuked by Monroe; his efforts were not authorized by US law and his powers were later revoked immediately on receipt of the letter on May 9, 1812.[56] Mathews's grandiose plans to press on from a captured St. Augustine to Mobile and Pensacola and disrupt Spanish control of West Florida were an essential element in Madison's decision to withdraw US support from the Patriots.[57] Shortly afterward, Governor David Brydie Mitchell of Georgia was put in control of East Florida under the United States to negotiate a peaceful resolution with Spain.[58] Nonetheless, Mitchell continued US occupation of East Florida and tangentially supported the Patriots.[59]

On June 18, 1812, the United States declared war on Great Britain, and this new political and military situation only strengthened calls for greater US control in the Floridas.[60] By July 1812, the siege of St. Augustine was at a standstill.[61] About 400 US troops under Lieutenant Colonel Smith were stationed outside the city, and Governor Kindelán had about 800 within the most impressive military structure in the province, the Castillo de San Marcos adjacent to the city.[62]

This was not a propitious moment to promulgate a constitution. Until then, as a military force, the Patriots had little need of governmental structure. Patriot proclamations and statements bore signatures of ad hoc officers.[63] By mid-July 1812, the situation had changed dramatically. General Mathews no longer had credible US support, the United States had declared war against Great Britain, and the Castillo de San Marcos was under new command with more Spanish troops.

Under these new conditions, on July 10, 1812, the Patriots sought to reassert their claims to legitimacy and established a government for East Florida.[64] John Houston McIntosh, as president, led an assembly of fifteen men to draft a document that expressed the Patriots' disenchantment with Spain and their desire for political independence.[65] William Hamilton served as secretary; Lodowick Ashley, William Craig, and Buckner Harris were notable members of the convention.[66] The Patriot Constitution was passed on July 17, 1812.[67]

The following week, on July 25, 1812, a plebiscite selected McIntosh as "director of East Florida" and fifteen men were selected to serve on the legislative council, the legislative body under the constitution.[68] The new government held its first session the next day.[69] On July 30, 1812, Director McIntosh wrote President Madison and Secretary of State Monroe requesting formal recognition of the country of East Florida.[70] None was forthcoming, and local relations between the Patriots and US forces became tense.[71] US forces did as much as possible to avoid recognizing the Patriots as an authority acting in East Florida.[72]

Official US claims to East Florida lost ground in Washington. On February 12, 1813, an act of Congress did not, as some hoped, provide support for military action against Spanish East Florida.[73] About a month later, on March 7, 1813, Spain extended a pardon to Patriot collaborators if they returned to live as loyal subjects.[74] And over the preceding few months, the Patriot cause and their number had diminished significantly.[75] In light of the pending withdrawal of the United States, Buckner Harris, president of the Legislative Council of the Territory of East Florida, and the remaining Patriots defended their claim to East Florida.[76] John Houston McIntosh was given dictatorial powers to manage financial and political affairs.[77] The Patriots ineffectively raised concerns for the safety and the property of their supporters.[78] Toward the end of April 1813, General Pinckney effected the process for a US evacuation of East Florida.[79] East Florida surged into its new Spanish constitutional regime under the Constitution of Cádiz after it was promulgated in St. Augustine on October 17, 1812, and in Fernandina on May 8, 1813.[80] With the US withdrawal, John Houston McIntosh left East Florida through St. Marys and pressed his claims for damages against the United States.[81] He returned to St. Marys in September 1813 and left public life.[82]

The Patriots soon disintegrated. A splinter group of Patriots unsuccessfully attempted to create a separate territory in the Alachua District near present-day Gainesville.[83] In April 1814, the United States disavowed recognition of the Patriots' claim in Alachua, and their Director Buckner Harris was killed by Spanish-backed Seminoles on May 5, 1814, effectively ending any chances for the Patriots and their Republic of East Florida.[84]

The Patriot Constitution is a simply constructed document of approximately 2,600 words. It consists of a preamble, three articles subdivided into paragraphs by ordinal numbers, and a closing paragraph.[85] The recitations in the preamble claimed to speak for "the people of the province of East Florida" and compared the difficulty of living under Spanish rule with the better conditions found in the United States.[86] Religious differences were recited; Patriots did not "idolize[] their priest[s]," a clear criticism of Spanish-American Roman Catholicism.[87] Spanish maladministration and apparent concern about the instability of Spain, however, formed the central complaint.[88] Spain was blamed for oppressive laws and tyrannical and corrupt local royal officials.[89] The governor and, implicitly, the governor's power over and involvement with judicial affairs—no doubt a clear lack of separation of powers in the mind of the Patriots—were important elements averred by the revolutionaries.[90] The Patriots applauded the then-recent movements toward independence in South America and expressed their worry that East Florida would be sold to Great Britain, then an active belligerent against the United States.[91] Revolution and independence, as required for legal cession to the United States, were the only courses of action left to these inhabitants, who wished to be "citizens of a Territory of the United States."[92]

After separating the powers of government into executive, legislative, and judicial branches, article I addressed the legislative power institutionalized through the Legislative Council of East Florida.[93] The legislative council was a fifteen-member body composed of elected free, white men over the age of twenty-one with property.[94] There were additional requirements of residency and active participation in the revolution for soldiers to be members of the council.[95] Like the constitution, the legislative council was a transitional institution that would cease on the territory's incorporation into the United States.[96] The council was empowered to make laws, to establish courts, to appoint officials, to tax and to spend, and to serve as a court of impeachment.[97] The council also was granted the power to confirm resolutions and ordinances established before its existence and to establish compensation for officers.[98]

Article II of the constitution established the executive under a director, again a transitional officer, "until this Country shall be received by the United States."[99] The director had to have played an active part in the revolution, to be at least thirty years old, and to possess land and other property.[100] If the director was unable to serve, the president of the legislative council would exercise executive powers.[101] The director had the power of reprieve, of calling elections, of convening the legislative council, and of reviewing legislation.[102]

Article III is not about the judiciary but contains miscellaneous provisions. The judicial power under the Patriot Constitution was relegated to one paragraph in article I that gave the legislative council the power to create courts.[103] In addition to hearing and trying all manner of actions, the courts were given the power to execute their judgments and to administer oaths.[104] Instead of incorporating English common law, as one might expect, article III, subsection 1, stating that Georgia law was known best by the inhabitants of East Florida, specifically received the laws of Georgia and the United States.[105] This was, of course, a self-serving fiction. It was the Patriots and their leaders who were most familiar with Georgia law. This provision provided a quiet yet effective method to ensure that laws recognizing and enforcing slavery in Georgia and the United States would become the laws of East Florida.[106]

The concluding paragraph stated that the Patriot Constitution established a government while reiterating that the government was temporary and was "intended to exist and be in operation only until the United States shall acknowledge this Territory as part of the United States."[107] With cession to the United States as its primary goal, the Patriot Constitution was a temporary governing document that contained many structural and institutional gaps. The constitution made reference to elections for members of the legislative council and director, but provided no mechanism for such elections.[108] The Patriot Constitution had no enumeration of rights, evidently piggybacking on its incorporation of Georgia and US law for such important features of constitutional government.[109] Nonetheless, the drafters of the Patriot Constitution thought some rights had to be expressed in the text. The constitution provided for trial by judge and for freedom of the press in one article under the articles dealing with the executive.[110] Both manuscript versions of the Patriot Constitution use the expression "trial by judge" rather than the common "trial by jury," as found in the Georgia constitutions.[111] This was either a scribal error or it reveals the Patriots' realization that Patriot judicial institutions would not function long enough to establish a mechanism for juries or their frustration with the Spanish legal process, in which the governor often sat as the judge of the tribunal. Again, following the Georgia constitutions, the writ of habeas corpus was specifically listed as a right belonging to "all persons."[112] The whole document has a haphazard organization and a contingent quality that fit the overall plan of a temporary and transitional government. It contained minimal expectations.

The transitory nature of the document is evident throughout its provisions. Even the name of the new entity created by the Patriot Constitution varied within the text. At some places the newly independent state was named a "Province" and in other places a "Territory."[113] The text of the constitution referred only twice to East Florida as a "country."[114] Indeed, the ambiguity of the precise nature of the entity created was revealed in one manuscript of the Patriot Constitution where the word "country" was struck out and replaced with "territory."[115] Not once does the Patriot Constitution use the appellation "Republic of East Florida," which was used by the Patriots elsewhere. By adopting the term used by the United States for regions that were part of it before gaining statehood, the constitution's use of the term "territory" was consistent with the Patriots' goal of annexation by the United States and reinforced the transitory nature of the government established under the constitution.[116]

There is similar imprecision in terminology elsewhere in the text. For example, the legislative power is usually labeled the legislative council, yet one article states that laws will govern "until altered by Legislative Authority."[117] Even the choice of the term "Legislative Council" seems to have been specifically pointed toward the incorporation of the territory into the United States, as the United States used this term for legislative bodies within US territories. The term "Legislative Council" was in fact the term adopted for the legislative body of the Territory of Florida in 1822.[118] The concluding passages of the constitution reiterate the transitory nature of the constitution and its government. The government was intended "to exist and be in operation only until the United States shall acknowledge this Territory as part of the United States," and the constitutional delegates had confidence that the United States would ratify the Treaty of Cession.[119] Several provisions called for the terms of office or provisions to run only until the territory became part of the United States. The legislative council would cease to exist on the territory's joining the United States.[120] The chief executive officer of the territory, the director, was to hold office "until this Country shall be received by the United States."[121] Those impeached and removed from office under the Patriot Constitution might still be tried under the laws of the United States.[122] Thus, the Patriot Constitution employed a variety of terms to signal its instrumental and transitory nature as a document leading to annexation by the United States.

As a transitional document, the Patriot Constitution sought to shift sovereignty from Spain to the United States. Georgia, on the border with East Florida and the home of most of the Patriots, had a special status. George Mathews had served as governor of Georgia in three terms from 1787 to 1788 and from 1793 to 1796.[123] It is likely that when he turned to the task of reviewing constitutional language for East Florida, he gravitated toward the language of the Georgian constitutions. As governor in Georgia during these years, Mathews would have observed firsthand the functioning of the state under the Georgia Constitution of 1789.[124] It also appears that those charged with preparing the Patriot Constitution made substantial use of the

Georgia Constitution of 1798. McIntosh, a former member of the constitutional convention that drafted the Georgia Constitution of 1798, was directly involved in the preparation of the Patriot Constitution.[125] And drafters are not ones for reinventing the wheel, or in this case, a constitution.

The text of the Patriot Constitution was prepared from provisions of the Georgia Constitutions of 1789 and 1798, with several provisions being drafted specifically to meet the needs of the moment. The Patriot Constitution's borrowing of constitutional provisions was consistent with the unusual status of the Patriot Constitution as an admittedly transitional document and one that incorporated Georgia and US law when consistent with the Patriot Constitution.[126] Of the Patriot Constitution's twenty-nine articles, twenty either draw their inspiration from the Georgia Constitutions of 1789 and 1798, adopt and modify the language of these constitutions, or repeat their language verbatim. Table 2.1 notes the correspondence of the Patriot Constitution's provisions with those of the Georgia constitutions.

The table reveals that the Patriot Constitution borrowed heavily in structure and substance from the Georgia Constitution of 1798 and, to a slightly lesser extent, from the similar Georgia Constitution of 1789, especially in the Patriot Constitution's articles setting out the legislative and executive functions. As an example, two articles from the Patriot Constitution and the Georgia Constitution of 1798 may be compared. The Patriot Constitution provided the director with the following power:

> He shall issue writs of Election to fill all vacancies that may happen in the Legislative Council; & shall have power to convene the Legislative Council on extraordinary occasions, And shall give them from time to time information of the state of the Territory & recommend to their consideration such measures as he may deem necessary & expedient.[127]

The Georgia Constitution of 1798 stated of the governor:

> He shall issue writs of election to fill up all vacancies that happen in the senate or house of representatives; and shall have power to convene the general assembly on extraordinary occasions; and shall give them, from time to time, information of the state of the republic, and recommend to their consideration such measures as he may deem necessary and expedient.[128]

Table 2.1. The Patriot (1812) and Georgia (1789 and 1798) Constitutions

Patriot Constitution	Georgia Constitution	Subject of Article
Art. I, § 1	Art. I, § 1 (1798)	separation of powers
Art. I, § 2	Art. I, § 2 (1798)	composition of legislature
Art. I, § 3	Art. I, § 2 (1789) Art. I, § 3 (1798)	election and term of legislators
Art. I, § 4	Art. IV, § 1 (1798)	qualification to vote
Art. I, § 6	Art. I, 7 (1798)	territorial apportionment of legislators
Art. I, § 10	Art. III, § 1 (1798)	erecting courts
Art. I, § 11	Art. I, § 16 (1789) Art. I, § 22 (1798)	legislative powers
Art. I, § 12	Art. I, § 5 (1789)	impeachment of officers
Art. I, § 13	Art. I, § 4 (1789) Art. I, § 13 (1789) Art. I, § 13 (1798)	judge of elections to legislature and power to make internal rules
Art. II, § 1	Arts. II, §§ 1–2 (1789) Arts. II, §§ 1–2 (1798)	election and term of executive office, director or governor
Art. II, § 2	Art. II, § 3 (1789) Art. II, § 4 (1798)	qualification to serve as executive office
Art. II, § 3	Art. II, § 4 (1789) Art. II, § 4 (1798)	succession of executive office on death
Art. II, § 4	Arts. II, §§ 6–7 (1789) Arts. II, §§ 6–7 (1798)	executive official as commander in chief and power to pardon
Art. II, § 5	Art. II, § 8 (1789) Art. II, § 8 (1798)	power to convene legislature
Art. II, § 6	Art. II, § 10 (1789) Art. II, § 10 (1798)	veto power and two-thirds override
Art. II, § 7	Art. II, § 11 (1789) Art. II, § 13 (1798)	great seal of the territory or state
Art. II, § 9	Art. IV, § 3 (1789) Art. II, § 9 (1798)	trial by judge and freedom of the press
Art. II, § 10	Art. IV, § 3 (1789) Art. IV, § 9 (1798)	habeas corpus
Art. III, § 3	Art. I, § 20 (1798)	convicts not eligible for public office

The third article of the Patriot Constitution deviates substantially from the Georgia models because the Patriots did not see the need to create a lasting system of courts as covered by the Georgia constitutions.

The most interesting articles are those original provisions that were created out of whole cloth to meet the transitional and international demands of the moment. These provisions addressed the transitional concerns of ceding East Florida to the United States and thus operated on an international level. The Patriot Constitution adopted a rhetoric of revolution. The Patriots did not admit to being an invading group of Georgians, but pretended to be Spanish subjects justly casting away the yoke of oppressive Spanish domination.[129] They sought to repeat the paradigm of 1776. Thus, the Patriot Constitution spoke of revolution. The franchise was limited to "free white m[e]n . . . and every soldier who [had] taken an active part in our Revolution."[130] Similar qualifications were required for membership in the legislative council or for holding the office of director.[131] Citizenship was extended to volunteers who engaged in the revolution.[132] Thus, the Patriot Constitution tied valid political action to participation in a "revolution" that defined the polity and provided a path to the constitution.[133] The Patriots asserted that they were part of a larger international movement of necessary revolution against Spain. Thus, the Patriots declared themselves "free and independent" with the further and unique hope expressed in a constitution to "become a Territory and a Component part of the Government of the United States."[134] It was only in the interim period of independence before cession to the United States that some government of the territory was needed and therefore expressed in the articles of the Patriot Constitution.[135]

The constitution served an international purpose and sought to address an international audience, particularly after the United States disavowed General Mathews's actions. The constitution signaled to the United States and to other nations that the Patriots had established some form of a legally cognizable international entity, even if the Patriot Constitution could not come to consistent terminology about what it had in fact created. As Stagg notes on this point, "In March 1812, the Patriots were no more than 'a set of men, in an inchoate state of revolution,' and as such they were not a 'local authority,' whereas they could be so regarded after having 'gone thro[ugh] all the forms by which the U.S. themselves have arrived at a complete state of organization.'"[136]

In this regard, the Patriot Constitution serves as an example of the international dimension of American constitution-making recently explored in the work of David Golove and Daniel Hulsebosch.[137] The Patriot Constitution reached the US federal government when the United States itself was still constructing and negotiating the international effects of its own Constitution.[138] Hulsebosch asserts that "American constitution-making began as an international process. All the American constitutions of the Founding Era, state and federal, were made with foreign, as well as domestic, audiences in mind."[139] The expectation for a "revolutionary portfolio" of related constitutional and international documents essential to international support for the United States during its founding helps explain the collection of documents McIntosh used to promote his international goals of East Floridian independence from Spain and subsequent cession to the United States.[140] The Patriot Constitution may be read as a constituent part of a package of Patriot revolutionary documents directed toward several audiences on several levels, from local property owners (including those claiming property in enslaved human beings) to international actors and heads of state. Similar to the portfolio of documents Americans unwrapped when seeking European help, the Patriots constructed their own portfolio to bolster recognition of independence, legal statehood, and commercial trustworthiness.[141] The early US portfolio consisted of early state constitutions, the Declaration of Independence, the Articles of Confederation, and the Model Treaty of commerce.[142] The Patriot portfolio consisted of the Patriot Manifesto (Declaration of Independence), the Patriot Constitution, and the Patriot Articles of Cession. As mentioned previously, we know little about the Patriot Manifesto, although it seems likely the language found in the preamble of the Patriot Constitution reflected the sentiments that such a declaration contained. Mathews stated that he sent a copy of the "Declaration of Independence" and a "certified copy of an original declaration" to James Monroe on April 16, 1812.[143]

This indicates that Mathews used a separate document other than the constitution, sometimes called the Manifesto and sometimes called the Declaration of Independence, in his international dealings with the United States. As Hulsebosch notes, declarations of independence set the stage for characterizing armed conflict under international law.[144] He further observes that declarations of independence, like declarations of war, have a typical structure of setting out grievances recording the patience of the oppressed people, and as a result, justifying a declaration of a change in status. Declarations were one step toward shifting a rebellion to a justified war. A proper war had internationally recognized rules for maintaining neutral trade and for establishing the status of other countries.[145]

If the assertions of the Patriot Manifesto (Declaration of Independence) can be extrapolated from the preamble of the Patriot Constitution, several grievances were averred to justify the Patriot revolution. The Patriots claimed an unsupportable bondage under Spain, oppressive Spanish laws, tyrannical rule, corrupt justice, and fears of East Florida being sold to another foreign power.[146] Religious oppression also appeared as a theme, but only secondarily. One portion of the preamble complains that the Patriots saw a common nature in all people and did not "idolize[] their priest[s]," presumably as Roman Catholics did.[147]

The extent of the contemplated religious settlement was expressed only in the Patriot Articles of Cession.[148] One provision of the Patriot Articles of Cession guarantees East Floridians under the United States "the full and free enjoyment of religious toleration either agreeable to the rites of the Roman Catholic Church or any other form of adoration that may suit their conscience."[149] Another portion of the Patriot Articles of Cession guaranteed that priests would continue to enjoy the same subvention they received from Spain for life or as long as they resided in East Florida while performing their religious function.[150] Such concessions to Roman Catholicism were most likely contemplated as necessary appeasements to East Florida's Roman Catholic population despite the Patriots' apparent disdain of Roman Catholicism's links to the Spanish monarchy.

Thus, the Patriot Constitution reflected the Patriots' awareness that documents were needed to establish sufficient international legal personality to engage in cession negotiations with the United States. Decades earlier, American revolutionaries (perhaps among them General George Mathews) knew a constitution was central to claims of independence and international recognition for the United States.[151] As Hulsebosch writes:

> Almost all revolutionaries agreed it was important to latch onto written constitutions as a way to make a claim for nationhood. To act and to be seen as a nation, a polity had to have a constitution, and the brand-new revolutionary states seeking diplomatic relations could not easily make their case based on local scripts of customary or ancient constitutions.[152]

When McIntosh wrote Monroe on July 30, 1812, he explicitly adopted this explanation for the recent promulgation of a constitution, stating:

> Firmly confiding in the assurances and declarations of General Mathews and in the full belief that we and our country want to be taken under the protection of the United States, a temporary form of

Government was adopted merely to prevent confusion and to enable us to make a cession to the United States. This form answered our intention, until lately, when it was thought advisable to establish a more detailed one, lest the first should not be considered as sufficient to authorize a cession.[153]

The challenges were similar, at least from the perspective of a colony seeking not to conquer the imperial power and take over its entire realm but rather to shear off a portion of territory that would be recognized as independent and internationally autonomous. Hulsebosch notes that Adams's solution was a revolutionary portfolio of documents establishing international autonomy.[154] In a move calculated to mirror US independence under the parallel and historically rich title of "Patriot," McIntosh similarly produced documents to effect this surgical excision of sovereignty for a portion of an empire.

Hulsebosch soundly reminds us that commerce and property, in addition to domestic politics and international relations, were essential parts of such portfolios.[155] Just as the US portfolio contained the Model Treaty, the Patriot portfolio contained the Articles of Cession that addressed several aspects of commerce and property related to the transfer of East Florida to the United States. The Model Treaty sought to protect neutral shipping during war and open trade during peace.[156] The Patriot Articles of Cession covered several issues not addressed in the Patriot Constitution, but as part of the Patriot revolutionary portfolio, the Patriot Articles of Cession completed the constitutional package propounded by the Patriots. Issues addressed in the Patriot Articles of Cession included religion, property rights, the transfer of Spanish officials and soldiers to equivalent US positions, shipping, the permission for dissenters from cession to emigrate, planned hostilities against Pensacola and Mobile, and the possibility of East Florida rejoining Spain by majority vote of East Floridians in the future.[157]

The property and trade provisions of the Patriot Articles of Cession reveal the commercial side of the Patriots' revolutionary portfolio. They guaranteed titles obtained from Spain or through processes valid under Spanish law.[158] Licenses to cut timber, an important economic benefit, would be respected until May 1, 1813.[159] The Articles of Cession also made provision for revolutionaries who had not received lands from Spain in the same amount such individuals were expecting from Spain.[160] The trade provisions were even more important from the international standpoint. Subject to ordinarily imposed duties, East Florida would be open to "a liberal intercourse with

Great Britain or any other nation" until May 1, 1813.[161] Property owners wishing to leave East Florida were granted a year to remove their property, including enslaved humans unless going to a free state, and to appoint agents to sell their property.[162]

The Patriot portfolio also recognized the interests that international traders and local property holders asserted over land, trade, and human beings through slavery. The process of shifting East Florida from Spanish to US sovereignty necessarily had to account for foreign owners and actors in the region. As the United States moved toward war with Great Britain in 1812, it recognized the utility of good relations with the British merchants who traded with Indians in the area.[163] These traders had established an extensive network of trading posts, stores, and facilities that extracted substantial wealth from Native communities through the fur and pelt trade.[164] Holding a de facto monopoly on this trade was Panton, Leslie, and Company, whose partners were Scots merchants, including William Panton, John Leslie, and John Forbes.[165] The trading house was known under various combinations of these names at different times and locations.[166] Eschewing political complications in commerce, the Patriots tolerated Forbes's activities as a merchant.[167] Forbes, too, had assurances from Mathews that his company would be protected if East Florida were occupied by the United States.[168] These concerns were directly addressed in the provision of the Articles of Cession addressing free trade.[169]

From the US standpoint, the Patriot Articles of Cession were unexpectedly conciliatory on the subject of trade, especially because Great Britain would be one of the beneficiaries of open ports in US East Florida. Patriot and US interests alike sought to maintain good relations with traders, even British traders such as John Forbes, who could keep the wheels of commerce turning and could ensure relatively peaceful interactions with Native populations.[170] In this light, article IV of the Articles of Cession required that ports of East Florida remain open to Great Britain until at least May 1813. Mathews later argued for May 1814.[171] Stagg observes that the provision would have had a doubly beneficial effect for the Patriots and the cession of East Florida to the United States. First, it would remove the concerns of "local merchants and planters, whose prosperity was heavily dependent on British trade."[172] Second, it would have the practical effects of permitting John Forbes and Company to continue its operations.[173] Protecting the House of Panton and Forbes was also a personal benefit to Mathews, who had sought to purchase land from Forbes.[174]

Thus, the Patriots' revolutionary portfolio addressed the same concerns and topics found in the American revolutionaries' documents. The Patriot Manifesto served as a declaration of independence and set out East Florida as a separate sovereign for purposes of establishing international recognition and appropriate treatment in war. The Patriot Constitution provided internal government and a written document setting out the foreign-relations law of East Florida. The Patriot Articles of Cession addressed important questions of trade, commerce, property, and religion. The East Florida Patriots were following a pattern established by the American Patriots several decades earlier, or, in the words of their chief executive, Director John Houston McIntosh, "as some of their forefathers had done in '76."[175]

Modeling their actions on revolutionary practices at the birth of the United States provided the Patriots with an intellectual structure of "documentary constitutionalism," to use Billias's term.[176] There were, however, additional regional constitutional pressures at play. On March 19, 1812, Spain promulgated the Constitution of Cádiz, which was to serve as the basic text of its constitutional monarchy until 1814 on the Iberian Peninsula and in the Americas, including East Florida.[177] If Spain found a written constitution useful as it faced a French invasion and an absent throne, how much more would this band of a few hundred soldiers and adventurers benefit from written documents? The Patriot revolutionary portfolio, with the Patriot Constitution as its centerpiece, sought to establish the legitimacy of its government in the process of asserting independence and negotiation with the United States. Despite their small numbers, questionable status, and relative legal and political simplicity, the Patriots could not ignore the pressures of the age of constitutions in the Americas.[178] Without a constitution, the Patriots must have felt like an illegitimate actor surrounded by great powers with recently written constitutions. The Patriot Constitution was essential in their international goal of splitting East Florida from Spain and attaching it to the United States.

The Patriot Constitution was the product of the perceived political necessity of justifying the Patriots' military actions with a document that would clothe their conduct in the rhetoric of justified rebellion. The Patriots had first relied only on their Manifesto or Declaration of Independence, but as US support for their enterprise waned and eventually collapsed, the Patriots turned to a fuller expression of their sovereignty and independent political action through a constitution. The Patriot Constitution increased the likelihood that the executive it established would be recognized by officials of other governments, particularly the United States. It sought to transform a group of military adventurers from Georgia into a nation capable of conducting foreign relations.

The Patriot Constitution could only go so far. The preamble of the Patriot Constitution gave a relatively cursory list of grievances against Spain and its tyranny over East Floridians. The Patriots expressed their feelings of bondage, particularly when comparing their lot to citizens of the United States. Spain was divided and under attack and might even offer East Florida up for sale. Without specificity, the Patriots noted Spain's oppressive laws, the tyranny of its governor, and the corruption of its judges. Based on these grievances, the Patriots declared their independence. It was not, however, to be a lasting independence. The Patriots sought to create a transitional territory that would immediately be subsumed into the United States.

The drafters of the Patriot Constitution relied heavily on the Georgia constitutions of 1789 and 1798. Mathews and McIntosh would both have been familiar with these texts, and indeed, the Georgian majority within the Patriots might also have found these provisions comfortably familiar, especially as they related to the legality and regulation of slavery.

The United States is mentioned several times in the Patriot Constitution as the ultimate goal of East Florida's independence, and indeed, the Patriot Constitution claims that the signers wished to be "citizens of a territory of the United States."[179] Despite the sensibilities of the Patriots, political considerations on the part of the United States meant that it was unable to assist the Patriots and their claim of an independent East Florida anxious to join the United States. The greater political structure afforded by the Patriot Constitution was too little and too late.

The Patriot Constitution speaks to broader questions concerning the use and development of constitutions in early nineteenth-century America. Hulsebosch and others have written about packages of documents that serve internal, domestic constitutional aims and external, international goals. The Patriot Manifesto (Declaration of Independence), the Patriot Articles of Cession, and the Patriot Constitution formed a "constitutional portfolio" that reflected the international constitution-making of the period.

Notes

1 This chapter was previously published as M.C. Mirow, "The Patriot Constitution and International Constitution Making," *Texas Review of Law & Politics* 21, no. 3 (September 20, 2017): 477–517. The original article appeared with an appendix of

the text of the Patriot Constitution of 1812. That is missing in this republication as is the one sentence in the introduction that mentions the appendix, which originally followed the article. While the citations and any abbreviations to sources remain as they appear in the original publication, they have been updated with available information.

2 Robert L. Tsai, *America's Forgotten Constitutions: Defiant Visions of Power and Community* (Cambridge: Harvard University Press, 2014), 6–7 (observing that while "[s]ome [constitutions] . . . were embraced by the people[,] . . . [m]ore numerous were constitutions rejected by officials or put into practice incompletely by followers").

3 See George Athan Billias, *American Constitutionalism Heard Round the World, 1776–1989: A Global Perspective* (New York: New York University Press, 2009), xi (arguing that American constitutionalism, expressed in the Constitution, early state constitutions, the Declaration of Independence, the Articles of Confederation, The Federalist, and the Bill of Rights, had [and has] a "substantial and stable" international influence); David M. Golove and Daniel J. Hulsebosch, "A Civilized Nation: The Early American Constitution, the Law of Nations, and the Pursuit of International Recognition," *NYU Law Review* 85 (2010): 932, 934 (arguing that "the United States' founding instrument is best understood, in historical perspective, as a fundamentally international document"); Daniel J. Hulsebosch, "The Revolutionary Portfolio: Constitution-Making and the Wider World in the American Revolution," *Suffolk University Law Review* 47 (2014): 759, 760–61 (observing that "Americans and their historians have long viewed constitution-making in the Founding Era as a local event with global repercussions[,]" when in fact "American constitution-making began as an international process"). See generally David Armitage, *The Declaration of Independence: A Global History* (Cambridge: Harvard University Press, 2007) (discussing global influence on the creation of the Declaration of Independence and the Declaration's influence on the world).

4 See Robin F. A. Fabel and David L. Schafer, "British Rule in the Floridas," in *The History of Florida*, ed. Michael Gannon (Gainesville: University Press of Florida, 2013), 144–46 (explaining that East Florida was then the region roughly corresponding to Florida's peninsula and that the division between East and West Florida was created during Florida's British period, from 1763 to 1783).

5 See James G. Cusick, *The Other War of 1812: The Patriot War and The American Invasion of Spanish East Florida* (Athens: University of Georgia Press, 2003), 3–4 (remarking on President Madison's efforts to acquire East Florida while avoiding open hostilities with Spain).

6 Cusick, *The Other War of 1812*, 4–5.

7 Cusick, *The Other War of 1812*, 4–5.

8 See Rembert W. Patrick, *Florida Fiasco: Rampant Rebels on the Georgia-Florida Border 1810–1815* (Athens: University of Georgia Press, 1954), 1–3 (characterizing President Madison "as anxious to annex these Spanish provinces to the United States").

9 Patrick, *Florida Fiasco*, 1–3.

10 Patrick, *Florida Fiasco*, 20–21.

11 Patrick, *Florida Fiasco*, 20–21.
12 See Patrick, *Florida Fiasco*, 21 (noting that, rejection of the Pinckney Treaty by the Spanish Cortes notwithstanding, the United States held her claims substantiated by the signature of the Spanish foreign minister).
13 Patrick, *Florida Fiasco*, 27.
14 See Patrick, *Florida Fiasco*, 21–22.
15 See Patrick, *Florida Fiasco*, 22 (discussing the negative ramifications of Spain's retrocession of Louisiana to France).
16 Patrick, *Florida Fiasco*, 63.
17 J.C.A. Stagg, *Borderlines in Borderlands: James Madison and the Spanish-American Frontier, 1776–1821* (New Haven: Yale University Press, 2009), 90–91; J.C.A. Stagg, "George Mathews and John McKee: Revolutionizing East Florida, Mobile, and Pensacola in 1812," *Florida Historical Quarterly* 85, no. 3 (2007): 269, 277.
18 J.C.A. Stagg, "James Madison and George Mathews: The East Florida Revolution of 1812 Reconsidered," *Diplomatic History* 30 (2006): 23, 33; see also Stagg, *Borderlines in Borderlands*, 43 (noting that "rather than simply seizing East Florida," the United States offered to assume on behalf of its citizens the claims arising from Spain-abetted "French spoliations" and to attach East Florida as fulfillment thereof).
19 Stagg, *Borderlines in Borderlands*, 54.
20 See Stagg, *Borderlines in Borderlands*, 33 (noting that seizure of East Florida by the United States risked armed hostilities).
21 Patrick, *Florida Fiasco*, 30–31.
22 Patrick, *Florida Fiasco*, 31; see also 183–84 (noting the relative freedom that Black people experienced under Spanish rule and how that "[c]ontinued freedom depended on Spanish retention of East Florida"); and 251 (referencing the contemporary fear that "war would bring an invasion of the South by the black militia of Spain").
23 For a brief description of the Treaty of San Lorenzo, see Treaty of San Lorenzo/Pinckney's Treaty, 1795, history.state.gov, https://history.state.gov/milestones/1784-1800/pickney-treaty [https://perma.cc/P6MU-MKER] (last visited March 6, 2017). For the text of the treaty, see Treaty of Friendship, Limits, and Navigation Between Spain and the United States; October 27, 1795, The Avalon Project, http://avalon.law.yale.edu/18th_century/sp1795.asp [https://perma.cc/G83F-JAPP] (last visited March 6, 2017).
24 Patrick, *Florida Fiasco*, 3–4.
25 Patrick, *Florida Fiasco*, 4; Stagg, *Borderlines in Borderlands*, 34–35.
26 Patrick, *Florida Fiasco*, 11–15, 57.
27 Patrick, *Florida Fiasco*, 29.
28 For information on development in West Florida, see Séan Patrick Donlan, "Entangled up in Red, White, and Blue: Spanish West Florida and the American Territory of Orleans, 1803–1810," in *Entanglements in Legal History: Conceptual Approaches*, ed. Thomas Duve (Frankfurt am Main: Max Planck Institute for European Legal History, 2014), 213–50; Andrew McMichael, *Atlantic Loyalties: Americans in Span-*

ish West Florida, 1785–1810 (Athens: University of Georgia Press, 2008), 149–75; Stagg, *Borderlines in Borderlands,* 52–86.

29 Stagg, *Borderlines in Borderlands,* 31. Reflecting the practices of the independence of the United States, the West Florida process included a declaration of independence and constitution for the "State of Florida." See Donlan, "Entangled up," in Duve, *Entanglements in Legal History,* 234–42; McMichael, *Atlantic Loyalties,* 164–68; Stagg, *Borderlines in Borderlands,* 62–68. For the Constitution for West Florida of 1810, see David A. Bice, *The Original Lone Star Republic: Scoundrels, Statesmen, and Schemers of the 1810 West Florida Rebellion,* 207–32 (Clanton, AL: Heritage Pub. Consultants, 2004) (providing facsimile copy); James A. Padgett, "The Constitution of the West Florida Republic." *Louisiana Historical Quarterly* 20 (1937): 881–94. The Patriot Constitution did not borrow text from the Constitution of West Florida. See Stagg, *Borderlines in Borderlands,* 76–77, 77 n86 (describing the features of the West Florida Constitution, features at variance with those of the Patriot Constitution).

30 See Gene Allen Smith and Silvia Hilton, "Introduction," in *Nexus of Empire: Negotiating Loyalty and Identity in the Revolutionary Borderlands, 1760s–1820s,* ed. Gene Allen Smith and Silvia L. Hilton (Gainesville: University Press of Florida, 2010), 3–6 (sketching in brief the tumultuous political history of the regions along the US southern border); Samuel C. Hyde, Jr., "Introduction: Setting a Precedent for Regional Revolution: The West Florida Revolt Considered," *Florida Historical Quarterly* 90 (2011): 121–26 (providing an overview of the prevailing political situation).

31 Patrick, *Florida Fiasco,* 56.

32 For biographical details of George Mathews, see generally G. Melvin Herndon, "George Mathews, Frontier Patriot," *Virgina Magazine of History and Biography* 77 (1969): 307.

33 Patrick, *Florida Fiasco,* 56; Cusick, *The Other War of 1812,* 68.

34 Cusick, *The Other War of 1812,* 59.

35 Cusick, *The Other War of 1812,* 75; see also Stagg, *Borderlines in Borderlands,* 104–5.

36 Patrick, *Florida Fiasco,* 49.

37 Patrick, *Florida Fiasco,* 49.

38 Cusick, *The Other War of 1812,* 83.

39 Cusick, *The Other War of 1812,* 89. For the date of the Manifesto, see Copy of Letter from Gen. John Floyd to Crawford (March 21, 1812), in *Miscellaneous Letters of the Department of State 1780–1906,* microformed on National Archives Microfilm Publications, Microcopy No. M 179, Roll 25, f. 149 (National Archives Records Service).

40 See Letter from George Mathews to James Monroe, Secretary of State (March 14, 1812), in State Department Territorial Papers, Florida Series 1777–1824, microformed on National Archives Microfilm Publications, Reel 2, Jan.–Dec. 1812, f. 102 (National Archives Records Service). The letter states that it encloses "the Manifesto and Declaration of Independence of East Florida." No documents are found with the letter. Stagg, *Borderlines in Borderlands,* at 291 n61. The Patriot Manifesto was called the "Declaration of Independence" by Mathews in a letter of April 16, 1812. The letter lists a declaration, an original declaration, and the Articles of Cession as

separate enclosed documents. The reel containing the letter does not include the documents. Letter from George Mathews to James Monroe, Secretary of State (April 16, 1812), in State Department Territorial Papers, Florida Series 1777–1824, microformed on National Archives Microfilm Publications, Reel 2, January–December 1812, f. 128 (National Archives Records Service).

41 Patrick, *Florida Fiasco,* 72 n2.
42 Cusick, *The Other War of 1812,* 90.
43 Patrick, *Florida Fiasco,* 72 n2, 105.
44 See Letter from George Mathews to James Monroe, Secretary of State (March 21, 1812), in Miscellaneous Letters of the Department of State 1789–1906, microformed on National Archives Microfilm Publications, January 1–June 30, 1812, M179, Roll 25, f. 117 (National Archives Records Service).
45 See Letter from George Mathews to James Monroe, Secretary of State (March 21, 1812), in Miscellaneous Letters of the Department of State 1789–1906, microformed on National Archives Microfilm Publications, January 1–June 30, 1812, M179, Roll 25, f. 117 (National Archives Records Service).
46 See Letter from George Mathews to James Monroe, Secretary of State (March 21, 1812), in Miscellaneous Letters of the Department of State 1789–1906, microformed on National Archives Microfilm Publications, January 1–June 30, 1812, M179, Roll 25, f. 117 (National Archives Records Service).
47 Cusick, *The Other War of 1812,* 132.
48 Cusick, *The Other War of 1812,* 121–25.
49 Cusick, *The Other War of 1812,* 127.
50 Cusick, *The Other War of 1812,* 127.
51 Cusick, *The Other War of 1812,* 84.
52 Cusick, *The Other War of 1812,* 150.
53 Cusick, *The Other War of 1812,* 149–50; Patrick, *Florida Fiasco,* 103–4.
54 See Patrick, *Florida Fiasco,* 103–4 (providing the text of Mathews's formal surrender demand).
55 Cusick, *The Other War of 1812,* 166.
56 Patrick, *Florida Fiasco,* 121, 125.
57 Stagg, *Borderlines in Borderlands,* 284–92.
58 Cusick, *The Other War of 1812,* 139–40.
59 Patrick, *Florida Fiasco,* 133–37.
60 Cusick, *The Other War of 1812,* 209.
61 Cusick, *The Other War of 1812,* 187.
62 Cusick, *The Other War of 1812,* 187; Patrick, *Florida Fiasco,* 143.
63 See Patrick, *Florida Fiasco,* 103 (referring to a "chairman" and a "Board of Officers of the Constituted Authority of East Florida").
64 Cusick, *The Other War of 1812,* 212.
65 Cusick, *The Other War of 1812,* 212.
66 Patrick, *Florida Fiasco,* 165.
67 Cusick, *The Other War of 1812,* 212.
68 Cusick, *The Other War of 1812,* 212.

69 Cusick, *The Other War of 1812,* 212.
70 Letter from John McIntosh to James Monroe, Secretary of State (July 30, 1812), in State Department Territorial Papers, Florida Series 1777–1824, microformed on National Archives Microfilm Publications, Reel 2, January–December 1812, ff. 212–213 (National Archives Records Service).
71 Patrick, *Florida Fiasco,* 166–167, 71, and 168–69.
72 Patrick, *Florida Fiasco,* 168–69.
73 Cusick, *The Other War of 1812,* 254; Stagg, *Borderlines in Borderlands,* 130–31.
74 Cusick, *The Other War of 1812,* 259; Patrick, *Florida Fiasco,* 255.
75 Patrick, *Florida Fiasco,* 259, 75, and 259–60.
76 Patrick, *Florida Fiasco,* 259–60.
77 Patrick, *Florida Fiasco,* 260–61.
78 Patrick, *Florida Fiasco,* 261–63.
79 Cusick, *The Other War of 1812,* 263–65; Patrick, *Florida Fiasco,* 258–65.
80 M.C. Mirow, "The Constitution of Cádiz in Florida," *Florida Journal of International Law* 24 (2012): 271, 280, 289.
81 Patrick, *Florida Fiasco,* 268, 272–75.
82 Patrick, *Florida Fiasco,* 275.
83 Patrick, *Florida Fiasco,* 268–69.
84 Cusick, *The Other War of 1812,* 290–91.
85 See generally *Patriot Constitution of 1812.*
86 *Patriot Constitution of 1812,* pmbl., para. 1.
87 *Patriot Constitution of 1812,* pmbl., para. 1.
88 *Patriot Constitution of 1812,* pmbl., para. 2.
89 *Patriot Constitution of 1812,* pmbl., para. 2.
90 *Patriot Constitution of 1812,* pmbl., para. 2.
91 *Patriot Constitution of 1812,* pmbl., para. 2.
92 *Patriot Constitution of 1812,* pmbl., para. 2.
93 *Patriot Constitution of 1812,* art. I.
94 *Patriot Constitution of 1812,* art. I, §§ 2–3, 7.
95 *Patriot Constitution of 1812,* art. I, §§ 2–5, 7.
96 *Patriot Constitution of 1812,* art. I, § 3.
97 *Patriot Constitution of 1812,* art. I, §§ 9–12, 15.
98 *Patriot Constitution of 1812,* art. III, §§ 2, 4.
99 *Patriot Constitution of 1812,* art. II, § 1.
100 *Patriot Constitution of 1812,* art. II, § 2.
101 *Patriot Constitution of 1812,* art. II, § 3.
102 *Patriot Constitution of 1812,* art. II, §§ 4–6.
103 *Patriot Constitution of 1812,* art. I, § 10.
104 *Patriot Constitution of 1812,* art. I, § 10.
105 *Patriot Constitution of 1812,* art. III, § 1.
106 Compare Patrick, *Florida Fiasco,* 225 (noting that recruits in the 1812 invasion of East Florida had an interest in maintaining slavery as "a necessary method of control"); Patrick, *Florida Fiasco,* 289 (noting that contemporary English law prohibited

slavery); and William S. Coker and Thomas D. Watson, *Indian Traders of the Southeastern Spanish Borderlands, 1783–1847* (Gainesville: University Presses of Florida, 1986), 292–93 (similarly acknowledging that contemporary British law did not recognize slavery); with *Georgia Constitution of 1798*, art. IV, §§ 11–12 (which formally recognized the existence of slavery).
107 *Patriot Constitution of 1812*, art. III, § 4, para. 2.
108 See *Patriot Constitution of 1812*, art. I, § 3 (referencing the election of legislative-council members); *Patriot Constitution of 1812*, art. II, § 1 (noting that the director "shall be elected by a majority of the voters present" but neglecting to specify the particulars of such a vote).
109 See generally *Patriot Constitution of 1812* (making no mention of individual rights).
110 *Patriot Constitution of 1812*, art. II, § 9.
111 *Georgia Constitution of 1789*, art. IV, § 3; *Georgia Constitution of 1798*, art. IV, § 5.
112 *Patriot Constitution of 1812*, art. II, § 10.
113 *Patriot Constitution of 1812*, pmbl., para. 2 (referring both to "Province" and "Territory"); *Patriot Constitution of 1812*, art. III, § 4, para. 2.
114 *Patriot Constitution of 1812*, art. I, § 7; *Patriot Constitution of 1812*, art. II, § 1 (referencing "Territory").
115 *Patriot Constitution of 1812*, art. II, § 2, in State Department Territorial Papers, Florida Series 1777–1824, microformed on National Archives Microfilm Publications, Reel 2, January–December 1812, f. 203v (National Archives Records Service).
116 Patrick, *Florida Fiasco*, 166.
117 *Patriot Constitution of 1812*, art. III, § 1.
118 An Act for the Establishment of a Territorial Government in Florida, 17th Cong., 1st Sess., Sec. 5, reprinted in *The Federal and State Constitutions, Colonial Charters, and Other Organic Laws of the State and Territories, and Colonies Now or Heretofore Forming the United States of America*, ed. Francis Newton Thorpe (Government Printing Office, 1909), 658.
119 *Patriot Constitution of 1812*, art. III, § 4.
120 *Patriot Constitution of 1812*, art. I, § 3.
121 *Patriot Constitution of 1812*, art. II, § 1.
122 *Patriot Constitution of 1812*, art. I, § 12.
123 Stagg, *Borderlines in Borderlands*, at 271, 282 n36.
124 See *Georgia Constitution of 1789*, art. II, § 6 (stating that the governor "shall be commander-in-chief in and over the State of Georgia and of the militia thereof").
125 Patrick, *Florida Fiasco*, 56.
126 *Patriot Constitution of 1812*, art. III, § 1.
127 *Patriot Constitution of 1812*, art. II, § 5.
128 *Georgia Constitution of 1798*, art. II, § 8.
129 Patrick, *Florida Fiasco*, 64–68.
130 *Patriot Constitution of 1812*, art. I, § 4.
131 *Patriot Constitution of 1812*, art. I, § 7; *Patriot Constitution of 1812*, art. II, § 2.
132 *Patriot Constitution of 1812*, art. I, § 5.

133 *Patriot Constitution of 1812*, pmbl.; *Patriot Constitution of 1812*, art. II, § 2; see Horst Dippel, "A Nineteenth-Century 'Truman Doctrine' Avant la Lettre? Constitutional Liberty Abroad and the Parliamentary Debate about British Foreign Policy from Castlereagh to Palmerston," in *Constitutionalism, Legitimacy, and Power: Nineteenth-Century Experiences*, ed. Kelly L. Grotke and Markus J. Putsch (Oxford: Oxford University Press, 2014), 23 (exploring the relationship between revolution and constitution and arguing that "[m]odern constitutionalism is the result of revolution"); Horst Dippel, "Modern Constitutionalism: An Introduction to a History in Need of Writing," *The Legal History Review* 73 (2005): 153–69 (further exploring the foundations of constitutionalism).
134 *Patriot Constitution of 1812*, pmbl.
135 *Patriot Constitution of 1812*, pmbl.
136 Stagg, *Borderlines in Borderlands*, at 54 n99 (quoting Crawford to Monroe, August 6, 1812), in James Monroe Papers (Library of Congress).
137 See Hulsebosch, "The Revolutionary Portfolio," *Suffolk University Law Review* 47 (2014): 759–822 (observing that the drafting of the US Constitution was a diplomatic and cultural endeavor designed to encourage Europe to view the United States as a legitimate nation); see generally Golove and Hulsebosch, "A Civilized Nation," *NYU Law Review* 85 (2010) (arguing that a primary purpose of the US Constitution was to obtain recognition and acceptance in the international community).
138 Golove and Hulsebosch, "A Civilized Nation," *NYU Law Review* 85 (2010): 1015–18 (noting that these effects lasted until at least the end of the War of 1812).
139 Hulsebosch, "The Revolutionary Portfolio," *Suffolk University Law Review* 47 (2014): 761.
140 Hulsebosch, "The Revolutionary Portfolio," *Suffolk University Law Review* 47 (2014): 761.
141 See Golove and Hulsebosch, "A Civilized Nation," *NYU Law Review* 85 (2010): 1016 (noting that US diplomats to European countries often provided a copy of the US Constitution).
142 Hulsebosch, "The Revolutionary Portfolio," *Suffolk University Law Review* 47 (2014): 761, 764; see also Armitage, *The Declaration of Independence*, 35; Golove and Hulsebosch, "A Civilized Nation," *NYU Law Review* 85 (2010): 1063.
143 Letter from George Mathews to James Monroe, Secretary of State (April 16, 1812), in State Department Territorial Papers, Florida Series 1777–1824, microformed on National Archives Microfilm Publications, Reel 2, January–December 1812, f. 128 (National Archives Record Service).
144 Hulsebosch, "The Revolutionary Portfolio," *Suffolk University Law Review* 47 (2014): 772–75.
145 Hulsebosch, "The Revolutionary Portfolio," *Suffolk University Law Review* 47 (2014): 791–93; see also Armitage, *The Declaration of Independence*, 14, 21, 31–35, 141; Billias, *American Constitutionalism*, 16–22; Golove and Hulsebosch, "A Civilized Nation," *NYU Law Review* 85 (2010): 941–43.
146 *Patriot Constitution of 1812*, pmbl.

147 *Patriot Constitution of 1812,* pmbl.
148 See *Patriot Articles of Cession,* art. II.
149 *Patriot Articles of Cession,* art. II.
150 *Patriot Articles of Cession,* art. IV.
151 See Golove and Hulsebosch, "A Civilized Nation," *NYU Law Review* 85 (2010): 935 ("[A] core purpose of American constitution-making was to facilitate the admission of the United States into the European-based system of sovereign states."); Golove and Hulsebosch, "A Civilized Nation," *NYU Law Review* 85 (2010): 981–82 (discussing how the framers balanced their twin goals of "popular sovereignty and international respectability in the design of the new constitutional system").
152 Hulsebosch, "The Revolutionary Portfolio," *Suffolk University Law Review* 47 (2014): 766.
153 Letter from John McIntosh to James Monroe, Secretary of State (July 30, 1812), in State Department Territorial Papers, Florida Series 1777–1824, microformed on National Archives Microfilm Publications, Reel 2, January–December 1812, f. 212 (National Archives Records Service).
154 Hulsebosch, "The Revolutionary Portfolio," *Suffolk University Law Review* 47 (2014): 799–800.
155 Hulsebosch, "The Revolutionary Portfolio," *Suffolk University Law Review* 47 (2014): 763.
156 Hulsebosch, "The Revolutionary Portfolio," *Suffolk University Law Review* 47 (2014): 795–98.
157 *Patriot Articles of Cession,* arts. II–VI.
158 *Patriot Articles of Cession,* art. III.
159 *Patriot Articles of Cession,* art. IV.
160 *Patriot Articles of Cession,* art. III.
161 *Patriot Articles of Cession,* art. IV.
162 *Patriot Articles of Cession,* art. IV.
163 Stagg, *Borderlines in Borderlands,* 276–77.
164 Coker and Watson, *Indian Traders,* 31–35.
165 Coker and Watson, *Indian Traders,* 15.
166 Coker and Watson, *Indian Traders,* 1–30.
167 Stagg, *Borderlines in Borderlands,* 276, 167, and 283–284; Stagg, *Borderlines in Borderlands,* 117.
168 Stagg, *Borderlines in Borderlands,* 283–84; and 117.
169 *Patriot Articles of Cession,* art. IV.
170 Stagg, *Borderlines in Borderlands,* 276–77.
171 Stagg, *Borderlines in Borderlands,* 288 n55 (citing Letter from George Mathews to President James Madison [April 16, 1812], in Madison Papers: Presidential Series 4: 327 [Library of Congress]).
172 Stagg, *Borderlines in Borderlands,* 289.
173 Stagg, *Borderlines in Borderlands,* 289 (citing a March 21, 1812, letter from George Mathews to James Monroe).
174 Stagg, *Borderlines in Borderlands,* 293–94.

175 Letter from John H. McIntosh to James Monroe, Secretary of State (July 30, 1812), in State Department Territorial Papers, Florida Series 1777–1824, microformed on National Archives Microfilm Publications, Reel 2, January–December 1812, ff. 212v–213 (National Archives Record Service).
176 Billias, *American Constitutionalism*, 8.
177 See generally M.C. Mirow, *Florida's First Constitution, The Constitution of Cádiz: Introduction, Translation, and Text*, (2012); M.C. Mirow, "The Constitution of Cádiz in Florida," *Florida Journal of International Law* 24 (2012): 271.
178 M.C. Mirow, "The Age of Constitutions in the Americas," *Law and History Review* 32 (2014): 229, 233–34 (explaining the influence that American institutions have had on Latin American constitutional developments).
179 *Patriot Constitution of 1812*, pmbl., para. 2.

3

Florida's First State Constitutional Convention in 1838

JAMES M. DENHAM

As Florida prepared for the opening of a constitutional convention in the Gulf Coast boomtown of St. Joseph on December 3, 1838, preparatory to a bid for statehood, the territory reeled in crisis. Most visibly, the Second Seminole War (1835–1842) continued to wreak havoc in the peninsula. Economic catastrophe also stalked the land. The national economic depression known as the Panic of 1837 sent the territory's shaky banking structure reeling. Even so, the mood as the convention opened was festive. Cosam Emir Bartlett, the editor of the *Apalachicola Gazette* and himself a delegate representing Franklin County observed that the "city of the Saints presented quite a hustling appearance this morning. Most of the members of the constitutional convention have come in and may be seen at different corners of the streets, on the piazzas of the boarding houses. . . . solemnly engaged in electioneering for the important offices of president, clerk, or doorkeeper of the convention." Bartlett's sources told him that the two contenders for president of the convention was former Governor William P. DuVal and Judge Robert Raymond Reid of St. Augustine. "It would be premature at this time," Bartlett reported, "to decide in whose favor the majority of the convention will decide. As usual in such cases, the friends of both parties are sanguine."[1]

From December 3, 1838, to January 11, 1839, fifty-six men met in St. Joseph, Florida, and wrote a Constitution for a state of Florida.[2] For one month the delegates jostled over personal ambitions, debated political principles, and drafted a constitution that restrained Florida's wildcat banking system and protected Florida's and the antebellum South's most treasured domestic institution—slavery.

Ten months earlier on February 2, 1838, territorial Governor Richard Keith Call signed an act into law calling for a constitutional convention, and prescribing the number of delegates per county. Florida's Middle District received the most delegates with twenty. East Florida received seventeen. South Florida had three members (two from Monroe and one from Dade County), and West Florida had sixteen. The county with the largest number of delegates was Leon with eight. Election for delegates to attend the convention was set for the second Monday of October 1838. Also at that election voters selected members for the two houses of the legislative council.[3] The legislative session was to begin immediately following the convention.

A year before, voters had voiced their preferences for or against statehood, and the results reflected substantial regional divisions in the territory. The total vote was 2,214 for "State" and 1,274 for "No State." Of the four districts, Middle Florida overwhelmingly supported statehood, while voters in West Florida also supported the measure. In East Florida voters opposed statehood by more than a two-to-one margin.[4] East Florida's opposition to statehood was based on its suffering condition during the Second Seminole War, the cost of state government, and the likelihood that a state government would be dominated by more populous, and financially powerful, Middle Florida.

Boosters of St. Joseph scored a coup when Florida's legislative council voted to have the Gulf Coast town adjacent to Apalachicola host Florida's constitutional convention. Due to the extensive lobbying of Territorial Delegate Joseph White, William P. DuVal, and Richard C. Allen (the latter two men served as delegates to the convention), Congress authorized creation of companies to create links between St. Joseph Bay and the Apalachicola and Chipola Rivers. Allen, the president of the Lake Wimico and St. Joseph Canal and Railroad Company asserted that the envisioned road "forms the first link in the great line which is to extend from the Atlantic Ocean, across the peninsula of Florida, and the Gulf of Mexico."[5] In 1838 the rivalry between St. Joseph and Apalachicola, the town at the mouth of the river, was at fever pitch. At stake was the possibility of securing the lion's share of the commerce on the Apalachicola and Chattahoochee River systems, providing Gulf access to some of the richest planting regions of Alabama and Georgia. Securing the convention gave the new town the stamp of legitimacy.[6]

In 1838 Florida was a divided territory with diverse regions, economic conditions, and points of view. Its roughly 47,000 inhabitants divided into Western, Middle, Eastern, and Southern districts, each with its own unique demographic and economic characteristics. Florida's population was so scattered, and travel so difficult, that at times any kind of unity seemed beyond anyone's grasp. Judge Robert Raymond Reid, a person who took a leading role in the convention noted three years earlier, "There is an Eastern, and Western, and Middle Party, a Call Party, a White Party, a Nuttall, a Gadsden—the whole community from the point of the Peninsula to the St. Mary's and Pensacola split up into bits. This should not be so," he observed, "the parties should divide on principle. No body can tell when we shall get into the Union but 'tis to be regretted that there are not separate Governments for East and West Florida."[7]

The territory's most populous and prosperous district was Middle Florida, the plantation-rich region between the Apalachicola and Suwannee Rivers. The region boomed after the founding of Tallahassee in 1824. Middle Florida contained roughly half the territory's population, and the region was tied to the antebellum South's chief distinctive institution—slavery. Everywhere in Florida slavery existed, but in the Eastern District, it was less stringent. There, Spanish traditions ameliorated the institution, in ways that were out of accord with the antebellum South's laws and customs. The Adams-Onis Treaty (1821) transferring Florida from Spain to the United States, guaranteed free persons in Florida the same rights and privileges as other citizens of the United States. Traditions of some racial mixing and easy manumissions existed there.[8] Even so, by 1838, failed court battles, a harsh slave code passed in 1828 and 1832 preventing manumission and imposing other proscriptions against free blacks, had the effect of forcing all blacks firmly within the same condition of unfreedom as that experienced throughout the other slaveholding states.[9] Because East Florida lands were more sparsely settled and more suited to cattle raising and subsistence agriculture, plantation slavery, in the traditional sense, would not take root there until the 1850s.

At the time of the St. Joseph convention, territorial politics had reached a fever pitch. The constitutional convention's conclusion marked the fall of the "Nucleus," a faction that had dominated territorial politics since the middle 1820s. The Nucleus derived its power from the political patronage of the Jackson administration (1828–1836). Current Governor Richard K. Call, former Governor William P. DuVal (1822–1834), and George T. Ward—aka the "land office crowd"—owed their positions to the political coattails of Old Hickory. For roughly fifteen years, the Nucleus monopolized the most lucrative political offices. By the time of the convention, with Andrew Jackson out of the picture, this grouping composed primarily of well-to-do planting interests had coalesced into a nascent Whig political party, based on support of internal improvements, canal building, and especially banks. Antagonistic to this group were aggressive, anti-corporate and anti-bank Democrats, called Locofocos by their enemies. These two antagonistic groups would battle each other in St. Joseph.[10]

In 1838, Florida's unstable banking system was on the verge of collapse, and the convention's timing made territorial banking the most contentious issue. In the years preceding the convention the Democrats (anti-bank) and Whigs (pro-bank) battled it out at the polls, the stump, and in print. Beginning in 1834, the territorial legislative council had chartered several banks over the vociferous objections of the territory's anti-bank politicians. Over expansion, badly secured loans, evidence of political cronyism, and a bad national economic picture precipitated by the Panic of 1837, made for a volatile political situation. There were already signs that the territory's economic situation was shaky, and this cast a shadow over deliberations at St. Joseph. The validity of "faith bonds" (whether or not the full faith and credit of the future State of Florida would back the bonds that these institutions had issued) became the most controversial issue of the convention. One commentator spoke the obvious when he stated that the main question of the convention was whether the "State will assume the Territorial faith pledged for the Union and Pensacola Banks."[11] As you will see later, debates over banking provisions were acrimonious.[12]

From 1828 to 1838, Florida's territorial legislative council chartered sixteen banks. By the time of the convention, only three were of any consequence. The Union Bank of Florida commenced its operation on January 16, 1835. It was empowered to sell bonds of up to $1 million, and this amount increased as time went on. Middle Florida planters who mortgaged their land and their slaves in exchange for stock were the institution's largest investors. Within a month, nearly one hundred shareholders invested in $925,900 worth of stock.[13] The two other banks of significance were the Bank of Pensacola (chartered in 1831) and the Southern Life Insurance and Trust Company (chartered in 1835) that operated out of St. Augustine.[14]

Another issue that cast an ominous cloud on the convention's deliberations was the Second Seminole War. By 1838 the Second Seminole War was in its third year. The conflict pitted Seminoles, Creeks, and other Native Americans in alliance with maroons (sometimes called Black Seminoles), against the combined strength of the region's whites, the US Army, and volunteer units from as far away as South Carolina, Tennessee, and Missouri. To many white Floridians, the fighting represented nothing less than a massive slave revolt and race war, a direct threat to the wealth and economic underpinnings of more-settled plantation areas between the Apalachicola and Suwannee Rivers. Some in their panic claimed to foresee the rise of a free state in the east. East Florida bore the brunt of the war, which devastated farms and settlements in the interior. Travel was all but impossible. Courts shut down. So did trade. Many settlers died, or became refugees fleeing to Jacksonville, St. Augustine, or into the hastily built forts that dotted the landscape.[15] The devastation the war wrought was real enough, but the conflict further exacerbated the chronic tensions between East Florida and Middle Florida. This especially proved true because of the latter region's domination of the territorial legislative council.

Many in East Florida opposed statehood based on financial reasons, claiming that a new state government would create an unnecessary economic burden on them. Taxes would rise. Citizens in East Florida questioned whether they could support a state government. "At present our Territorial expenses are paid by the General Government," one East Florida opponent of statehood declared. "Large annual appropriations are made for the improvement of our country—roads and bridges cut and built; our Territorial taxes are comparatively light, though sufficiently burthensome, and we have the privilege of electing our representatives and enacting our own laws. We have judicial tribunals also supported by the General Government." On the other hand, if Florida joined the Union it would be compelled to pay for all these officers and "our sparse population [would] be taxed beyond our means for these purposes. . . . The people will, by accepting the form of a state government, impose upon themselves burthens which they may not be able to bear. The name of a state may by pleasing for a time and the idea will take with many, but in our opinion, the form and dignity of a State Government without the wherewithal to support them, will not compare with our present situation as a Territory." Heavy taxes would impede immigration. "East Florida now is but a wild waste and depopulated region, and anything which would in the slightest degree, have the effect of checking the settlement of the country we deprecate. In becoming a state, we have all to lose and nothing to gain, under the present circumstances, and until we have a population able to bear the increased expense, we shall consider this question as premature."[16]

While a majority of East Florida settlers opposed creating a new state, most also favored dividing the territory at the Suwannee River.[17] "Division" was the natural outcome of the anti-statehood sentiment in East Florida. After all, the idea made sense based on precedent: the Spanish and the British had divided the territory into two colonies. By 1838 things had changed. Tallahassee, the territorial capital, had been founded in 1824 between the two isolated settlements of St. Augustine and Pensacola. And many attempts to link the territory together through roads and canals were moving forward. Even so, division made sense from a national standpoint. Pro-slavery advocates pointed to the possibility of creating two or maybe three slave states out of Florida. There was also significant support for division in West Florida. Some advocated dividing the territory at the Apalachicola River, or even perhaps having Alabama annex that portion of the territory.

Division sentiment was emblematic of the sectional divisions within the territory. One commentator argued that for East Florida to "consent to be taxed under such circumstances would be suicidal. . . . We ask to remain a SEPARATE AND DISTINCT TERRITORY." (Plus many in East Florida chaffed at the idea of a future state of Florida being dominated by Middle Florida.) "EAST FLORIDA is content to remain a while longer in leading strings not to Middle and West Florida, but of the General Government. To the friends of State Government we say 'we seek no change, but least of all such change as they would bring us.'"[18]

As time for holding the convention grew closer, these voices grew louder. Throughout the year citizens in East Florida held public meetings and petitioned the Congress opposing statehood, and calling for division of the territory.[19] The St. Augustine *Florida Herald* took up the cause with enthusiasm.[20] In one of many petitions to Congress, the citizens of East Florida proclaimed, "Nature never intended that East Florida should be formed into a State with Middle and West Florida—Its geographical position presents an insurmountable objection. It is only necessary to cast the eye over the Map, to see that at no distant day a separation must from necessity take place."[21]

By late November, delegates and visitors began arriving in St. Joseph by stage and via the Apalachicola River and Gulf of Mexico in order to secure accommodations for the opening session on December 3. Among those on the scene was Louis Goldsborough, former naval officer and son-in-law of former US Attorney General William Wirt. Goldsborough was angling to succeed Richard C. Allen as president of the St. Joseph and Lake Wimico Company, and he was attending a stockholders' meeting in the town. Goldsborough offered his observations on the convention and its participants to his wife in Baltimore. St. Joseph presents a "dreary aspect and judging from all I see, I think its business has declined since I last visited it. . . . My heart quails at the idea of living here. . . . The convention here." He continued,

"I regret to say is, in the majority for Agrarianism, Loco-Focoism, Fanny Wrightism, &c, &c. A desperate effort is making to tear the Union Bank to pieces, with [James] Westcott at the Head of the party—poor dirty, insignificant creature." Goldsborough was not impressed with the makeup of the delegates. Besides DuVal, who in his mind was the "first man among them," there were no others who stood out.[22]

The delegates represented varying degrees of skill, backgrounds, educational levels, and outlooks. Delegates were natives of thirteen of the twenty-six states of the Union but the place of origin of the vast majority of the delegates skewed heavily toward the South. Forty-two of the delegates hailed from slaveholding states: South Carolina (14), Georgia (10), Virginia (8), North Carolina (5), Kentucky (2), Maryland (2), and Tennessee (1). Only three of the fifty-six men were Florida-born. The group contained mostly planters and lawyers, but there were "two ministers of the gospel, two newspaper editors, three doctors, an innkeeper, a sea captain and fisherman, and a merchant in the group. More than a third of the delegates had had legislative experience."[23] William P. DuVal and Robert Raymond Reid had served in the US Congress. Also, in Reid and Richard C. Allen the convention had two sitting US District judges.

Delegates of the Florida Constitutional Convention

Western District

Jackson—Thomas Baltzell, Samuel C. Bellamy, Alfred L. Woodward, Richard H. Long
Escambia—Jackson Morton, Benjamin D. Wright, Thomas M. Blount, Walker Anderson
Walton—John McKinnon, Daniel G. McLean
Washington—Stephen J. Roche, E. Robbins
Calhoun—William P. DuVal, Richard C. Allen

Middle Florida

Leon—George T. Ward, John Taylor, Thomas Brown, Samuel Parkhill, James D. Westcott, Leigh Read, Leslie A. Thompson, William Wyatt
Gadsden—Banks Meacham, John W. Malone, John M. G. Hunter, Samuel B. Stephens
Jefferson—Abram Bellamy, John M. Partridge, Joseph McCants, E. Carrington Cabell

Madison—John C. McGehee, Richard J. Mays
Hamilton—Joseph B Watts, William B. Hooker
Franklin—A. G. Semmes, C. E. Bartlett

East Florida

St. Johns—Joseph S. Sanchez, Robert Raymond Reid, David Levy, Edwin T. Jencks
Duval—A. W Crichton, Oliver Wood, Samuel T. Garey
Alachua—Isaac Garrison, E. K. White, E. Bird
Columbia—John F. Webb, Wilson Brooks, George E. McClellan
Nassau—James G. Cooper, William Haddock
Mosquito—William H. Williams

Southern District

Hillsborough—William Cooley [elected but did not serve]
Monroe—William Marvin, Joseph B. Brown
Dade—Richard Fitzpatrick

As Goldsborough indicated, the most controversial issue of the convention was territorial banking. At least fourteen of the elected delegates were stockholders of the Union Bank or one of the other banks operating in Florida at that time.[24] When the delegates met, John Gamble's bank as well as other Florida banking institutions were under attack, and the convention became a battleground among its supporters and opponents. As Herbert J. Doherty has written, "Florida banks had suspended specie payments in May and June of 1837. It was foreseen that the territory might be called upon to make good the bonds which it had endorsed for the broken banks, and it was upon this issue that the election hinged in East Florida." Banks were "such a clear-cut issue in the divisionist East, however, the voters there lost sight of the fact that the anti-bank men whom they sent to the convention were also supporters of statehood, which most of the eastern voters opposed."[25] Given the timing of the convention, it is not surprising that the forum became a battleground among supporters and opponents of the territory's banking institutions. Florida's state constitution was unique in that, as one scholar has noted, it was the first state constitution to attempt the "constitutionalization of detailed economic legislation."[26]

The first battle over banking came in the selection of the convention's presiding officer. Leon County delegate, Samuel Parkhill, one of the largest shareholders of the Union Bank, nominated ex-governor DuVal for the post. As a correspondent to the *Floridian* reported, Parkhill "alluded to the past service of the nominee in various official stations in Florida. As Judge, as Governor for upwards of twelve years, and as a citizen, his course has been such as to commend him the grateful feelings of every Floridian. He was one of the earliest emigrated to Florida, and had encountered as many privations as any other citizen." Other Middle Florida delegates quickly fell in line with DuVal's nomination. Tallahassee's Thomas Brown added his endorsement. "The oldest and the youngest citizen of Florida, when they heard his name, called to mind his eminent services and moral worth." It was only proper, Brown added, that this position of honor "should be conferred upon one of the oldest residents and public servants of Florida; who had done his duty faithfully, who was well known to the people, and in whom they had the fullest confidence."[27]

DuVal's nomination drew a swift rejoinder. Leon County's Gen. Leigh Read, a rising star in the anti-bank faction of the Democratic Party, nominated Judge Robert Raymond Reid. In a flamboyant speech, Leon County delegate James Westcott seconded Reid's nomination, asserting that no man "had a claim or pre-emption right, for any services, however eminent, to any station." A spirited debate followed. As an anti-bank Democrat, confidant of President Martin Van Buren's secretary of state, John Forsyth, the St. Augustine resident seemed the perfect candidate for Middle Florida anti-bank statehood advocates. Westcott's speech favoring Reid betrayed personal animus against DuVal. According to one observer, "considerable feeling appeared to exist between some of the delegates" in the contest between DuVal and Reid, "but nothing unpleasant occurred."[28]

Dorothy Dodd has speculated that Reid's candidacy emerged out of a deal struck between anti-bank delegates from Middle Florida and the East Florida delegation, who they feared might break up the convention unless Reid became leader. The Eastern delegation, combined with delegates from Madison and Hamilton Counties; John M. Partridge and Abram Bellamy of Jefferson County; James Westcott, Leigh Read, and Leslie Thompson of Leon; Cosam Emir Bartlett of Franklin, and William Marvin of Monroe voted for Reid. The final tally that came on December 4 was twenty-seven for Reid and twenty-six for DuVal.[29] The election was only the first of many battles fought between pro-bank and anti-bank forces, and the anti-bank forces clearly won this first skirmish.

Once elected, Reid graciously accepted the results and made a speech encouraging harmony and an end to political divisions. "We stand here, fellow-citizens, upon an eminence, and the eyes of men upon us. I am sure you will bring to your deliberations candor, calmness, and an enlightened intelligence. I trust this place will be considered too holy for the introduction of party, or partisan politics."[30]

Robert Raymond Reid's election over former Florida Governor William P. DuVal was a coup for anti-bank forces. DuVal, a strict constructionist from Virginia by way of Kentucky, had been opposed to territorial banking. As Florida's territorial governor, he had vetoed numerous bank bills in the twelve years he was in office. Yet bank forces in the territory were overwhelming, and many of them were his friends and business associates. In his last few months as governor, DuVal signed the Union Bank Bill into law.[31] Within a short time, DuVal became a stockholder and firm supporter of the Union Bank. By the time of the convention, he also represented the institution in court.

The key figure in forging this anti-bank, pro-statehood alliance was James D. Westcott. Working with pro-statehood East Floridian David Levy, an associate of Reid, Westcott skillfully undercut DuVal who came to the convention as the territory's best-known politician. There was a good bit of personal animus between DuVal and the younger Westcott, stemming from numerous clashes when Westcott served as territorial secretary during DuVal's last several years in office. A talented operator, the New Jersey native enjoyed the backing of President Van Buren, whose influence had sent him to Florida in 1830. Since that time, Westcott's career had blossomed. In 1834, he became US attorney for the Middle District of Florida. His legal practice had also prospered, and he was angling to become the leader of Florida's Democratic Party. Several years before the convention, Reid had taken the measure of this young, talented politician. Observing him in Tallahassee in 1833, the judge confided to himself in his diary that Westcott was "rough, factious, and egotistical." Two years later, he amended his appraisal. He observed that Westcott "drinks, gambles, studies, speculates, swears, and yet has character."[32]

In Robert Raymond Reid, the convention had a pro-statehood, anti-bank East Floridian. Both in public and privately in his diary Reid had expressed his reservations about banks. Five years before he attended the convention, Reid mused, "There is a passion for bank making existing at present in this Territory, which must prove injurious to the general interests. Banks must be founded on capital and superstructure." Any other "basis," the judge noted to himself, was "erroneous. Such schemes are fit only for the brains of speculators who care not who loses so [long] as they make a lusty hit.... In this free country Banks... favor monopoly, make aristocracy, and create slaves."[33]

For now, the convention seemed ready to begin its deliberations, but disagreement over whether the territory was ready to come into the Union almost derailed the convention before it even got started. The fireworks began on December 5, when Richard Fitzpatrick of Dade County introduced a resolution calling for immediate formation of a state government no matter what Congress might decide. Some delegates proposed to vote immediately on the resolution to determine whether there was a majority favoring state government. The resolution was aimed at East Florida delegates who supported division or some measure other than immediate statehood. Jackson County's Samuel Bellamy asserted that "it was too late to debate the duties of this convention, and the policy and right of our admission into the Union." Their task, he insisted, was simply to create a state constitution, and nothing else.[34]

At that point DuVal joined the debate. He asserted that he had come to the "convention with straight forward purposes; he came here to do his humble part in aiding Florida to take that stand in the Confederacy to which she is of right entitled." The population question was irrelevant to the task at hand. It was time, he said, to present "our claim for admission in the halls of Congress." DuVal challenged those who agreed with him to raise their hands. "It is time for the advocates of a State Government to know who are the friends of Florida," he stated. DuVal admitted that his call for the resolution was a test, and he did not hesitate to avow it.[35]

> Richard Long of Jackson County suggested that for delegates not to favor state government was tantamount to perjury. But DuVal dissented vehemently to this insinuation. Intending to cast no imputations upon gentlemen who differed from him, least of all did he insinuate perjury against any honorable member of that body. What sir, are we to be told, that because the people had elected delegates to the convention, that therefore the persons so elected were bound to vote for and advocate a State form of government or be taunted with the charge of perjury? I say no such thing and repel the insinuation as groundless and illiberal. Gentlemen here are sent to speak for the parts, as well as the whole of this Territory, and if the constituents of any member on this floor believe it impolitic and ruinous for Florida at this time to seek admission into the Union, he for one, would

never censure that member for faithfully representing their wishes. It is a new and strange doctrine sir that every man here is bound to advocate a State Government because he has sworn to do his duty as a member of this convention.[36]

DuVal reminded other delegates that each delegate could eventually vote for or against the finished version of the document as his conscience directed.

> Mr. Chairman, on a subject of so much importance as the organization of a new state, a diversity of opinion as to the mode, time and policy of the measure must be expected. If the gentlemen from the East—representing their constituents are not ready for the application; If the East borne to the dust by long continued calamity, and suffering under the privations of a barbarous war are not prepared for the change—are we, honorable Delegates to be taxed with perjury because they may utter the language of their constituents? When was the free voice of the American people ever restrained by a construction so arbitrary. Sir, upon this subject all opinion must be heard—all views fairly considered. If Middle and West Florida are in favor of the measure and East Florida from her particular condition opposed to it—let her be heard. I for one am not disposed to trample upon the rights to stifle her voice, and say to her Delegates you must go in for a State right or wrong, because you have sworn to do your duty as member of this convention—That duty may require them to oppose it.

DuVal then asserted that all that was "aimed by the resolution was to know if there is a majority of this convention in favor of State Government—if there is, let us say so and go on to form a constitution for the new State. If there is a majority opposed to the measure, let us know it—or it is unnecessary to consume the time and money of the people if no good is to result from our deliberations."[37]

Lengthy debate on the resolutions followed until Reid took the floor. Speaking for the East Florida delegates, Reid recognized the "disadvantageous circumstances" of East Florida. "She is depressed and suffering—she is bleeding at every pore, and yet exercising a magnanimity and disinterestedness ... she has determined to aid you in effecting your object of admission into the Union. And it is be tolerated, that such conduct as this should be met here, with suspicion and reproach? The representatives from the

East, Sir are now and ever, prepared to perform their duty to themselves and to the People of Florida."[38] The debate went on. David Levy opposed the resolution. William Marvin and Richard C. Allen favored it. So did Samuel Bellamy of Jackson County.

In a final attempt to secure passage of the resolution, Bellamy used the trump card of state's rights (in this case territorial rights) against the power of Congress over Florida. He was "sick, tired and disgusted with this state of vassalage," and was "unwilling longer to hold his property at the mercy of the General Government, . . . and the monstrous claim set up by the Abolitionists to a certain class of Southern property . . . rendered a prompt action on the part of the people of Florida, essential to their security." Thus, Bellamy asserted that only statehood status protected Florida from Congress's tampering with its domestic institutions. He opposed any right of the convention to "question or talk about expedience of forming a State Government; it was enough for him that the people had willed it. He was for going into the Union at once. If denied admission we should set up for ourselves, join Texas, or for himself individually, he would even join the cantons of Switzerland, rather than longer occupy our present position. . . . He represented a high minded and intelligent people; their interest was identified with Florida, and with her they must sink or swim. He therefore went for Florida first, Florida last, Florida right or wrong." At long last, a vote to dismiss further consideration of the resolution passed by a vote of thirty-nine to fifteen, and the matter was dropped. At that point, the delegates began the work of writing a state constitution.[39]

Abram Bellamy of Jefferson County offered a resolution that the Alabama state constitution be used as a kind of template for the convention's work, and that it may be taken up "and considered article after article, and altered and modified to suit the State of Florida."[40] Historian Stephanie Moussalli notes that while they used Alabama's constitution as their guide, the delegates also consulted those of Kentucky, Tennessee, Pennsylvania, Indiana, and several New England states.[41]

On December 6 Reid submitted committee appointments. Among the seventeen committees, a few of the most important stood out. Of these DuVal chaired the Executive Department Committee; Westcott chaired the Banking Committee; and five delegates made up the Committee on General Provisions, which dealt with the issue of "Domestic Slavery."[42] While there were conflicts over most issues, when it came to the institution of slavery the sad fact is that there was no disagreement among the delegates that the institution was essential, the natural condition of Black people, and vital to

Florida's growth and prosperity. Nearly all the delegates were slaveholders or had a close relationship with the institution. Given the context of the time, there were several references in the debates to abolitionists, fanatics, and the dangers of northern hostility to slavery. In several instances, some delegates in an effort to score points against their opponents resorted to attacks suggesting that this or that point of view threatened slavery. In a sense, slavery became a kind of litmus test for issues.

Article XVI, section 1, of the final version of the Constitution asserted that the General Assembly "shall have no power to pass laws for the emancipation of slaves." Section 2 barred the General Assembly from preventing emigrants to Florida from bringing slaves into the state. The section also empowered the assembly to pass laws to "prevent free negroes, mulattoes, and other persons of color, from immigrating to this State, or from being discharged from on board any vessel, in any of the ports of Florida." The initial Report of the Committee on General Provisions, including the subject of slavery, reported elements meant to ameliorate the harshness of slavery, at least from a paternalist point of view, but these provisions were not included in the final draft.[43] Slavery also encroached into the question of representation in the legislature. The convention adopted the three-fifths clause of the Constitution, counting blacks for purposes of representation. This had the effect of giving Middle Florida counties more representatives in the legislative council.[44]

Personal animus between William P. DuVal and the younger James Westcott became one of the dominant motifs throughout the entire convention. The first sharp exchanges between the two came after DuVal's Committee Report on the Executive Department when Westcott questioned the number of years of residence necessary to become governor of Florida. DuVal interpreted his remarks as both a personal attack and as an attempt to take over the work of the convention. After a series of heated exchanges, it was clear that DuVal's contempt of Westcott was palpable. After a lengthy Westcott monologue, DuVal sneered that all would admit that the member from Leon "deserves thanks for his universal action and unlimited efforts to conduct the entire business of this body, and give to the country a constitution worthy.... of the high principles, purity and wisdom of the distinguished legislator from Leon. No member of this house admires more than myself, a genius so rare—a wisdom as profound, and a devotion and love of country, so sincere as is constantly manifested by that generous and candid member," DuVal intoned.[45]

The battle between DuVal and Westcott grew more intense once Westcott's Banking Committee made its report on December 13. Eight days later on December 21, DuVal, Westcott, and the other delegates took up the report and sparred on banking resolutions.[46] At issue was whether the charters of the Union Bank and the other financial institutions in operation at the time (and their financial obligations) would be carried forward or could be repudiated by the future state. As Dorothy Dodd explains, DuVal and banking advocates insisted that there was no "question either of the validity of charters and bonds or of the essential soundness of the financial theory on which they rested. Anti-bank men, such as Westcott, [Leslie] Thompson, Marvin, Levy, and Abram Bellamy, contended either that charters were illegal in the first place or that, even if the bonds were valid, a primary convention of the people had the right to repudiate them."[47] Conflicts over banking provisions became so intemperate that it nearly resulted in breaking up the convention.[48]

Pro-bank men vehemently opposed any tampering with the bank charters or corporations as they existed at the time. In defense of this proposition, they argued that the honor of the territory and its future was at stake. William P. DuVal declared the issue was not one of mere "local interests . . . but general principles. . . . of preserving the inviolability of contracts" as opposed to "breaking the solemn pledge of the state and its people." Canals, railroads, and banks operated under the clear mandate of the legislature under terms fully agreed to by both parties. "If, after money was loaned and improvements made, the Legislature could step in, under pleas of supremacy of the law, and destroy all the privileges it had granted there would be an end of all public improvements. It would be a death blow to corporations, nobody would put faith in, or lend money, upon such a hazardous condition. The House should deliberate coolly, and weigh well the consequences of its decision." Nothing should be done, DuVal asserted, that would "imply an intention of bad faith or infringe upon the character of the State. For the good of the State he would give corporations power to improve the country and protect both their privileges and the privileges of the people under the shield of the Constitution."[49]

DuVal said he "would have it the law of the land that the obligation of contracts could not be impaired by the proposed clogs; it might be understood that the Legislature might impair these obligations. . . . We know not when or for what occasion the faith of the State might be required, but it might be when they had neither money nor credit to enable them to defend their wives and children or their hearths."[50] Duval offered the example of the War of 1812 when the United States' credit helped stave off defeat. "She triumphed, and triumphed nobly but could she have raised the means, had her credit been a matter of speculation or if perfidy had been anticipated? When we want credit or means, what would be our character with such a condition in our constitution as that proposed by the member of Leon? In event of a foreign war, Florida would be the theatre of naval operations, and the scene of a deadly and terrible conflict, with a servile population, more formidable in our midst, than a legitimate contest with a most powerful nation." If such circumstances occurred and Florida was in need of credit "what could we affect with a blighted name . . . and tarnished reputation? The example of the U.S. was worthy of consideration. To insist upon clogs and qualifications would destroy all chance of our becoming a State. Let the House, therefore, leave local details for the present, and meet the question of the inviolability of contracts, face to face."[51] Louis Goldsborough was present in the galleries that day. DuVal's speech, he asserted to his wife, contained "sound and solid arguments, such as have been felt by all present and such too, as have provided the greatest effect."[52]

In a stiff rejoinder to DuVal and others, Delegate Richard Long of Jackson County stated that he disapproved of many of the provisions in the Union Bank charter, "particularly that feature which makes the Territory the *principle,* rather than the *security,* on the Bonds. Does the Territory receive money negotiated by these bonds, or is she in any way benefited by the sale? Not one dollar, sir, from all her responsibility, goes into the Treasury. There has been an unequal division between the Bank and the Territory. The former is entitled to, and draws the *money*—the latter draws the *liability.*"[53]

As a way of sidestepping the volatile issue, Long and his fellow Jackson County delegate, Thomas Baltzell, offered a resolution for the convention to send the charter to Congress and "ask them to revise, amend, and annul the charter of this great Bank, so far as the interests of the people may demand, and our own previous obligations may allow. . . . Congress can settle this matter between the Banks and its people, with a more becoming temper, with more light and experience than this convention."[54]

As previously noted, the sanctity of protecting Florida's most treasured domestic institution (i.e., slavery) hovered over the convention like a mist. Leon County Delegate William Wyatt's rejoinder to Long and Baltzell's offered proof of this miasma. Wyatt professed that he did not care one way or another about banking but fundamentally opposed Long and Baltzell's idea of turning the banking issue over to Congress. On its face the resolution's "doctrines are monstrous. They assume all the grounds contended for by the abolitionists of the North, in relation to the powers of Congress over Territories, and their right to abolish slavery in the Territory of Florida—Slaves are property, and that acquired under acts of incorporations, is held by virtue of the laws of the Territorial Government." This statement brought numerous outbursts from the gallery suggesting that Wyatt was accusing those supporting the resolution of "treason" to the South. Wyatt disclaimed the assertion but added that "if an avowed abolitionist was to entertain such doctrines in this place, it would be denounced by every Southerner as treason, and I sir, would not answer for his life." Cheers echoed throughout the gallery. Wyatt warned the delegates that if Florida's constitution allowed Congress to tamper with its bank charters, it was implicitly surrendering its rights regarding its peculiar institution. "Every southerner will deny the right of Congress to abolish slavery in Florida, but the abolitionists will meet them and say, this right has been conceded, by the very convention of the people of Florida, who ask admission into the Union." In essence, Wyatt opposed attempts to push the matter to Congress, or any attempt of the convention to alter, change, or annul banking or any other corporate charters. That issue must be left to the General Assembly of the State of Florida, Wyatt asserted. In the end Wyatt lost his point. Baltzell and Long's resolution passed on January 3 by a vote of thirty-eight to eighteen.[55]

As the forum reached its final days, most observers of the deliberations noted the lack of unanimity on banking or many other issues. Louis Goldsborough, after witnessing body's contretemps wrote his wife, "The convention gets on very slowly and very badly."[56] Another spectator noted as the sessions came to a close that "little or nothing has been done." Eighteen committees had made their reports and the "misfortune is that they do not agree, and cannot be easily dovetailed together. You have no conception of the amount of wind which has been used here."[57]

In the end, the anti-bank advocates prevailed. They were able to put numerous restrictions on banking activity in the final version of the document. Historian Arthur Thompson has called Article XIII of the Florida Constitution "Banks and other Corporations," a "sweeping indictment of the territorial banking system and repudiation of the economic tactics of the Nucleus." The article contained numerous provisions restricting banking. Bank officers were banned from holding state office. Banks could not deal in real estate and manufacturing and were subject to regular legislative investigations. Stockholders of banks, in case of forfeiture of its charter were individually liable for payment of all debts in proportion to the stock they owned. Most importantly, the finished version of the constitution prohibited a future state from pledging its faith for any bank liability. If antibanking forces had not succeeded in voiding the territory's obligations to the current institutions, the door seemed open on that score.[58]

On January 11, the final day of the convention, there were last-ditch efforts to strike the article on banking from the final draft. Richard Fitzpatrick and E. Carrington Cabell entered protests against including the article. Fitzpatrick charged that there was no quorum present in the final readings. Cabell protested Baltzell's resolutions, insisting that the "interposition of Congress to alter, repeal, amend or modify the charters. . . . was calculated to affect prejudiciously the vested rights and interests of certain Banking and Railroad institutions, now in successful operation." The protests recorded, the delegates cast their votes on the final version. The total was fifty-five to one, with Richard Fitzpatrick the lone dissenting voice, upon which Reid proclaimed "this to be the Constitution of the State of Florida."[59]

In a concluding address Reid congratulated the delegates on their "fortitude, zeal and untiring industry." He predicted that the citizens of Florida would approve the constitution. While no one could be certain when Florida would join the Union, he urged the delegates not to "embarrass the country and evince disrespect to the General Government, by a hasty and rash attempt to supersede the Federal authorities . . . You will proceed slowly perhaps, but surely; adding strength to strength, until at last, your admission in the Union of states, will be secured by that public opinion, which shall rally on your side."[60]

When the convention closed, Reid's friends David Levy, James Westcott, Leigh Read, and other anti-bank Democrats emerged from the body in a strong position. A casualty of the convention was Thomas Baltzell, who lost a close election for territorial delegate to Congress to Charles Downing, a pro-bank statehood supporter from East Florida. The most prominent issue in the race was Baltzell's resolution in favor of turning the banking question over to Congress.[61] Angry attacks in the partisan press on both pro-bank and anti-bank forces grew more frequent in the months ahead. The subsequent legislative council session, which began its deliberations only days after the meeting concluded, contained a majority to move against banking interests, and they were successful in continuing the momentum toward this end. They were determined to use their new majority to dismantle the territory's banking system. Despite a lot of hot air, violence in the streets and on the dueling ground, they were in large part unsuccessful.[62] What actually sent the banks crashing down was more the degenerating economy than legislation. In the months ahead, Florida's economy hit rock bottom.

The delegates hardly had time to leave St. Joseph before prominent voices began lobbying members of Congress on issues the convention had grappled with. Missouri Senator Thomas Hart Benton proved receptive to these entreaties. In January 1839, Benton introduced a bill to divide the territory.[63] Later that year he offered a resolution to have the "President of the United States" request from the "constituted authorities in Florida, a statement of all the Territorial bonds issued, and authorized to be issued in that Territory" along with all other relevant documents regarding the establishment of banks.[64]

The voters approved the constitution by a vote of 2,070 to 1,975, with an overwhelming majority in favor of the constitution coming from Middle Florida. The narrow margin of passage and the sizable majorities cast in East and West Florida for "No Constitution" demonstrated the fundamental lack of consensus among Floridians regarding the St. Joseph Constitution as well as a whole myriad of issues surrounding the question. Even so, on October 21, 1839, Robert Raymond Reid proclaimed the constitution approved and ratified by the people.[65]

The time, manner, and circumstances that Florida would come into the Union depended on Congress. Sectional tensions at the national level augured against admission of Florida any time soon. Not surprisingly, opponents of statehood used the deteriorating economic situation, the uncertainty at the national level, and the challenges of the Second Seminole War, to argue for division. For the next six years, until Florida entered the Union, dividing the territory at the Suwannee River continued as a popular proposal for East Floridians. Beginning with the legislative council session that met immediately following the constitutional convention, petitions from East Florida citizens for dividing the territory came forward continuously.[66] Supporters of that course advocated allowing Middle Florida to become a state, and then permitting East Florida to join the Union as an independent state on its own time. For example, "Truth" in a letter to the editor of the St. Augustine *Florida Herald* asserted, "the Territory of Florida should not be bounded by a *single* State. She has every constituent element for *two States*. The one East and the other West of the Suwannee." Once the Indian war ended, Truth predicted, "Who can doubt that" all Floridians would not favor creating "two free and independent States to the National Confederacy. Our politicians know that we speak the TRUTH."[67] Anti-division leaders in Middle Florida used all manner of arguments to thwart division. They even went so far as to accuse East Floridians who favored division as being in league with, or the dupes of abolitionists.[68] Though proponents of division bitterly denied that their goals had anything to do with abolition or outside influences, the assertions continued.[69]

The years ahead proved tumultuous, as Florida's economic picture moved toward meltdown. One year after the convention, President Van Buren appointed Robert Raymond Reid territorial governor. Domestic unrest, the degenerating Indian war, and the economic fallout associated with Florida's fragile banking system consumed Reid's brief tenure until the next president removed him.[70] Reid died soon thereafter. William P. DuVal served in the next two legislative councils before resigning to attend to his law practice. Even so, he remained a staunch advocate of division, working with John C. Calhoun and other national leaders for admission of Florida, not as one, but two slave states. For Levy and Westcott, future political prospects were bright. Levy won election as Florida's delegate to Congress in 1841 where he used his ample talents to push Florida toward statehood. Levy's efforts enjoyed success in 1845 when he and Westcott became the first two senators of the State of Florida. In the end, national considerations dictated the time and the manner that Florida joined the Union. In the winter of 1845, Iowa was ready for admission as a free state, and in March, both entered the Union simultaneously.[71]

For the next fifteen years Florida was part of a Union that argued about—but also tolerated and accommodated—slavery. In 1860, when Abraham Lincoln, a member of a party whose platform opposed the expansion of slavery, was elected president, Florida and six other states seceded from the Union. William P. DuVal joined other white Southerners in the belief that the Union rested in the rights of slaveholders to take their property into the territories without obstruction. "The slave question is the rock which will certainly dash the Constitution into fragments," he wrote his friend John Crittenden in 1848.[72] DuVal's prediction proved true.

Notes

1 *Apalachicola Gazette,* December 8, 1838, quoted in Walter Sidney Martin, *Florida During Territorial Days* (Athens: University of Georgia Press, 1944), 267–68.
2 Reports of the daily sessions and debate of the work of the convention delegates appeared in the *Tallahassee Floridian* and the *St. Joseph Times.* In 1926, historian James Owen Knauss brought together and edited surviving newspaper editions of the debates that were available at that time, edited them, and published them in a work on territorial Florida journalism. See "Extracts from the *Times* and the *Floridian,* Reports of the Convention," 125–226, in James Owen Knauss, *Territorial Florida Journalism* (Deland: Florida Historical Society, 1926). A year after the con-

vention the *St. Joseph Times* published *Journal of the Proceedings of a Convention of Delegates to form A Constitution for the People of Florida Held at St. Joseph, December 1839*. But this version did not include debates. The contents of this *Journal* were published in what is still the standard work on the state constitution, Dorothy Dodd, *Florida Becomes a State* (Tallahassee: Florida Centennial Commission, 1945), 132–303. The most recent account of the 1838 St. Joseph Florida Constitution is Stephanie Moussalli, "Florida's Frontier Constitution: The Statehood, Banking, and Slavery Controversies," *Florida Historical Quarterly* 74 (Spring 1996): 423–39. See also Edward E. Baptist, *Creating an Old South: Middle Florida's Plantation Frontier before the Civil War* (Chapel Hill: University of North Carolina Press, 2002), 160–61; James M. Denham, *Florida Founder William P. DuVal: Frontier Bon Vivant* (Columbia: University of South Carolina Press, 2015), 252–62. Other older works are F. W. Hoskins, "The St. Joseph Convention: The Making of Florida's First Constitution," *Florida Historical Quarterly* 16 (July 1937): 33–43; (October 1937): 97–109; (April 1938): 242–50; 17 (October 1838): 125–31; James B. Whitfield, "Florida's First Constitution," *Florida Historical Quarterly* 17 (October 1938): 73–83; Emily Porter, "The Reception of the St. Joseph Constitution," *Florida Historical Quarterly* 17 (October 1938): 103–24. See also Canter Brown, Jr., *Ossian Bingley Hart: Florida's Loyalist Reconstruction Governor* (Baton Rouge: Louisiana State University Press, 1997), 38–40; Arthur W. Thompson, *Jacksonian Democracy on the Florida Frontier* (Gainesville: University of Florida Press, 1961), 9–16; Herbert J. Doherty, Jr., *The Whigs of Florida*, (Gainesville: University of Florida Press, 1959), 4–7; Martin, *Florida During Territorial Days*, 266–72.

3 "Act to Call a Convention for the Purpose of Organizing a State Government," Acts of the Legislative Council of the Territory of Florida (1838), 15–16.

4 See totals in "Proclamation of Governor Call and Returns of the 1837 Election," July 27, 1837, in Dodd, *Florida Becomes a State*, 109–12.

5 Petition to Congress by the Lake Wimico and St. Joseph Canal and Railroad Company, January 2, 1838; Clarence Carter, ed. *Territorial Papers of the United States*, 26 vols. (Washington, DC: US Government Printing Office, 1934–1962), 25: 42–53. Hereinafter TP.

6 On the boomtown of St. Joseph and its rivalry with Apalachicola, see William W. Rogers, *Outposts on the Gulf: Saint George Island & Apalachicola from Early Exploration to World War II* (Gainesville: University Press of Florida, 1987), 10–15; Denham, *Florida Founder*, 244; Willoughby, *Fair to Middlin': The Antebellum Cotton Trade on the Chattahoochee and Apalachicola River Valley* (Tuscaloosa: University of Alabama Press, 1993), 12; Martin, *Florida During Territorial Days*, 176–80; James Owen Knauss, "St. Joseph: An Episode of the Economic and Political History of Florida," *Florida Historical Quarterly* 17 (October 1938): 84–102; Robert R. Hurst, "Old St. Joseph, Its Railroads and Environs," *Florida Historical Quarterly* 39 (April 1961): 354–65.

7 Diary of Robert Raymond Reid, February 27, 1835, State Library of Florida, Dorothy Dodd Room, R. A. Gray Building, Tallahassee, Florida.

8. On the differing traditions of slavery in East Florida see Jane Landers, *Black Society in Spanish Florida* (Urbana: University of Illinois Press, 1999), 7–28; Larry Rivers, *Slavery in Florida, Territorial Days to Emancipation* (Gainesville: University Press of Florida, 2000), 1–15; Canter Brown, *Florida's Peace River Frontier* (Orlando: University of Central Florida Press, 1991), 63–74; Canter Brown, "Race Relations in Territorial Florida, 1821–1845," *Florida Historical Quarterly* 73 (January 1995): 287–307; Frank Marotti, *Heaven's Soldiers: Free People of Color and the Spanish Legacy in Antebellum Florida* (Tuscaloosa: University of Alabama Press, 2013), 46–60; Daniel L. Schafer, *Zephania Kingsley Jr. and the Atlantic World: Slave Trader, Plantation Owner, Emancipator* (Gainesville: University Press of Florida, 2013), 157–76.
9. Free Black rights in East Florida under the Adams-Onis Treaty were highly contested in the courts in the 1820s. For an overview of this struggle, see Craig Buettinger, "Free Blacks, Citizenship, and the Constitution in Florida Courts, 1821–1846," *Florida Historical Quarterly* 98 (Summer 2019): 1–22.
10. For Florida politics at this time, see Thompson, *Jacksonian Democracy on the Florida Frontier*; Doherty, *The Whigs of Florida*; Herbert J. Dohery, Jr., *The Whigs of Florida* (Gainesville: University of Florida Press, 1959); Baptist, *Creating an Old South*, 96–119; Denham, *Florida Founder*, 106–262.
11. "From Our Correspondents," December 6, 1838, in *Tallahassee Floridian*, December 15, 1838.
12. Summaries of debates on banking provisions in the convention are in J. D. Dovell, *History of Banking in Florida* (Orlando: Florida Bankers Association, 1955), 33–40.
13. J. D. Dovell, *History of Banking in Florida*, 14; John G. Gamble to the Secretary of the Treasury, February 21, 1835, TP, 25: 109–12.
14. For information on the operations of these three banks, see Dovell, *History of Banking in Florida*, 15–29; Martin, *Florida During Territorial Days*, 144–64.
15. For the Second Seminole War, see John K. Mahon, *History of the Second Seminole War, 1835–1842* (Gainesville: University Press of Florida, 1985); John Missall and Mary Lou Missall, *The Seminole Wars: America's Longest Indian Conflict* (Gainesville, University Press of Florida, 2004); C. S. Monaco, *The Second Seminole War and the Limits of American Aggression* (Baltimore: Johns Hopkins University Press, 2018); William S. Belko, ed. *America's Hundred Years War: U.S. Expansion to the Gulf Coast and the Fate of the Seminoles, 1763–1858* (Gainesville: University of Florida Press, 2011); Joe Knetsch, *Florida's Seminole Wars, 1817–1858* (Charleston: Arcadia Publishing, 2003).
16. *St. Augustine Florida Herald*, April 12, 1837.
17. For the statehood and "division" question in Florida, see Sidney Walter Martin, "The Proposed Division of the Territory of Florida." *Florida Historical Quarterly* 20 (January 1942): 260–76. See also Martin, *Florida During Territorial Days*, 258–77; Doherty, *The Whigs of Florida*, 4–5; Dodd, *Florida Becomes a State*; Baptist, *Creating an Old South*, 159–61.
18. *St. Augustine Florida Herald*, February 17, 1838.
19. Memorial to Congress of Inhabitants of St. Augustine, February 5, 1838, in Dodd, *Florida Becomes a State*, 122–26.

20 See *St. Augustine Florida Herald*, June 2, 16, 30, September 1, 1838.
21 See Memorial to Congress by Citizens of East Florida, February 5, 1838, TP: 25: 469–75.
22 Louis M. Goldsborough to Elizabeth Goldsborough, December 13, 21, 1838, Louis M. Goldsborough Papers, vol. 4, Library of Congress.
23 Dodd, *Florida Becomes a State*, 47. See also *St. Augustine Florida Herald*, April 25, 1839.
24 Union Bank stockholders at the time of the St. Joseph convention were George T. Ward (Leon), Thomas Brown (Leon), Samuel Parkhill (Leon), William Wyatt (Leon), Banks Meacham (Gadsden) Joseph McCants, (Jefferson), E. Carrington Cabell (Jefferson), John C. McGehee (Madison), Joseph B Watts (Hamilton), William P. DuVal (Calhoun), Samuel Bellamy (Jackson), Richard C. Allen (Calhoun), John Taylor (Leon). Meacham, Allen, and Leslie Thompson (Leon) were stockholders in the Central Bank of Florida. List of stockholders drawn from John G. Gamble to the Secretary of the Treasury, February 21, 1835, TP, 25: 109–12 and Benjamin Chaires to the Secretary of the Treasury, August 25, 1834, TP, 25: 46–49; "List of Stockholders in the Union Bank of Florida," January 12, 1838, in Message of the President of the United States in Compliance with a Resolution of the Senate in Relation to the Bonds Issued by the Territory of Florida, May 7, 1840, Senate Document, First session, Twenty-Sixth Congress, vol. 7, 77–86.
25 Doherty, *Whigs of Florida*, 5.
26 G. Alan Tarr, *Understanding State Constitutions* (Princeton, NJ: Princeton University Press, 1998), 115, n97.
27 *Tallahassee Floridian*, December 4, 1838.
28 *Tallahassee Floridian*, December 6, 1838.
29 Dodd, *Florida Becomes a State*, 48.
30 *Journal of the Proceedings of a Convention of Delegates to Form a Constitution for the People of Florida Held at St. Joseph, December 1838* (St. Joseph: Times, 1839), in Dodd, *Florida Becomes a State*, 136–37.
31 Denham, *Florida Founder*, 215–16. On the Union Bank of Florida, see Baptist, *Creating a New South*, 65, 112–19; Dovell, *History of Banking in Florida*, 16–19; Caroline Mays Brevard, *A History of Florida from the Treaty of 1763 to Our Own Time* (DeLand: Florida State Historical Society, 1924–1925), 202–17; Kathryn T. Abbey, "The Union Bank of Tallahassee: An Experiment in Territorial Finance," *Florida Historical Quarterly* 15 (April 1937): 207–31.
32 Robert Raymond Reid Diary, February 18, 1833, February 27, 1835, Special Collections, R. A. Gray Building, Tallahassee, Florida.
33 Robert Raymond Reid Diary, February 18, 1833; Stephen Miller, ed., *Bench and Bar in Georgia: Memoirs and Sketches* (Philadelphia: J. B. Lippincott and Company, 1858), 2: 205–6.
34 Reports of the Convention, in Knauss, *Territorial Florida Journalism*, 139–41.
35 Reports of the Convention, in Knauss, *Territorial Florida Journalism*, 141.
36 Reports of the Convention, in Knauss, *Territorial Florida Journalism*, 142–43.
37 Reports of the Convention, in Knauss, *Territorial Florida Journalism*, 144.

38 Reports of the Convention, in Knauss, *Territorial Florida Journalism*, 148–49.
39 Reports of the Convention, in Knauss, *Territorial Florida Journalism*, 150–53; *Tallahassee Floridian*, December 15, 1838. See also *St. Joseph Times*, quoted in *Tallahassee Floridian*, December 22, 1838. For an overview of these divided views and their impact on first few days of the Convention, see Dodd, *Florida Becomes a State*, 47–51.
40 *Journal of the Proceedings of a Convention of Delegates*, in Dodd, *Florida Becomes a State*, 143.
41 Moussalli, "Florida's Frontier Constitution," 423.
42 *Journal of the Proceedings of a Convention of Delegates*, in Dodd, *Florida Becomes a State*, 146–47.
43 Dodd, *Florida Becomes a State*, 170–71.
44 Moussalli, "Florida's Frontier Constitution," 433–35.
45 Debates in the Constitutional Convention, December 17, 1838, from *St. Joseph Times*, printed in *Tallahassee Floridian*, January 12, 1839. See also Reports of the Convention, in Knauss, *Territorial Florida Journalism*, 184–186.
46 *Journal of the Proceedings of a Convention of Delegates*, in Dodd, *Florida Becomes a State*, 177–79, 198. For the extensive debate on the banking, see Reports of the Convention, in Knauss, *Territorial Florida Journalism*, 180–84.
47 Dodd, *Florida Becomes a State*, 56–57, 447, n47.
48 Some years later accusations were made that the "faith bond bank faction became more and more violent, denunciatory, and abusive. Especially [at issue] was the course of the clique managed by Lot Clark, Charles Downing, Peter Sken Smith, Thomas Douglas, and Samuel L. Burritt, in East Florida, rancorous toward Judge Reid and Mr. Levy, and they were well abetted by the Union Bank Junto, headed by their attorney Ex-Governor Duval, Charles H. Dupont, a director of the Union Bank, and others in Middle Florida. While the Convention was in session, the Bank minority held on a Sunday a caucus, to decide whether they should not break up the Convention, unless the Democrats yielded their opposition to the recognition of the Faith Bond Banks. Fortunately, the meeting was heard of and attended by a leading Democrat who made the chief movers ashamed of their course. Ex Gov. DuVal was one of the prime getters up of this meeting, which might justly be called a blood cousin to the Hartford Convention." "The Lawlessness of the Times," *St. Augustine Florida Herald and Southern Democrat*, September 12, 1840. Soon after he became governor, Robert Raymond Reid relayed essentially the same information in a letter to the secretary of state. Robert Raymond Reid to John Forsyth, December 10, 1840, quoted in Martin, *Florida During Territorial Days*, 157. See also Arthur Thompson, *Jacksonian Democracy on the Florida Frontier* (Gainesville: University of Florida Press, 1961), 14.
49 Reports of the Convention, in Knauss, *Territorial Florida Journalism*, 171–73.
50 Reports of the Convention, in Knauss, *Territorial Florida Journalism*, 171–73.
51 Reports of the Convention, in Knauss, *Territorial Florida Journalism*, 171–73.
52 Louis M. Goldsborough to Elizabeth Goldsborough, December 21, 1838, Goldsborough Papers, vol. 4, Library of Congress.
53 Reports of the Convention, in Knauss, *Territorial Florida Journalism*, 180–81.

54 Reports of the Convention, in Knauss, *Territorial Florida Journalism*, 180–82.
55 Reports of the Convention, in Knauss, *Territorial Florida Journalism*, 192–95. *Journal of the Proceedings of a Convention of Delegates*, in Dodd, *Florida Becomes a State*, 233–34.
56 Louis Goldsborough to Elizabeth Goldsborough, December 21, 1838, Louis Goldsborough Papers, vol. 4, LC.
57 *Pensacola Gazette*, January 5, 1839.
58 Thompson, *Jacksonian Democracy on the Florida Frontier*, 15; "A Constitution, or Form of Government, for the People of Florida," in Dodd, *Florida Becomes a State*, 322–24; Larry Schweikart, *Banking in the American South from the Age of Jackson to Reconstruction* (Baton Rouge: Louisiana State University Press, 1987), 174; Baptist, *Creating an Old South*, 160–61; Dovell, *History of Banking in Florida*, 37–40.
59 *Journal of the Proceedings of a Convention of Delegates*, in Dodd, *Florida Becomes a State*, 296–98. A number of delegates left the convention early and voted for the final version by proxy and thus did not sign the final document. They were Jackson Morton, Benjamin D. Wright, Thomas M. Blount, William P. DuVal, John Taylor, Thomas Brown, Samuel Parkhill, Leslie A. Thompson, Samuel B. Stephens, Richard J. Mays, A. G. Semmes, Samuel T. Garey, and James G. Cooper. Dodd, 298–99.
60 Dodd, 301–2.
61 Baltzell set out his views on his resolution in a letter to a constituent, Thomas Baltzell to Joseph McBride, March 15, 1839, in *St. Joseph Times*, March 30, 1839. See also "Delegate's Election" in *St. Joseph Times*, May 4, 1839. For the election totals, see *St. Augustine Florida Herald and Southern Democrat*, August 22, 1839.
62 James M. Denham, "Read-Alston Duel and Politics in Territorial Florida," *Florida Historical Quarterly* 68 (April 1990): 427–46; James M. Denham, "Robert Raymond Reid," in R. Boyd Murphree and Robert A. Taylor, eds. *The Governors of Florida* (Gainesville: University Press of Florida, 2020), 56–61; Denham, *Florida Founder*, 269–83; Baptist, *Creating an Old South*, 169–72; Clifton Paisley, *Red Hills of Florida, 1528–1865*. (Tuscaloosa: University of Alabama Press, 1989), 99–102.
63 Joseph Hernandez urged Benton to offer a bill to divide the territory claiming that the "country east of the Suwannee River is capable of sustaining an immense population and must in the political order of things, eventually form a state separate from that of Middle and West Florida, and greatly to their advantage and that of the country." See Joseph Hernandez to Thomas Hart Benton, January 16, 1839, M200, RG 46, Territorial Papers of the Senate, Reel #11; "Eastern Territory of Florida," *St. Augustine News*, January 26, 1839.
64 *Richmond Enquirer*, December 31, 1839.
65 Proclamation of Robert Raymond Reid, President of the Convention Lately in Session at St. Joseph, in *St. Augustine Herald and Southern Democrat*, November 14, 1839; TP, 25: n470.
66 These petitions are compiled in Dodd, *Florida Becomes a State*, 336–414. See also Sidney Walter Martin, "The Proposed Division of the Territory of Florida." *Florida Historical Quarterly* 20 (January 1942): 266–76; Emily Porter, "The Reception of the St. Joseph Constitution," *Florida Historical Quarterly* 17 (October 1938): 103–24.

67 *St. Augustine Florida Herald,* January 26, 1839.
68 According to the plot, Peter Sken Smith, Lot Clark, and other abolitionist migrants from the North were conspiring with East Florida planter Zephania Kingsley to make East Florida a free state. "Disunite them [the sections] and we shall have the germ of an Abolitionist State in East Florida, in less than five years; it will be a receptacle for runaway slaves from the contiguous States, more dangerous than the Seminole nation has been. Hordes of immigrants from the North, gathered up by colonizing emissaries and agents, are waiting but for the Indians to give place to make settlements, and not a few of these emigrants will be infected with the Abolition monomania. Many will be from Europe." Much of East Florida was "literally shingled with Spanish grants, confirmed and unconfirmed, genuine and forged, honest and fraudulent." Much of the land would eventually fall into the hands of wealthy speculators from New York who will be the means by which "emigrants *of this sort"* will come to Florida. "Under a State Government, united with Middle, West, and South Florida, no danger is to be apprehended. The soundness of these sections, and their control in the State Legislature, would secure the State from taint. It would only be in the Eastern member that the disease would lurk. It could not be cured. We would not impute to those who now compose the population of East Florida, that they are now subject to such accusation, but only to express the fear—nay, the conviction, that in a short time, they would be outnumbered by the immigration to that section brought through the channels we have alluded to. . . ." The leading abolitionist print in the North, the *Emancipator,* has repeatedly alluded to East Florida as the *point d'appui* in their assaults upon the South, and boast that it should be a "FREE STATE." *Tallahassee Floridian,* April 4, 1840. See also *St. Joseph Times,* April 1, 1840.
69 On these denials, see *Jacksonville East Florida Advocate,* May 12, 1840. On the June 24 St. Augustine public meeting endorsing division, see *Quincy Sentinel,* July 17, 1840.
70 Denham, "Robert Raymond Reid," 57–65.
71 Franklin A. Doty, "Florida, Iowa, and the National Balance of Power, 1845," *Florida Historical Quarterly* 35 (July 1956): 30–59.
72 William P. DuVal to John J. Crittenden, November 26, 1848, John Jordan Crittenden Papers, Reel 6, Library of Congress.

4

The Constitution of 1861

Florida's Confederate Constitution

R. Boyd Murphree

The Constitution of 1861 lived and died with secession. Created in the weeks following Florida's withdrawal from the United States on January 10, 1861, the constitution ceased to be the fundamental law of the state when Union troops occupied Florida and imposed martial law in May 1865. If Florida's role in the American Civil War has been called a "forgotten front," legal scholars, Florida historians, and Civil War–era historians have given even shorter shrift to the story of the creation, implementation, and significance of Florida's Confederate constitution after the passage of the Ordinance of Secession. The traditional reason for this neglect has been the view that beyond declaring Florida's secession, the Constitution of 1861 did little more than substitute "Confederate States" for "United States" in the provisions of the Constitution of 1838. As one of Florida's top legal historians observed, the Constitution of 1861, with some exceptions, was "a mere copying of the 1838 Constitution with language changes to reflect the displacement of the United States by the Confederacy as the national government."[1]

This chapter takes a different view. Although the Constitution of 1861 was short-lived, it was a significant governing document. A constitution that made changes in Florida law to implement secession, join the Confederate States, and prepare for the likelihood of war with the Union, the Constitution of 1861 met those requirements without making extensive revisions to Florida's existing constitutional law. Like its federal counterpart, the Constitution of the Confederate States, the Constitution of 1861 was produced and implemented quickly in a crisis and was important "not so much for what was done as for what was not done." Both documents maintained most of the features of their model documents, the Constitution of the United States for the Confederacy, and the Constitution of 1838 for Florida, while making changes that reinforced the dominant Southern governing philosophy of states' rights grounded on the pillars of slavery and state sovereignty.[2]

Beyond what the Constitution of 1861 did or did not do, the secession convention that created the constitution held that its ordinances, which were attached to the published revised state constitution, had the authority of the constitution, the supreme law of the state. In Ordinance 14, an ordinance amending the constitutional oath of all state civil and military officers and legislators, such officials were required to swear to "preserve, protect, and defend the Constitution of this State, and the ordinances adopted by this Convention." The convention also enshrined its sole authority to amend the constitution by passing a constitutional amendment requiring the convening of a new convention to authorize any future amendments. These developments conflicted with the Florida legislature's role as the lawmaking body of the state, including its traditional power to amend the constitution. The convention's intervention also challenged the authority of the governor in state defense and other issues. In 1862, the convention created an executive council that, by ordinance of the convention, was supposed to function along with the governor as the executive body of the state. Political conflict between the chief executive and the convention came to a head when Governor John Milton challenged the constitutionality of the convention's involvement in legislative and executive affairs. Combined with the convention's ordinances, the Constitution of 1861 proved to have a significant impact on state policies during the Civil War.[3]

Florida left the Union less than sixteen years after becoming a state on March 3, 1845. The new state was born at the beginning of the sectional crisis that culminated in the secession of Southern states in 1860–1861. When he took the oath of office, Florida's first state governor, William D. Moseley, did so standing next to an unofficial state flag that bore the inscription "Let Us Alone" as a statement that Florida would oppose federal intervention in its internal affairs. Moseley enunciated this declaration by invoking John C. Calhoun's doctrine of state sovereignty.[4]

Originally applied against what Calhoun saw as the unconstitutionality of the tariff of 1828, Calhoun's doctrine proposed that the states never gave up their original sovereignty when they agreed to delegate certain enumerated powers to the federal government in the Constitution. Whenever the federal government passed a law that went beyond its enumerated powers, it was violating sovereign powers that the states had retained when they agreed to the federal compact. A state threatened by such an unconstitutional law had the right, through an elected convention representing the sovereignty of the state through its people, of interposition or nullification to reject the unconstitutional federal law.[5]

In his inaugural address, Governor Moseley pointed to nullification as an essential sovereign state right to address unconstitutional federal intervention: "That among the most important and highly cherished of the reserve rights, is the right of *State interposition,* under its constitutional authorities, as the *legitimate* remedy for such an act of usurpation on the part of the National Government." When he spoke those words in July 1845, Moseley targeted federally funded internal improvements and tariffs as the main threats to state sovereignty. However, just a year later, the US House of Representatives passed the Wilmot Proviso that called for the exclusion of slavery from any territory that the United States acquired from its war with Mexico. Now the defense of slavery, which since the American Revolution Southern leaders had argued was essential for white liberty and social stability, was reinforced as the focus of states' rights politics. Except for Whig Governor Thomas Brown, who opposed the extreme Southern states' rights position, all of Florida's governors between 1845 and 1865 embraced Calhoun's philosophy of state sovereignty.[6]

Following Abraham Lincoln's victory in the presidential election of 1860 and fearing that Republican control of the federal government would end in the abolition of slavery, South Carolina, on December 20, 1860, became the first Southern state to take Calhoun's ideas to their logical conclusion by seceding. Governor Madison Starke Perry of Florida, a South Carolinian by birth and a Calhounist at heart, called for the election of delegates to a state convention that would convene to decide if Florida would follow South Carolina out of the Union. Perry had no doubts about what his state would do, declaring to South Carolina's secession convention that "the gallant little State of Florida will follow your lead." After the election of convention delegates on December 22, Governor Perry proclaimed that the "Convention of the People of Florida" would convene on January 3, 1861, in Tallahassee to vote on secession.[7]

A study of the sixty-nine men who filled the convention seats in the chamber of the Florida House of Representatives on January 3 reveals the following facts: the median age was forty-three; less than 10 percent were Florida born; the majority were native Georgians and South Carolinians; most were farmers and merchants; fifty-one delegates owned enslaved persons and averaged about thirty-six slaves per delegate; and a typical delegate had $25,000 in real and personal property. These were the men who would vote on Florida's secession and create a revised state constitution.[8]

Governor Perry and most of the convention delegates wanted Florida to secede as soon as possible after convening the convention. Like South Carolina's secessionists, they believed that delaying secession for the sake of convening a convention of all the slaveholding states or even a convention of lower South states would inevitably lead to a waning of secessionist enthusiasm as time passed. That the immediate secessionists were running the convention was clear by the election of John C. McGehee as convention president. A Florida fire-eater, McGehee had long advocated for secession and the creation of a separate Southern nation. His opening address to the convention was in the same vein. He declared that abolitionism had seized power in the North and now controlled the federal government. The abolitionist government "threatens annihilation to slavery . . . the element of all value" for the South. When the Republican Party assumed power in Washington, McGehee said it would be "driven on by an infuriated fanatical madness" that would "destroy every vestige of right growing out of property in slaves." If Florida remained in the Union, "our doom is decreed."[9]

Opposing McGehee and the delegates for immediate secession were delegates who wanted to delay Florida's secession until the state could secede jointly with other Southern states, especially the neighboring states of Alabama and Georgia. These "cooperationist" delegates offered amendments in the convention that would have led to Florida delaying secession until Alabama and Georgia acted and even having the convention delay a vote on secession until the question was put to the voters of Florida. Of the sixty-nine delegates, 60 percent supported immediate secession. Given their numbers, it was not surprising that the immediatists defeated the cooperationist resolutions that would have delayed secession; however, the fact that 40 percent of the delegates wanted to postpone secession shows there was significant resistance in the state against the radical step of immediate secession. Aware of this sentiment, the immediatists were not willing to put the question of secession on a statewide ballot.[10]

The immediatists won the day on January 10, 1861, when the convention passed the Ordinance of Secession. A straightforward statement of the state's departure from the United States, the document declared Florida's withdrawal from the United States, broke any political connection to the government of the United States, declared Florida's status as a sovereign nation, and repealed all ordinances and laws recognizing Florida's former union with the United States. While historians have given the ordinance passed on January 10, 1861, considerable attention, that document was not the first ordinance of secession presented to the convention.[11]

On January 9, the secession convention's Select Committee on Ordinances presented an ordinance that was so innocuous in its language that it hardly qualified as a declaration of secession. The ordinance stated that the laws and treaties of the United States would remain in force in Florida until such time as the convention repealed them. Committee chair John P. Sanderson, a reluctant secessionist, submitted the unremarkable ordinance after presenting the committee's arguments for the legality of secession. Although the select committee did not include reasons for secession in the ordinance, it did preface the submission of the ordinance with a statement arguing for the legality of secession. The committee used standard secessionist arguments based on Jeffersonian Republican and Calhounist political theory. As contracting sovereign polities to the federal union, the states had the right to break from that compact when the union could no longer guarantee the states' citizens their fundamental rights to life, liberty, "property," and the pursuit of happiness. Since the federal union no longer secured those rights for Florida, the state had a right and obligation to withdraw from the compact known as the United States of America. The committee recommended that Florida "secede now, and re-assume all the rights by her delegated to the Federal Government . . . and declare herself to be a Sovereign and Independent Nation."[12]

After the reading of the initial ordinance, it was obvious that the document did not rise to the gravity of the question of secession. The tepid reception to the ordinance moved the convention to take the responsibility for the creation of a new ordinance out of the hands of the Committee on Ordinances and place it under the Committee on Judiciary. Delegate Sanderson was also a member of that committee but not its chair. After an hour of work, chair William G. M. Davis reported that his committee had prepared a substitute ordinance, which was the ordinance the convention passed on January 10.[13]

How does Florida's Ordinance of Secession compare with the secession ordinances of the six other states that together with Florida formed the Confederate States of America? South Carolina, Mississippi, Georgia, and Louisiana passed ordinances similar to Florida's ordinance. These ordinances declared that the state was withdrawing from the United States, abrogated all laws that recognized the state's membership in the federal union, and declared the state's sovereignty and full independence. Looking to the future, Mississippi's ordinance declared the state's willingness to join other seceding states in a new federal union.[14]

Alabama and Texas were the only original secession states to include language in their ordinances justifying secession. Texas's ordinance accused the federal government of not protecting Texans living in its frontier regions and, alluding to the victory of Lincoln and the Republican Party in 1860, stated that "recent developments in Federal affairs" had made the federal government into a weapon to be used to abolish slavery, assaulting the slaveholding states rather than protecting them "against outrage and aggression." Alabama's ordinance was even more explicit in identifying Lincoln and the Republicans as the impetus for the state's secession, declaring their electoral victory "a political wrong of so insulting and menacing a character" that the state had no option but secession as the means to defend itself from future federal aggression. In addition, Alabama, like Mississippi, called for the creation of a new federal union consisting of all the slaveholding states and invited those states to send delegates to Montgomery in February 1861 to consult on the formation of such a union.[15]

Following secession, South Carolina, Georgia, Mississippi, and Texas published documents stating their reasons for secession. The authors of these "Declarations of Causes" devoted the overwhelming portions of their texts to the defense of slavery. They argued that the federal government under the political and economic control of the Northern states had violated the equal rights of the slaveholding states in the Union by undermining their constitutionally protected right to own slaves, a right that the recently elected sectional Republican Party sought to abolish. The documents pointed to the crucial economic and societal interest of the slaveholding states in maintaining slavery and their constitutional right to establish the institution in the territories held in common by all the states.[16]

Florida did not publish a declaration of causes. The secession convention did, however, authorize the appointment of a five-man committee to draft such a declaration. Created on January 21, 1861, the committee was to report during the next session of the convention. During that session, on March 1, 1861, committee member Thompson Bird Lamar asked that the committee be discharged without further work on the question of Florida's reasons for secession. Although the committee's work was not published, a copy of one draft survived in the papers of Governor Perry.[17]

Consisting of six handwritten pages marked "Treatise," the document begins by stating that Florida made the decision for secession after the "utmost deliberation" and due to "immeasurable necessity." The first of the causes of secession was the Northern states' responsibility for John Brown's raid through Northern support and sympathy for Brown's violent actions against a fellow slaveholding state. This accusation is followed by a condemnation of Northern states for undermining the fugitive slave act by not enforcing the law and encouraging the release and support of runaway slaves. Ironically, the document attacks those states for nullifying the fugitive slave act even though the doctrine of nullification was central to the extreme states' rights philosophy of Florida and the other seceding states. The next argument accuses the abolitionist North of carrying on a campaign of insulting and degrading the slaveholding states through violent language in the halls of Congress, the spread of abolitionist literature, denying the admission of any new slaveholding states into the Union, and electing a president, "an obscure and illiterate man," and political party that seeks the ultimate elimination of slavery. These actions represent a torturous "death by a slow fire" that will lead to the submission of the slaveholding states unless they resist: "Men who can hesitate to resist such aggression are slaves already and deserve their destiny."[18]

Turning to economic grievances, the authors submit that the slaveholding states contributed more than their fair share to the cost of acquiring new territory for the United States, and that it was due mainly to Southern blood and leadership that the nation won the war with Mexico. The South had also ended up paying for much of the general revenue of the federal government through the payment of import duties. In a unique economic justification for secession, the Florida declaration maintains that through its control of federal legislation, the North enjoys a monopoly on the fishing trade off the coasts of Southern states. The document closes with a reaffirmation of Florida's determination to resist the degradation of its rights under the Constitution and submission to the tyranny of a sectional, abolitionist party by separating from the United States of America.[19]

Convention ordinances, declarations of causes, ceremonies, and celebrations of secession—a public signing of the Ordinance of Secession occurred on January 11, 1861, at the state capitol—temporarily obscured the grim reality that Florida and the other seceding states would have to use force to secure their independence from the United States. Even before the convention voted on secession, Governor Perry ordered state militia companies to seize control of federal military properties across the state. The units occupied without violence the federal arsenal at Chattahoochee, Fort Marion in St. Augustine, and Fort Clinch on Amelia Island. On January 12, the commander of the US naval yard at Pensacola surrendered that facility to Florida and Alabama militia—Governor Perry had requested that Alabama, which had seceded on January 11, send the units—however, a Union contingent held and refused to surrender Fort Pickens at the mouth of Pensacola Harbor. Florida also failed to occupy Union-controlled Fort Taylor in Key West and Fort Jefferson on the Dry Tortugas. The Union remained in control of these strategic posts for the duration of the Civil War.[20]

It was in this emergency atmosphere that Florida's secession convention took up the task of revising the original 1838 Constitution to meet Florida's new status as a seceded state and in anticipation of joining the other secession states in the creation of an independent Southern nation. Whereas the Confederate convention that assembled in Montgomery, on February 4, 1861, was initially focused on creating a provisional constitution for the new nation, a task the delegates completed in just four days, the Florida convention did not adjourn and convene a separate session devoted to constitutional revision. Instead, the convention remained in its regular session and passed ordinances amending the state constitution and organizing the new state government.[21]

The legal basis for the convention's ability to amend the state constitution and to pass ordinances in protection of the state rested in the act the legislature passed authorizing the convening of the convention. In addition to considering Florida's future position within the United States, the act gave the convention the power to take all measures "necessary and proper" to ensure the state's security as a result of its relationship with the federal union and to "amend the Constitution of the State of Florida" as necessary to implement those measures. Section 5 of the act gave the convention's ordinances extraordinary authority: "The ordinances of said Convention shall be the supreme law of the State of Florida." Armed with such a powerful mandate, convention delegates, who assembled as the "People of Florida," believed they had a right and duty to pass ordinances having the effect of laws and to amend the constitution to secure Florida's sovereignty.[22]

After passing the Ordinance of Secession, the Committee on Ordinances submitted ordinances organizing Florida's independent government. These ordinances included extending Florida's control over all federal defense installations in the state, the creation of state admiralty courts, regulating commerce and foreign trade, continuing the postal service, and having Florida join with other states to form a national government for the South. After submitting these foundational ordinances to the convention, the Committee on Ordinances proclaimed its work completed and turned over its ordinance-making function to the standing committees of the convention.[23]

The move to unite Florida with other states in a Southern confederacy was the convention's most important goal after secession. After several votes, the convention, which had resolved that three of its own delegates would represent Florida in the upcoming convention of slaveholding states in Montgomery, could not reach a majority vote on any of the candidates. A new resolution then gave the governor the authority to choose three persons from among the citizens and qualified voters of the state to represent Florida in Montgomery. Governor Perry chose Jackson Morton, James Patton Anderson, and James B. Owens, all three of whom were convention delegates. The Florida delegation was the smallest of all the state delegations in Montgomery. Anderson and Owens were part of the twelve-member committee appointed to create a provisional constitution for the new government. They and their fellow committee members worked into the night for four days to complete the provisional constitution. On February 9, Montgomery celebrated the adoption of the provisional Constitution of the Confederate States of America, including the creation of a provisional congress, army, and the election of Jefferson Davis as president and Alexander Stephens as vice president.[24]

In the days following the proclamation of the provisional Confederate Constitution, the provisional Confederate Congress moved on to prepare a permanent constitution. Two members of the Florida delegation, Morton and Owens, served on the new twelve-member committee to draft the constitution. As they had done with the provisional Confederate Constitution, the committee embraced the US Constitution as the model for the permanent Confederate Constitution, replacing "the United States" with "the Confederate States" throughout the document. The permanent Confederate Constitution embedded the doctrine of state sovereignty and absolute defense of slavery as the foundations of the new Southern nation. Declaring that the government was established by "each State acting in its sovereign and independent character" and that "no law denying or impairing the right of property in negro slaves shall be passed," the permanent Confederate Constitution was the culmination of the Calhounist political philosophy that had informed the work of the states' secession conventions. On March 11, 1861, the provisional Confederate Congress approved the permanent Constitution, which now went to the seven seceded states for ratification.[25]

The process of amending the Florida Constitution began weeks before the Florida delegation arrived in Montgomery. On January 11, the day of the signing of the Ordinance of Secession, the Committee on Ordinances submitted an ordinance calling for the General Assembly to amend the constitution as necessary for the state's executive, legislative, and judicial departments to assume the same functions and responsibilities that the three federal departments had exercised in the state. Ordinance 9, the ordinance that passed in its final form, had the convention, not the General Assembly, amending the constitution to allow the state executive and legislative departments to take over those functions from the same federal departments; however, the ordinance did not mention the judiciary. This omission may have been due to the more complex task of replacing the federal court system in Florida, which was divided into two district courts, one for the northern half of the state and one for the southern half, with the Southern District's court still under federal control at Key West.[26]

Including the ordinance discussed previously as well as the Ordinance of Secession, which became the preamble of the Constitution of 1861, the convention, in its initial weeks, passed eight ordinances amending the existing constitution, the Constitution of 1838. Two of the ordinances concerned military service. Ordinance 4 amended article 6, section 5, which excluded anyone from serving in a state office who had fought or participated in a duel. The ordinance allowed anyone who had previously been prevented from serving the state due to dueling to now enter civil or military state service. Ordinance 4 removed the old section 5 from article 6 in the revised constitution. Now, according to section 3, article 6, no one could hold public civil or military office if they participated in a duel after the passage of the revised constitution. Given the national crisis generated by secession and the possibility of war with the United States, the state needed volunteers to defend the state and to fill offices vacated by federal officials. By removing the dueling restriction, Florida would have a larger pool of men to draw on for military service, especially those from the upper classes who were the most likely group to have been in duels and who were potential officers. Ordinance 15 replaced the previous constitutional provisions on the state militia under article 7 with three new sections. The new provisions gave the legislature responsibility for electing militia officers, removing that power from local militia members. In addition, sections 2 and 3 specified that violations of the militia laws would be tried by courts-martial, and only a court-martial could remove an officer from his commission.[27]

Just as it had with Ordinance 4, the convention removed other sections of the constitution that restricted who could serve in state offices. In Ordinance 5, the convention annulled section 3, article 6, which had imposed an interval of a year before any officer or employee of a bank could be eligible to run for governor or for a seat in the General Assembly; the same ordinance also removed section 8 of the same article, a year interval on governors, supreme court justices, and judges being elected or appointed to other state offices. Removing these restrictions would allow experienced officials to be eligible for other offices as soon as possible during the uncertain months ahead in 1861.[28]

Ordinances 6 and 16 focused on the executive branch. When Florida became a state in 1845, Governor Moseley, who was elected that year, served his four-year term until the first Monday in October 1849, the day and month after four years that the constitution mandated would be the date for the inauguration of a new governor. That meant that Thomas Brown, who was elected governor in October 1848, could not take office until October of the next year. This lengthy transition period was awkward for both the sitting governor, who had a governor-elect waiting in the wings for a year, and for the governor-elect, who had to bide his time for a year before he could take office. Ordinance 6 removed the ungainly transition period. Beginning with the opening session of the General Assembly in 1865, the governor-elect would be inaugurated on the second Monday of that session after being elected on the first Monday in October 1865. However, what the convention gave with one hand it could take away with the other. Ordinance 16 reduced future gubernatorial terms from four years to two years. Like Ordinance 6, this ordinance was set to begin in 1865.[29]

The convention recessed on January 21, 1861, reassembling on February 26. President McGehee recalled the delegates to Tallahassee to consider ratification of the provisional Confederate Constitution. Although this second assembly of the convention lasted only four days, the delegates ratified the provisional Confederate Constitution and passed two ordinances amending the Florida Constitution. Ordinance 23 repealed section 10, article 6, which had barred members of the clergy from serving in the legislature and as governor. A much more consequential measure was Ordinance 26, which amended article 14, the article that governed the process of amending and revising the state constitution. The revised article 14 removed the power of amending the constitution from the General Assembly and gave it to the convention: "Sec. 1. No Part of this Constitution shall be altered, except by a Convention duly elected." Although this revolutionary amendment removing the legislature's historic role in amending the Florida Constitution passed the convention by an overwhelming majority—thirty-eight to two— there was an attempt to put a check on this power by allowing the voters of Florida to decide on the ratification of future convention amendments. Not willing to debate this ordinance, the convention laid the proposal on the table and moved on to other business. The convention was so intent on passing Ordinance 26 that it even voted down a motion to allow the newly formed select committee on amending the constitution to study and report on the ordinance. Other than Florida, Georgia was the only other secession state to give full amendment power to its convention.[30]

After voting to recess on March 1, the convention resumed its session on April 18, 1861. The delegates who took their seats that day now represented a state at war. Six days earlier, Confederate forces in Charleston, South Carolina, opened fire on Union-held Fort Sumter, launching civil war. The main order of business of the resumed session was to ratify the permanent Confederate Constitution as well as the revised Florida Constitution. In a unanimous vote on April 22, the convention ratified the permanent Confederate Constitution. Florida was the last of the original seven member states of the Confederacy to ratify. On April 27, the convention passed the Constitution or Form of Government for the People of Florida as Revised and Amended. The 1861 document kept the title of the 1838 Constitution but added "Revised and Amended" to signify the convention's changes to the original constitution. Unlike the Georgia and Virginia conventions, which created new constitutions in 1861, the Florida convention followed the path of the other secession states in maintaining their existing constitutions with amendments reflecting their new status as seceded states and members of the Confederacy. Also, unlike Georgia and Virginia, the Florida convention refused to allow the voters a chance to accept or decline ratification of the revised constitution. In a close vote, A. K. Allison, who had proposed the popular vote ordinance, and eighteen other reluctant secessionist and former cooperationist delegates supported the ordinance, but they lost to President McGehee and twenty-two more radical delegates.[31]

Given that Florida was now at war with the Union, which could be expected to invade the state, slave owners were worried that their enslaved persons might be more encouraged to rebel and attack them and other white Floridians in attempts to escape to Union-held territory or to Union naval vessels patrolling the coast. On April 19, the convention passed Ordinance 27 authorizing the General Assembly to create special local slave tribunals to try any "slaves, free negroes and mulattos" accused of committing felonies. The tribunals were originally to consist of two justices of the peace and twelve slave-owning male citizens who by a majority vote could pronounce judgment based solely on the statement of the offense in the arrest warrant without the calling of a grand jury. If the accused were found guilty of a crime warranting capital punishment, the state would reimburse the slave owner one half the value of the enslaved person or persons after the special court assessed their value. The convention, in Ordinance 40, later amended the ordinance by allowing any twelve qualified jurors to serve on the tribunals instead of limiting jury service to slave owners; the amended version also struck out the language requiring the state to reimburse slave owners for their loss. The ordinance became section 27, article 4, of the revised constitution.[32]

In instituting the slave tribunals, the convention was strengthening the state's constitutional restrictions on enslaved and free persons of color that Confederate Florida inherited from the territorial Constitution of 1838. Both constitutions barred the General Assembly from emancipating any enslaved person, and both documents gave the General Assembly the power to forbid free blacks, mixed raced persons, and "other persons of color" from immigrating into Florida. Article 16, section 2 of the Constitution of 1838 also barred the General Assembly from preventing citizens of other states from bringing enslaved persons with them into Florida. The revised 1861 constitution did away with this provision in conformity with the Confederate Constitution's broad protections of slavery, which turned over the power to bar enslaved persons from entering the Confederate States from states or territories outside the Confederacy to the Confederate government.[33]

The Constitution of 1861 also maintained the limited franchise of the 1838 Constitution. Voting was restricted to white males aged twenty-one or over who were citizens of the Confederate States at the time of voting and had resided in Florida for at least one year before voting, and who made their permanent home in the county of voting for at least six months before voting. Who was or who was not a citizen of the Confederate States were questions left to the Confederate Congress to decide. According to article 1, section 8, subsection 4, of the Confederate Constitution, Congress had the power "to establish uniform laws of naturalization." However, the Confederate government never passed laws establishing who was a Confederate citizen. That power was left to the individual Confederate States. While some Confederate States defined citizenship, Florida failed to do so. The convention's Ordinance 11, which passed in January 1861, gave the General

Assembly the power to determine state citizenship and to set the terms for Florida citizenship for people from "the late American Union." Ordinance 39, which passed on April 27, two weeks after the Civil War began, detailed penalties for disloyalty to Florida and the Confederate States, including being "forever disqualified from the privileges of citizenship in this State."[34]

In December 1862, the Florida Senate passed a bill entitled "an act relating to citizenship," concerning the military service of "unnaturalized persons." Seeking to encourage the continued military service of foreign nationals, including men from Union states living in Florida who were loyal to the Confederacy, the bill gave state citizenship to "all unnaturalized persons who were in the State at the time of the passage of the Ordinance of Secession, and who have entered the army of the State or Confederate States." The Florida House, however, voted down the measure. Even without a legal definition of state citizenship, the state constitutional provisions upholding white male supremacy in terms of the franchise, the ability to hold public office, serve in the military, and the right to bear arms, among other qualifications, made it clear that only free white persons were considered real citizens of the state. As in the United States, white men, not white women, even though they were legal residents of Florida and citizens of the Confederate States, inhabited a higher level of citizenship that allowed them to vote, hold public office, etc.[35]

Another addition to this hierarchy of state and Confederate citizenship were those state residents who remained loyal to the Union during the Civil War. Although the level of Unionist sentiment in Florida was not as great as it was in the mountain regions of Confederate states, where low slave ownership and distance from state government fueled Unionism, there were strong enclaves of Unionist support in Florida, especially as the war lengthened and the likelihood of Confederate victory dwindled. Of course, the governments in Tallahassee and Richmond considered as traitors any Unionist who fought against the Confederacy or actively supported the Union through other measures. And the citizenship of any Floridian who voiced Unionist support or acted in suspicious ways was suspect.[36]

The Confederacy made broad use of sequestration of property to enforce loyalty and designate the disloyal as enemy aliens. In addition to property seizures authorized by Ordinance 39 (previously mentioned), which the convention designated as a permanent rather than temporary ordinance, Florida made sequestration or confiscation of enemy alien property part of the revised constitution. During the January 1862 session of the convention, delegates passed Ordinance 51, which amended article 6 of the state constitution by adding a section that denied any of the citizens from the states or territories of the United States that are at war with the Confederacy from "ever" becoming citizens of the State of Florida. The ordinance listed a wide range of rights and occupations that such a person was barred from practicing, including voting in elections, holding public office, or engaging in any kind of business, trade, or profession. If such a person were caught in any of these activities, the state had the right to confiscate their property.[37]

In April 1861, however, active Unionist support in Florida was submerged under the wave of excitement and patriotism for the Southern cause that followed the Confederate attack on Fort Sumter. It was in this heady atmosphere that the convention held its last meeting of the year. On April 27, 1861, the convention adjourned sine die and would remain adjourned unless the convention president convened the convention on or before December 25, 1861. As the year receded, on December 13, President McGehee announced that the convention would reconvene in Tallahassee on January 14, 1862. McGehee justified his decision by saying he had consulted with several legislators and concerned citizens who were appalled by the governor's management of the state's financial affairs and his use of funds designated for equipping units called into Confederate service. Florida's governor in December 1861 was John Milton, who had been inaugurated in October 1861 after winning the election in October 1860. A power struggle and constitutional crisis ensued between the convention and Governor Milton in 1862.[38]

Milton was an energetic governor who was determined to lead. He had spent much of his time during the months between the outbreak of war and his inauguration inspecting the state of Florida's defenses. What he found alarmed him. In a letter dated October 2, 1861, five days before his inauguration, Milton wrote to Confederate Secretary of the Navy Stephen Mallory that the state's defenses were "in a most deplorable condition" with poorly led and poorly placed units. He lamented that he was entering office during this "deranged state of affairs," but he was "resolved to place the State upon the best war footing." During the first months of his administration, Milton sounded the alarm to Confederate President Jefferson Davis and the Confederate War Department about the weakness of Florida's defenses and what he saw as the unsound policy of allowing the raising of units for incorporation into the Confederate army without his approval as the governor of Florida and commander in chief of the state's military forces. He believed the state had a right and duty to defend itself in cooperation with the Confederate government but not in subservience to federal power over states' rights.[39]

During his years as governor, Milton believed the state had to retain some of its own military forces for state defense since the Confederate government was intent on using most of Florida's military manpower for the war outside of Florida, which Richmond considered a low defense priority. It was Milton's insistence on maintaining a viable state-controlled defense force and exercising what he saw as his legitimate right as state commander in chief to manage state military affairs that became the crux of his political conflict with the state convention. Most members of the convention saw no need to expend limited financial resources on defense when the national government was responsible for the Confederate states' security. They wanted Governor Milton to turn over all responsibility for Florida's defense to the Confederate government and military as the institutions responsible for national defense.[40]

The financial irregularities that had been the original impetus for recalling the convention were sorted out in the first days of the convention. However, for Milton's opponents in the legislature, the convention, and the press, their impression of his mismanagement of financial affairs was only part of what they saw as Milton's mishandling of state affairs, especially military affairs. They did not like his attack on the Confederate War Department for allowing individuals to create units that were then accepted into Confederate service without state approval. Milton also infuriated his opposition when he attacked the competency of certain officers and blamed the previous administration of Governor Perry for the terrible condition of Florida's defenses. Early in the 1862 convention session, delegates passed a resolution calling for the disbanding of the state militia by March 10, 1862. Milton argued that it was imperative to maintain the state troops in defense of ports such as Apalachicola that were undefended by Confederate units. This weakness became even more acute following Confederate defeats at Forts Henry and Donelson in February 1862. The Confederate government responded to these disasters by withdrawing regiments from other Confederate states to reinforce the front in Tennessee. Most of the Confederate units in Florida were transferred to Tennessee. With Confederate forces leaving the state, Milton insisted that the militia was needed more than ever to defend key points along Florida's coast. The convention did not agree. Tired of his interference in what they saw as national military issues and convinced that his leadership was leading the state to ruin, the convention decided to create an executive council to restrain Milton's power and to ensure that the convention would have a hand in future executive decisions.[41]

In creating an executive council, Florida followed the lead of South Carolina, which created an executive council in the first week of January 1862. During the first week of the Florida convention in January 1861, Governor Perry agreed to appoint four "Counsellors of State" from the membership of the convention. These counsellors were to advise the governor "on all important matters of State"; however, there are no records of any meetings between the governor and the counsellors, and the convention resolution authorizing the counsellors did not become a permanent resolution. It was not until January 25, 1862, in the wake of the convention and General Assembly's criticisms of Governor Milton's management of the state's financial and military affairs, that the convention passed Ordinance 52: "An Ordinance for strengthening the Executive Department during the exigencies of the present war." The ordinance created what became known as the Florida Executive Council.[42]

The ordinance included the following provisions: the council was authorized to exist for the duration of the war or until the convention decided otherwise; the convention would appoint four Florida citizens to serve on the council, which would hold its first meeting with the governor no later than twenty days after the adjournment of the present convention at the invitation of the governor or on February 28, 1862, if the governor had not called the meeting; the council was to assist the governor in the exercise of his constitutional duties and the duties prescribed to him by the convention; acting as one body, the governor and the council had the power to declare martial law and issue emergency decrees in defense of the state; they had the power to mobilize "any part" of the state population (including enslaved persons) for public service; they were authorized to obtain weapons and ammunition for state defense; and they had power over state military appointments.[43]

Governor Milton opposed the creation of the executive council and refused to call a meeting of the council before the February 28, 1862, deadline for the first meeting. His opposition to the council was not just based on his undoubted wish to prevent the convention from interfering in executive affairs. Milton opposed the convention on constitutional grounds. He believed the convention existed for three purposes and only three purposes: the convention was assembled to vote on secession; after that vote, the convention had to organize and oversee the transition to an independent state government; and the convention needed to revise and amend the state constitution to comply with the fact of secession. The convention, Milton argued, had achieved those purposes by April 27, 1861, the day the convention approved the revised and amended constitution and adjourned sine die. There was no reason or legal authority to reconvene the convention in 1862, since the convention had achieved its lawful purposes and since, according to the convention's own language, any convening of the convention had to be done on or before December 25, 1861—convention president McGehee argued that by issuing the proclamation on December 13 for reconvening the convention in January 1862 he had conformed to the intent of the convention's language for reconvening.[44]

In addition to these positions, Milton presented the General Assembly and the citizens of Florida detailed constitutional arguments for opposing the convention's actions. He said the people of Florida never intended for the convention to have legislative powers. If the convention had legislative power, what was the check on such power? The convention did not recognize any right of the legislature over their ordinances or the right of the governor to veto those ordinances. Unchecked power meant despotism. Florida did not give up its organic government when the convention convened. And the state constitution did not exist at the pleasure of the convention. "The Convention," Milton said, "had no power to destroy the Government of the State as established by the Constitution, and thus hurl the people into a state of anarchy and confusion."[45]

Milton's low opinion of the convention did not bode well for the success of the executive council. During their first meeting with the governor on February 28, 1862, the council members listened as Milton blasted the convention. He said the convention had no right to legislate or further amend the constitution. However, for purposes of harmony in government during wartime, he would leave the constitutional questions to the judiciary and do his best to facilitate the council's work. Although the initial meeting of the council and the governor was stormy, Milton's willingness to continue meeting with the council and the council's pliability when it came to most of the governor's policies allowed both sides to work together to pass resolutions affecting state finances, the economy, governmental appointments, and state defense.[46]

The last subject was especially dear to Milton, who took his responsibilities as the state's commander in chief seriously. His vehement opposition to the convention's disbanding of the state militia has already been mentioned. Milton used his relatively good relations with the council members to get them to pass a resolution on April 4, 1862, that reorganized the state militia by requiring all able-bodied white males between the ages of sixteen and sixty who were not in an exempt status—there were exemptions for government officials and for men engaged in work vital to the economy such as operating railroads and making salt—to be subject to military service in the state. However, opposition to funding an expanded militia was still strong. Opponents insisted that the Confederate government was responsible for Florida's defense and that there were already too many Floridians subject to military service, especially after the Confederate Congress passed the Conscription Act on April 16. Faced with this pressure, the council, over Milton's objection, repealed the militia resolution on April 26. Florida did not have a militia until July 1864, when the General Assembly reestablished the militia in the face of growing Union military threats to the state.[47]

Milton was pleased that his lobbying for the reestablishment of the militia had finally paid off. However, bringing back the militia, which now consisted of old men and teenagers outside of the age requirements of the Confederate draft, was a sign of the growing desperation in Florida and other states of the Deep South as Union forces pushed into areas of the Confederacy hitherto largely untouched by the war. By April 1865, Union troops were on the cusp of taking Richmond as the war entered its final days. It was in this atmosphere of defeat and depression that Governor John Milton's term ended. On April 1, 1865, he took his own life at his plantation near Marianna, Florida.[48]

On May 10, 1865, Union troops entered Tallahassee. Union military occupation ended the authority of the Constitution of 1861. Except for the drafting and passage of the Ordinance of Secession, the rest of Florida's Confederate Constitution has been largely forgotten. However, during its four years as the state's governing document, the Constitution of 1861 fulfilled the basic requirements of its framers by recognizing Florida's secession and membership in the Confederate States. Beyond these fundamental steps and measures designed to strengthen Confederate Florida's external and internal security, such as revising previous restrictions on eligibility for military service and sequestration of Unionist property, the Constitution of 1861 exemplified the Calhounist philosophy of states' rights that placed the ultimate expression of a state's popular will in the hands of an elected convention of the people. In authorizing the secession convention, the legislature made the convention's ordinances the supreme laws of the state. The convention in turn used this extraordinary power to place itself over the legislature by removing that branch's right to amend the constitution. In 1862, the convention intervened in the executive branch by creating the

Florida Executive Council to manage executive affairs with the governor. These factors point to the Constitution of 1861 as being a consequential governing document in Florida's constitutional history, rather than just a slightly revised version of the Constitution of 1838 with a nod to the Confederacy.

The legal legacy of the Constitution of 1861 was minimal, but its philosophical influence endured. Legally, Florida's 1865 and 1868 constitutions annulled the Ordinance of Secession, and the Constitution of 1865 repealed all ordinances of the secession convention and laws passed from 1861 to 1865 with respect to Florida's membership in the former Confederate States. However, one original provision of the Constitution of 1861 that did come to fruition decades after its passage was article 3, section 21, which called for the establishment of an official residence for the governor. That initiative became reality in 1907 with the opening of the state's first governor's mansion.[49]

Union victory in the Civil War destroyed the Confederacy and saw the triumph of federalism over John Calhoun's doctrine of state sovereignty represented in Florida and the other Confederate states' secession ordinances and constitutions, but the outcome did not end the doctrine's influence on southern state governance. During and after Reconstruction, southern states insisted on their right to regulate race relations within their jurisdictions, which saw the creation of regimes of strict racial segregation and repression of civil, voting, and economic rights for Black people throughout the states of the former Confederacy. In the late 1950s, Florida and other southern states returned with renewed vigor to the doctrine of state sovereignty to resist federally mandated integration of public schools. At the same time, the original Ordinance of Secession hung on a wall of the state capitol, a forlorn relic. However, relics can hold great power for those who choose to believe in them. In 1957, state legislators once again embraced the document's call for state sovereignty and independence by adopting an interposition resolution in defiance of the US Supreme Court's order to begin the dismantling of public school segregation. Taking their cue from Calhoun, the resolution's authors proclaimed it was the legislature's right and duty to interpose itself between the Supreme Court and, in language that the 1861 secession convention could have written, the People of Florida when a federal act threatened state sovereignty. While the legislature's push to nullify federal law failed, its resolution was based on the same extreme states' rights philosophy that had fueled secession in 1861 and on a legacy of white supremacy that still poisons the politics of today.[50]

Notes

1 Seth A. Weitz and Jonathan C. Sheppard, eds., *A Forgotten Front: Florida During the Civil War Era* (Tuscaloosa: University of Alabama Press, 2018); Talbot D'Alemberte, *The Florida State Constitution: A Reference Guide* (New York: Greenwood Press, 1991), 5. General histories of Civil War Florida give little or no attention to the Constitution of 1861; however, the first major work on Civil War Florida, William Watson Davis, *The Civil War and Reconstruction in Florida,* although a product of the long-discredited white supremacist Dunning School of historians, does contain some details about Florida's Civil War constitutional revisions. See William Watson Davis, *The Civil War and Reconstruction in Florida: A Facsimile Reproduction of the 1913 Edition with Introduction by Fletcher M. Green* (Gainesville: University of Florida Press, 1964), 175–76.

2 Davis, *The Civil War and Reconstruction in Florida,* 175. Although they do not contain information on the Florida Constitution of 1861, these sources are indispensable for understanding the development of constitutional thought and state constitutions in the antebellum South: Don E. Fehrenbacher, *Constitutions and Constitutionalism in the Slaveholding South* (Athens: University of Georgia Press, 1989); Kermit L. Hall and James W. Ely Jr., *An Uncertain Tradition: Constitutionalism and the History of the South* (Athens: University of Georgia Press, 1989); G. Alan Tarr, *Understanding State Constitutions* (Princeton, NJ: Princeton University Press, 1998).

3 *Constitution or Form of Government for the People of Florida as Revised and Amended at a Convention of the People Begun and Held at the City of Tallahassee on the Third Day of January A. D. 1861, Together with the Ordinances Adopted by Said Convention* (Tallahassee: Office of the Floridian and Journal, 1861) (hereinafter *Constitution or Form of Government for the People of Florida, 1861*); *Journal of the Proceedings of the Convention of the People of Florida, Begun and Held at the Capitol in the City of Tallahassee, on Thursday, January 3, A. D. 1861* (Tallahassee: Office of the Floridian and Journal, 1861), 104 (hereinafter *Journal of the Proceedings of the Convention of the People, January 1861*). On the executive council, see William C. Havard, "The Florida Executive Council, an Experiment in Civil War Administration," *Florida Historical Quarterly* 33, no. 2 (October 1954): 77–96. Ordinance 14 was a temporary ordinance that was no longer law after the convention passed Ordinance 31 that instituted a new oath in article 6, section 7, of the state constitution that removed the requirement to defend the ordinances of the convention, replacing that language with the duty to "preserve, protect, and defend the Constitution of this State, and of the Confederate States of America." Ordinance 63 of January 27, 1862, detailed the convention ordinances that were considered of a permanent nature and those considered temporary in nature. Ordinances 1, 4–6, 10, 14–16, 23–28, 31–32, sections 1, 9, 34–36 of Ordinance 33, 36–37, 39–40, 49–51, 54–55, 57, 61–63, and resolutions 8, 29, and 36 were deemed permanent. Ordinances 2–3, 7–9, 11–13, 17–22, 29–30, 34–35, 38, 41–43, 45–46, and all resolutions except for 8, 29, and 36 were temporary. For Ordinance 63, see *Constitution or Form of Government*

for the People of Florida, as Revised and Amended at a Convention of the People Begun and Holden at the City of Tallahassee on the 3rd Day of January, A. D. 1861, and at a Called Session Thereof Begun and Held January 14th, A. D. 1862, Together with the Ordinances adopted by said Convention at said Called Session (Tallahassee, 1862) (hereinafter Constitution or Form of Government for the People of Florida, 1862); Library of Congress, Early State Records Project, Law Library Microfilm Collection, University of Florida Digital Collections, George A. Smathers Libraries, accessed on December 27, 2021, at https://original-ufdc.uflib.ufl.edu/AA00078692/00001?search=convention%200f%20the%20people. The journals of the secession convention and the published 1861 and 1862 versions of the state constitution contain most of the convention ordinances at the end of the publications, before the resolutions; however, not all the ordinances are in those publications. For original copies of all the convention ordinances, see Florida Convention of the People, Ordinances and Resolutions, 1861–1862, volume 1, Series 1457, Record Group 1000, State Archives of Florida, Tallahassee.

4   Francis R. Hodges and Richard Soash, "William Dunn Moseley," in R. Boyd Murphree and Robert A. Taylor, eds., *The Governors of Florida* (Gainesville: University Press of Florida, 2020), 78.

5   John Niven, *John C. Calhoun and the Price of Union: A Biography* (Baton Rouge: Louisiana State University Press, 1988), 158–62.

6   Patricia Lasche Clements, *Legacy of Leadership: Florida Governors and Their Inaugural Speeches* (Tallahassee, FL: Sentry Press, 2005), 4. A concise account of the sectional crisis is presented in Michael F. Holt, *The Fate of Their Country: Politicians, Slavery Extension, and the Coming of the Civil War* (New York: Hill and Wang, 2004). For a detailed account and analysis of the centrality of slavery to Southern politics, see William J. Cooper Jr., *Liberty and Slavery: Southern Politics to 1860* (Columbia: University of South Carolina Press, 2000; New York: Knopf, 1983). On Thomas Brown and the other antebellum governors of Florida, see Murphree and Taylor, ed., *The Governors of Florida*.

7   R. Boyd Murphree, "Madison Starke Perry," in Murphree and Taylor, eds., *The Governors of Florida*, 120.

8   Ralph A. Wooster, *The Secession Conventions of the South* (Princeton, NJ: Princeton University Press, 1962), 68–72.

9   John E. Johns, *Florida During the Civil War* (Gainesville: University of Florida Press, 1963), 14–16; *Journal of the Proceedings of the Convention of the People, January 1861*, 7–8; Eric H. Walther, *The Fire-Eaters* (Baton Rouge: Louisiana State University Press, 1992), 2. Although Walther does not include McGehee in his study, McGhee fits Walther's definition of a fire-eater as a Southerner who persistently advocated for secession.

10 Wooster, *The Secession Conventions of the South*, 68, 72–74; John F. Reiger, "Secession of Florida from the Union: A Minority Decision?," *Florida Historical Quarterly* 46, no. 4 (April 1968): 364–66.

11 *Journal of the Proceedings of the Convention of the People, January 1861*, 31–32. The original copy of the Ordinance of Secession and the minutes of the convention are

in the State Archives of Florida in Tallahassee: Florida Convention of the People Ordinance of Secession, 1861, Series 972, Record Group 1000; Florida Convention of the People Minutes, 1861–1862, S. 540, RG 1000.

12 *Journal of the Proceedings of the Convention of the People, January 1861*, 25–27.

13 *Journal of the Proceedings of the Convention of the People, January 1861*, 27.

14 J. L. Proctor, *Proceedings of the Mississippi State Convention, Held January 7th to 26th, A. D. 1861, Including the Ordinances as Finally Adopted, Important Speeches, and a List of Members, Showing the Postoffice, Profession, Nativity, Politics, Age, Religious Preference, and Social Relations of Each* (Jackson, MS: Power and Cadwallader, Book and Job Printers, 1861), 8–9, accessed on December 28, 2021, Documenting the American South, University Library, University of North Carolina at Chapel Hill at https://docsouth.unc.edu/imls/missconv/missconv.html; *Journal of the Public and Secret Proceedings of the Convention of the People of Georgia Held in Milledgeville and Savannah in 1861. Together with the Ordinances Adopted. Published by Order of the Convention* (Milledgeville, GA: Boughton Nisbet and Barnes, State Printers, 1861), 31–32, accessed on December 28, 2021, Documenting the American South, University Library, University of North Carolina at Chapel Hill at https://docsouth.unc.edu/imls/georgia/georgia.html; *Ordinances and Constitution of the State of South Carolina, with the Constitution of the Provisional Government and of the Confederate States of America*. (Charleston, SC: Evans and Cogswell, Printers to the Convention, 1861), 3, accessed on December 28, 2021, Documenting the American South, University Library, University of North Carolina at Chapel Hill at https://docsouth.unc.edu/imls/southcar/south.html; *Official Journal of the Convention of the State of Louisiana. By Authority* (New Orleans: J. O. Nixon, Printer to the Convention, 1861), 10, accessed on December 28, 2021, Internet Archive, Open Library at https://archive.org/details/officialjourna10010ui/page/10/mode/2up?ref=ol&view=theater.

15 William R. Smith, *The History and Debates of the Convention of the People of Alabama, Begun and Held in the City of Montgomery, on the Seventh Day of January 1861: In Which Is Presented the Speeches of the Secret Sessions, and Many Valuable State Papers* (Montgomery: White, Pfister and Co., 1861), 72, accessed on December 28, 2021, Internet Archives, Alabama Department of Archives and History, at https://digital.archives.alabama.gov/digital/collection/constitutions/id/119; "Texas Ordinance of Secession," *Texas Almanac*, accessed on December 28, 2021 at https://www.texasalmanac.com/articles/ordinance-to-dissolve-the-union-between-the-state-of-texas-and-the-other-states.

16 "Declarations of Causes of Seceding States: South Carolina, Mississippi, Georgia, Texas," *Causes of the Civil War*, accessed on December 28, 2021, at http://www.civilwarcauses.org/reasons.htm#SouthCarolina.

17 *Journal of the Proceedings of the Convention of the People, January 1861*, 91; *Proceedings of the Convention of the People of Florida at Called Sessions, Begun and Held at the Capitol in Tallahassee on Tuesday, February 26th, and Thursday, April 18th, 1861.* (Tallahassee: 1861), 10–11 (hereinafter *Proceedings of the Convention People of Flori-*

da, *February 1861 and April 1861*), Library of Congress, Early State Records Project, Law Library Microfilm Collection, University of Florida Digital Collections, George A. Smathers Libraries, accessed on December 27, 2021, at https://original-ufdc.uflib.ufl.edu/AA00078694/00001?search=convention%200f%20the%20people. Besides Lamar, the other members of the committee were William G. M. Davis, James Baird Dawkins, Summerfield Massillon Glenn Gary, and James Gettis.

18 "Treatise," Constitutional Convention 1861, box 1, folder 6, Series 577, State Governors' Incoming Correspondence, Record Group 000101, Territorial and State Governors (1820–1929), State Archives of Florida, Tallahassee.

19 "Treatise," Constitutional Convention 1861, box 1, folder 6, Series 577, State Governors' Incoming Correspondence, Record Group 000101, Territorial and State Governors (1820–1929), State Archives of Florida, Tallahassee.

20 Johns, *Florida During the Civil War*, 21, 24–33.

21 Emory M. Thomas, *The Confederate Nation: 1861–1865* (New York: Harper and Row, Harper Torchbooks, 1979), 57–58.

22 Attorney General Statutory Revision Department, *Florida Statutes 1941, Volume 3: Helpful and Useful Matter* (Tallahassee: State of Florida, 1946), 149–50.

23 *Journal of the Proceedings of the Convention of the People, January 1861*, 37–38.

24 *Journal of the Proceedings of the Convention of the People, January 1861*, 66–69, 72; William C. Davis, *"A Government of Our Own": The Making of the Confederacy* (New York, Free Press, 1994), 82–127.

25 Davis, *"A Government of Our Own,"* 124; Charles Robert Lee Jr., *The Confederate Constitutions* (Chapel Hill: University of North Carolina Press, 1963), 144–46, 150; Marshall L. DeRosa, *The Confederate Constitution of 1861: An Inquiry into American Constitutionalism* (Columbia: University of Missouri Press, 1991), 135, 141.

26 *Journal of the Proceedings of the Convention of the People, January 1861*, 37, 103.

27 *Journal of the Proceedings of the Convention of the People, January 1861*, 101, 105; Attorney General Statutory Revision Department, *Florida Statutes 1941, Volume 3: Helpful and Useful Matter*, 156; Bertram Wyatt-Brown, *Southern Honor: Ethics and Behavior in the Old South* (Oxford: Oxford University Press, 1982, Oxford University Press paperback, 1983), 350–51.

28 *Journal of the Proceedings of the Convention of the People, January 1861*, 105; Attorney General Statutory Revision Department, *Florida Statutes 1941, Volume 3: Helpful and Useful Matter*, 141.

29 R. Boyd Murphree, "Thomas Brown" in Murphree and Taylor, eds., *The Governors of Florida*, 95–96; *Journal of the Proceedings of the Convention of the People, January 1861*, 101–2, 105.

30 *Proceedings of the Convention People of Florida, February 1861 and April 1861*, 6; Attorney General Statutory Revision Department, *Florida Statutes 1941, Volume 3: Helpful and Useful Matter*, 140; *Constitution or Form of Government for the People of Florida, 1861*, 25–26; *Proceedings of the Convention People of Florida, February 1861 and April 1861*, 11; T. Conn Bryan, *Confederate Georgia* (Athens: University of Georgia Press, 1953, third printing, 1964), 14.

31 *Proceedings of the Convention People of Florida, February 1861 and April 1861,* 33, 65–66; George C. Rable, *The Confederate Republic: A Revolution Against Politics* (Chapel Hill: University of North Carolina Press, 1994), 41–42.

32 *Constitution or Form of Government for the People of Florida, 1861,* 27, 59–60; Attorney General Statutory Revision Department, *Florida Statutes 1941, Volume 3: Helpful and Useful Matter,* 154.

33 Attorney General Statutory Revision Department, *Florida Statutes 1941, Volume 3: Helpful and Useful Matter,* 144, 158; DeRosa, *Confederate Constitution of 1861,* 141.

34 Attorney General Statutory Revision Department, *Florida Statutes 1941, Volume 3: Helpful and Useful Matter,* 155–56; Paul Quigley, *Shifting Grounds: Nationalism and the American South 1848–1865* (Oxford: Oxford University Press, 2012), 157; Stephanie McCurry, *Confederate Reckoning: Power and Politics in the Civil War South* (Cambridge, MA: Harvard University Press, first Harvard paperback edition, 2012), 79–80; DeRosa, *Confederate Constitution of 1861,* 140; *Journal of the Proceedings of the Convention of the People, January 1861,* 103–4; *Constitution or Form of Government for the People of Florida, 1861,* 58–59.

35 *Journal of the Senate of the 12th General Assembly of the State of Florida; begun and held at the Capitol, in the City of Tallahassee, on Monday, the eighteenth of November, in the year of our Lord One Thousand Eight Hundred and Sixty-Nine* (Tallahassee, 1862), 136; Quigley, *Shifting Grounds: Nationalism and the American South 1848–1865,* 189; Paul Quigley, "Civil War Conscription and the International Boundaries of Citizenship." *Journal of the Civil War Era* 4, no. 3 (September 2914): 375–76, 379; A bill to be entitled an act in relation to citizenship, box 9. 1860/1861–182, Series 50, Senate Bill Files, 1845–1927, Record Group 95, State Archives of Florida, Tallahassee; *A Journal of the Proceedings of the House of Representatives of the General Assembly of the State of Florida at Its Twelfth Session, Begun and Held at the Capitol, in the City of Tallahassee, on Monday, November 17, 1862* (Tallahassee: Office of the Floridian and Journal, 1862), 182.

36 Johns, *Florida During the Civil War,* 154–59; T. W. Upchurch, "Perfectly Still No More: Unionists in Confederate Northeast Florida." *Florida Historical Quarterly* 93, no. 1 (Summer 2014): 2–3, 7, 12–13, 16, 23–24.

37 Daniel W. Hamilton, "The Confederate Sequestration Act," *Civil War History* 52, no. 4 (December 2006): 373–408; *Constitution or Form of Government for the People of Florida, 1861,* 58–59; *Constitution or Form of Government for the People of Florida, 1862,* 31.

38 *Proceedings of the Convention People of Florida, February 1861 and April 1861,* 70; *Journal of the Convention of the people of Florida at a Called Session, Begun and Held at the Capitol, in the City of Tallahassee, on Tuesday, January 14, 1862* (Tallahassee, 1862), 4–7 (hereinafter *Journal of the Convention of the people of Florida, 1862*), Library of Congress, Early State Records Project, Law Library Microfilm Collection, University of Florida Digital Collections, George A. Smathers Libraries, accessed on December 29, 2021, at https://original-ufdc.uflib.ufl.edu/AA00078695/00001?search=convention%200f%20the%20people.

39 R. Boyd Murphree, "Embattled Executive: Governor John Milton's Civil War," Weitz and Sheppard, eds., *Forgotten Front*, 89–114; John Milton to Stephen R. Mallory, October 2, 1861, *The War of the Rebellion: A Compilation of the Official Records of the Union and Confederate Armies*, series 1, volume 6 (Washington, DC: Government Printing Office, 1882), 288; R. Boyd Murphree, "Embattled Executive: Governor John Milton's Civil War," Weitz and Sheppard, eds., *Forgotten Front*, 95–98.

40 R. Boyd Murphree, "Embattled Executive: Governor John Milton's Civil War," Weitz and Sheppard, eds., *Forgotten Front*, 98–100.

41 R. Boyd Murphree, "Embattled Executive: Governor John Milton's Civil War," Weitz and Sheppard, eds., *Forgotten Front*, 96, 98, 100.

42 Charles Edward Cauthen, *South Carolina Goes to War, 1860–1865*, with a new introduction by J. Tracy Power (Columbia: University of South Carolina Press, 1950, new introduction, 2005), 139–51; *Journal of the Proceedings of the Convention of the People, January 1861*, 65; *Constitution or Form of Government for the People of Florida, 1862*, 32–33.

43 *Constitution or Form of Government for the People of Florida, 1862*, 32–33.

44 Havard, "Florida Executive Council," 84–89.

45 *Journal of the Convention of the people of Florida, 1862*, 36–42; Havard, "Florida Executive Council," 88–89.

46 Havard, "Florida Executive Council," 88–89.

47 Havard, "Florida Executive Council," 91–95; R. Boyd Murphree, "Embattled Executive: Governor John Milton's Civil War," Weitz and Sheppard, eds., *Forgotten Front*, 109.

48 R. Boyd Murphree, "Embattled Executive: Governor John Milton's Civil War," Weitz and Sheppard, eds., *Forgotten Front*, 109–10.

49 Attorney General Statutory Revision Department, *Florida Statutes 1941, Volume 3: Helpful and Useful Matter*, 152, 174, 191.

50 "Florida's Secession Articles Face Capitol Wall," *Tampa Tribune*, June 2, 1950, https://www.newspapers.com. Downloaded on May 20, 2024.

5

The 1865 Convention and Constitution

Robert Cassanello

The Florida Constitution of 1865 was born out of a period of military defeat and occupation. As a slave state and member of the Confederacy, the state leaders left standing after the Civil War had to contemplate the shape of state government after the abolition of slavery. In the summer and fall of 1865 the nation's eyes were on the South. The *New York Times* reported on the convention process in Florida with much skepticism. A reporter from the newspaper living in Tallahassee believed that northern transplants to Florida were leaving the state in anticipation of armed conflict and the fallout from the abolition of slavery. This prediction would be overstated for the era of Presidential Reconstruction, but because of this, the reporter recommended that the delegates create a strong state government that still recognized the authority of the federal government in addition to a system of criminal justice that would protect civil life for not only white people but for African Americans as well. On October 10, 1865, the state hosted elections for constitutional delegates for the convention to draft a document that would form the new government. The delegates created a stronger state government, especially a stronger chief executive, than existed during the antebellum period. The document that came out of the 1865 Constitutional Convention was closer to the antebellum constitution than a revision of it.[1] The 1865 Constitution was forward-looking in that it would create a blueprint for Black second-class citizenship, which lawmakers at the end of the nineteenth century would resuscitate after the federal government abandoned Congressional Reconstruction in Florida.

The first experiments in new Southern state constitution-making took place in the parts of the South either under US occupation or in the border states, which never seceded during the war. The US military in occupied parts of the South oversaw the return of local governments in places like New Orleans as early as 1863. In December 1863, President Abraham Lincoln announced his Ten Percent Plan, a policy for the return of states in rebellion to recognition and representation in the US Congress. When 10 percent of the voting population from the 1860 election swore a loyalty oath to the federal government and committed to abolishing slavery, then the state could launch the electoral and political processes to return to the United States. With the introduction of this plan, the policies of wartime Reconstruction gave way to Presidential Reconstruction first overseen by Lincoln. Lincoln was assassinated before he could execute his plan fully throughout the South under his authority. Before his death, abolitionists were critical of his plan because Lincoln was uncommitted to Black citizenship and full male suffrage, although his views on the matter were continuing to evolve. Lincoln's successor, President Andrew Johnson, shared some views of Reconstruction held by Lincoln including the idea that the Southern states could never legally secede. Johnson was a Southern Unionist from Tennessee and firmly believed in states' rights. Johnson believed that he was following Lincoln's policies when assuming office, although Johnson was much more lenient when it came to pardoning Confederate officials and sympathizers. As to Black citizenship and suffrage, Johnson said to one US congressman that "White men alone must manage the South."[2]

In the summer of 1865, President Johnson appointed provisional governors to Alabama, Georgia, Mississippi, South Carolina, Texas, and Florida, which was the last one appointed—William Marvin on July 14, 1865. Marvin had been a district judge and Unionist located in Key West during the war who resigned because of ill health in 1863. Key West was a hotbed of Unionists' politics and Johnson appointed his provisional governors from the ranks of Unionists. Johnson's governors were not of the same mind and temperament; some sought guidance from the president and others could be more combative. Governor Marvin and James Johnson of Georgia both turned out to be the most cooperative with the president. Johnson impressed upon the governors that new state constitutions must abolish slavery, repudiate Confederate debt, and never acknowledge a legal justification for secession. Johnson, too, advised his governors that while there should be no path to citizenship or suffrage for Black people, the states would need to oversee the rights of Black residents. Upon Johnson's directions, Marvin traveled the state and gave speeches preparing Floridians for establishing a new state government that included an election for a new constitutional convention.[3]

On October 25, the delegates for the 1865 Constitutional Convention had to decide how to approach the drafting of a new government. The government created in 1861 under the Confederate government of Florida was still primarily using the 1838 Constitution with updated language, so the previous constitution to refer to would have been the 1838 Constitution. One delegate, Allan H. Bush from Jackson County, initially offered a resolution that organized the committees, each of which would draft parts of the final document. G. Troup Maxwell from Leon County suggested the delegates start with the 1838 St. Joseph Constitution and just revise and substitute language as necessary in adapting that document to the conditions in 1865. This measure as presented was rejected by the body. D. G. Livingston, from Madison County and secretary of the convention, introduced a successful motion that required the 1838 Constitution, the last journal of the last state House of Representatives, and a copy of the Proceedings and Ordinances of the State Convention of 1861 be available to all delegates. Livingston gave the chairman of all standing committees these documents since there was a limited supply of printed journals and proceedings available to them.[4]

The clearest revision to the 1865 document was the legacy territorial language that existed in the 1838 Constitution. That constitution was drafted and conceived while Florida was still a territory of the United States and written with the objective that the territory one day would be admitted to the nation as a state. By 1865 Florida had been a state for twenty years, and during the Civil War organized as a Confederate state. The most glaring territorial revision to the 1865 Constitution was in defining the state's boundaries. The 1838 Constitution made reference to the Treaty of Amity, Settlement and Limits (Adams Onis Treaty), and the land ceded to the United States in 1819. There was also mention of the two-colony organization of East and West Florida. The 1865 boundary article only described Florida in geographic terms, pointing out in detail the western boundaries between Alabama and Georgia. The boundaries followed the Perdido, Chattahoochee, and Flint Rivers as well as the Gulf of Florida and Mexico and finally all islands less than three and a half miles from the state's shores.[5]

Article V of the 1838 Constitution would be the basis for the construction of Article V—the Judicial Department—in the 1865 Constitution. The Committee on the Judicial Department revised the previous constitution to adapt it for 1865. In their report the committee removed the antebellum circuit districts named Western, Middle, Eastern, and Southern Circuits. In 1865 the districts would be drawn, named, and defined later by the General

Assembly. The courts of chancery from the 1838 Constitution were stripped of their authority to supervise the courts of ordinary in matters of probate wills, grant letters of testamentary, and the settlement of estates. Instead, the circuit courts were granted that authority. A significant change to the judiciary was removing the sole authority of the legislature from appointing the chief justice of the state supreme court; instead the office would be appointed by the governor with the Senate given the right to "advice and consent." In addition, two associate justices would be appointed in the same fashion. Elections would be held for circuit court judges throughout the state, and their terms of service were increased from five years to six years. The system of impeachment and removal from office for justices in 1838 only applied to circuit court judges. In 1865 the delegates agreed to hold supreme court justices to a similar system of removal from office. Delegates drafted language so that the General Assembly could order the governor to remove a supreme court justice with a two-thirds vote. The 1865 Constitution also provided the governor with the authority to call an election when a judge from the chancery or circuit courts died in office or was removed, a power not prescribed in the 1838 Constitution. The appointment of clerks for the supreme court and the circuit courts were transferred from the General Assembly to the judges who oversaw those courts. The nature of the state attorney general would also change in the 1865 document. In the 1838 Constitution, the attorney general was elected by the General Assembly through a majority vote from both chambers. The attorney general could be removed with a two-thirds vote and their prescribed duties would be assisting the General Assembly with legislative paperwork, thus requiring them to attend the General Assembly as part of their official responsibilities. The 1865 revisions made the office an elected one and no longer required the attorney general to attend the General Assembly, with the General Assembly having the authority to remove an attorney general with just a majority vote of both chambers.[6]

The changes to the executive branch of the government were less significant than to the judicial branch. With the 1865 draft, the governor had the privilege to run for reelection, but in the 1838 draft the chief executive could only serve one term and could not serve again until an entire four-year term passed. The most significant change in the executive department was that of the succession of chief executive. The delegates added to the 1865 Constitution the position of lieutenant governor who would preside as president of the Senate ex officio. The lieutenant governor also would assume the governorship in the event of impeachment, death, or any other removal of office but only in a temporary capacity until a new election. Creating the office of lieutenant governor transformed the various powers should a governor be removed or die in office. Under the antebellum constitution, if the governor was removed or died, the responsibility of chief executive would move first to the president of the Senate, then if that person was unable to serve to the Speaker of the House. With the lieutenant governor assuming the office of the president of the Senate in 1865, succession went to their office and then the Speaker of the House. The antebellum system of overriding a governor's veto was a simple majority, but in 1865 that hurdle was raised to a two-thirds vote. Finally, the 1865 Constitution required the General Assembly to purchase a residence for the governor whereas in 1838 the governor was only required to reside in the city while the General Assembly was in session. Tallahassee residency could be required in the 1865 Constitution because in 1838 the delegates gave the General Assembly the power to move the capital of the territory after five years, with a commitment to fix the capital site after ten years.[7]

Changes in the legislative department of the 1865 Constitution reflected change from the previous decades of the antebellum General Assembly. In the 1865 Constitution, representatives from the House chamber would serve a two-year term; under the antebellum constitution, representatives would only serve a one-year term. The General Assembly initially met every two years in the 1840s but during the 1850s and Civil War years the General Assembly met almost every year. Qualifications for holding office were the same as during the antebellum period when white men over the age of twenty-one could serve as representatives, twenty-five for senators, along with similar state and local residency requirements. Under the antebellum constitution, half of all senators were elected during different years so when a term ended, half of the chamber would be replaced. This staggered process of filling the chamber was removed in the 1865 draft. The General Assembly could only meet up to thirty days unless a two-thirds majority agreed to extend the time of the session. More authority to the legislative department emerged during the convention. The constitution provided certain power to the legislature such as the regulation of tolls, the incorporation of towns, and organizations that were not commercial, industrial, or financial in nature, such as social and fraternal societies. Also, the legislature had the power to remove officers "for incapacity, misconduct or neglect of duty, in such manner as may be provided by law, when no mode of trial or removal is provided."[8]

The qualifications for suffrage changed only minimally. The 1838 Constitution was drafted toward the end of the Jacksonian era when universal white male suffrage was replacing any property requirements. In addition to reflecting that shift, the antebellum constitution also required white men to enroll in the state militia or forfeit their right to vote unless they were legally exempted from military service. The 1865 Constitution carried similar language to the 1838 Constitution concerning no property qualifications for voting as well as the right of all white men over the age of twenty-five to vote without regard to militia service. Another condition to suffrage that was transferred from the 1838 to the 1865 document was the authority of the Florida government to strip suffrage rights from citizens who were convicted of "bribery, perjury or other infamous crimes." Additionally, the General Assembly was given the power to not only exclude elected officials from office but also their suffrage rights for those convicted of bribery, perjury, forgery, or other high crime or misdemeanor. Of course, anyone found engaging in "undue influence," bribery, tumult, or other improper practices could face not only penalties but the right to vote stripped from them. Most of these suffrage conditions were originally part of the 1838 Constitution. What was debated but did not pass on the convention floor was language explicitly stating that state non-citizens—people living in the state but employed by the US government—and immigrants could not vote. Another restriction lost on the convention floor would have made it a requirement to have paid all state and county taxes to be eligible to vote, thus introducing a poll tax to the right of suffrage. In antebellum Florida, the General Assembly was more involved with registering electors as opposed to a supervisor of elections—that responsibility was removed from the 1865 Constitution.[9]

The language of apportionment did not change much between 1838 and 1865. The difference between the two constitutions was population growth and its impact on political geography. During the antebellum convention, most of the population was concentrated in the middle plantation belt, Leon County and the surrounding areas, with very few people living outside of that region comparatively. By 1865 and increasingly more so later, a concentration of people moved or migrated to the peninsular part of the state as well as the Panhandle. Under the antebellum Florida Constitution of 1838, there were restrictions to who could run for public office. Article VI, section 3, "No President, Director, Cashier, or other officer of any Banking company in this state, shall be eligible to the office of Governor, Senator or Representative to the General Assembly of this State" and former banking officials would have had to wait a year to run for office after leaving the employ of those banks. This language was stricken from the 1865 document more than likely because the suspicion of bankers and banking might not have been as contested in the 1860s as it was in the 1830s. Another election eligibility requirement stripped from the 1838 Constitution was the prohibition of any governor, justice, chancellor, or judge to run for any office, state, or federal position, until a year had passed since they left their elected office. Additionally, the prohibition of ministers and clergy from running for office was removed by the 1865 convention delegates. In 1865, delegates prohibited officeholders from holding two offices in the state unless directed by the General Assembly, and this provision was added to the constitution. The mechanics of voting, registering voters, and maintaining voting rolls evolved by legislation passed since the 1838 Constitution so those processes were more spelled out in the 1865 draft.[10]

What all post-emancipation state constitutions had to grapple with was how to definitively end the system of slave labor. President Andrew Johnson demanded that the recently reconstructed governments quickly abolish slavery as a precondition to rejoining the United States. In preparation for the 1865 Constitutional Convention, Governor William Marvin toured the state giving speeches about the conditions and expectations in the reconstruction of Florida in the late summer and early fall of 1865. During this tour he prepared white citizens for a new state government that would recognize and enshrine the end of slavery as a political, economic, and social institution. At some stops, such as the one in Quincy, Florida, he spoke to an exclusively Black audience. For them he explained that the war had been a "white man's war," which "unintentionally resulted in the abolition of slavery." He also issued a proclamation during this time that cemented the same points as his speech to formalize his blueprint for constructing a new state government. During these various speeches he would adapt and revise the language until he addressed the first day of the constitutional convention. He offered delegates these directions concerning the abolition of slavery, "You will affirmatively declare in the Constitution, that neither slavery nor involuntary servitude, except as a punishment for crime, whereof the party shall have been duly convicted, shall hereafter exist in this State." A Philadelphia newspaper, *The Daily Age*, also reported about Marvin and his directions, yet noted that most of the delegates were still proslavery and would never grant any privileges to African Americans, stating that Marvin had his work cut out for him.[11]

As the executive, Marvin charged delegates with this set of parameters around what the new government should look like concerning bondage and what he referred to as "civil rights and political privileges" concerning African Americans. The delegates to the convention adopted Marvin's recommendations fully. In each draft of the 1865 Constitution as well as the final document, delegates transposed the language from Governor Marvin's opening speech directly into the text of the constitution with little revision in each iteration. It finally read, "Whereas, slavery has been destroyed in this State by the Government of the United States; therefore, neither slavery nor involuntary servitude shall in future exist in this State except as a punishment for crimes, whereof the party shall have been convicted by the courts of the State, and all the inhabitants of the State, without distinction of color, are free, and shall enjoy the rights of person and property without distinction of color."[12] The prohibition on slavery and indentured servitude was not absolute but came with the language of possibly slavery (definitively indentured servitude) reincarnated as a penal condition birthed in a nascent system of convict labor. In early drafts of the constitution, delegates included language whereby either a misdemeanor or felony would make one susceptible to the conditions of forced convict labor; the final language only included crimes generally, which could mean the successful conviction of anyone through the state court system.[13] Florida followed other former slave states by preserving slavery within the penal system. Alabama, Arkansas, and Louisiana had similar, if not identical, language reconstructing the conditions of slavery as a legal punishment for crimes. In Florida's antebellum legislation, crimes could curb voting eligibility, but the specific crimes were spelled out and included with the language of "other infamous crimes" to suggest that all crimes inherently could not result in a loss of some citizenship rights. What accounts for the change in conditions was the fact that the delegates to the 1865 Constitution had to construct a legal document that included Black people in some form of quasi-citizenship. The language of convict leasing did survive in the 1865 Florida Constitution and beyond in the following language from the 1868 Florida Constitution, "Neither slavery nor involuntary servitude, unless for the punishment of crime, shall ever be tolerated in this State."[14]

Along with defining the conditions of slavery, the governor and delegates had to address the conditions and status of Black people as free people. The question circulating the convention was whether and to what extent were African Americans, in the absence of slavery as a social institution of control, citizens. They were free but not equal citizens, more something else, something lesser. Governor Marvin explained to the delegates that the rights of each race had to be well defined with the "governing power in the hands of the white race, but the colored race is to be free, and the government is to be administered in such a manner as not to infringe up its freedom."[15] Throughout 1865 there were national debates about what citizenship rights for Black people would mean in a country without slavery. President Andrew Johnson advised Southern governors that they should not enfranchise Black men. In the face of universal male suffrage from radical Republicans, Johnson recommended privately to Mississippi Governor William L. Sharkey that he consider opening suffrage to African Americans who were educated and property owners only. For Republicans in Congress, first they looked to the Guarantee Clause of the US Constitution, not only to protect a republican form of government but to protect a republican government that enshrined individual rights. In this debate Republican Congressmen Charles Sumner and Schuyler Colfax both argued that through the Guarantee Clause, the US government already had the authority to protect the rights of African American citizens in any of the states. This legal thought would be short-lived and eventually the Thirteenth and later the Fourteenth Amendments passed, not to mention the Civil Rights Act of 1866. These amendments and legislation would settle the question of Black citizenship during this period of Presidential and later Congressional Reconstruction.[16] Delegates drafted the Florida Constitution of 1865 before any federal constitutional revisions and national legislation would settle these questions of what rights were legal rights for Black residents in Florida.

In his address Governor Marvin recommended that the resulting constitution recognize the rights of both races of citizens equally, but at the same time "exclude the colored people from any participation in the affairs of the government." Marvin argued that this would not include the franchise or the right to hold office or sit on juries. He pointed to England at the time and mentioned that the English people are free yet only one tenth vote, the same with women and children in the United States who are citizens but do not vote. For the governor, Black men as a class of citizens had a freedom that could include owning property, the freedom of movement, and the freedom to an education, but they were not privileged to make decisions about who governs them. The delegates followed that sentiment. At the convention, on November 2, 1866, Silas L. Niblack issued an ordinance that read:

The people of the State of Florida in General Convention assembled, do ordain and declare, that while we recognize the freedom of the colored race, and are desirous of extending to them full protection in the rights of person and property, and in our legislation to secure their elevation and improvement in all that is calculated to promote human happiness, we declare it the unalterable sentiment of this Convention, that the laws of the State shall be made and executed by the white race.[17]

The constitutional convention did organize a Committee on General Provisions, which was tasked with all matters related to the "colored population" of the state. In the committee's report to the convention, it recommended that the constitution empower the General Assembly to pass future legislation that would outlaw "free negroes, mulattoes and other persons of color" from migrating to the state. This contradicted Marvin's suggestion that African Americans have freedom of movement, which to this committee was a protected right for Black residents within the state only. The General Assembly of 1866 did not pass this law during its session. It was the Committee on Census and Apportionment of Representation that recommended African Americans, as in the pre–Civil War US Constitution, count as three-fifths to each white inhabitant. This recommendation was adopted in the final draft of the constitution.[18]

The delegates recognized some rights for Black residents in Florida. The Committee on the Judicial Department advised the future General Assembly to recognize marriages between Black men and Black women, including those which would have transpired during slavery. The language went so far as to suggest that the legislation stipulates cohabitation be the proof of a legally recognized marriage. Cohabitation was the condition in the report for this recognition as any children born from two Black parents who were not cohabitating should legally be "deemed bastards." An amendment on the convention floor also changed the language of the report from using the words "freedmen and freedwomen" to "colored persons" to denote the end of slavery. During these debates, the Thirteenth Amendment abolishing slavery passed Congress but would be ratified soon after the state's constitutional convention. When the General Assembly met in 1866, the recommendations of this report became legislation both using the term "colored persons" and recognizing cohabitation as legal marriage and not criminal adultery. The legislation also made their children eligible heirs to any property. The delegates on the Committee on General Provisions did provide the right of African Americans to testify in court when the injured party was a Black person; if the injured party was a white person, African Americans could not serve on the jury. As rights were spelled out, delegates were careful to create a two-tiered system punctuating racial inequality. Marvin appealed to the delegates that while suffrage was too far a step, Black people needed rights before the law so that they could negotiate labor contracts with employers and not be taken advantage of. To the objection of some delegates, this was the rationale for the carve-out for African Americans to testify in court. Toward the end of the convention, the delegates passed a resolution ordering the provisional governor to remove all US Colored Troops from the state as soon as possible.[19]

Addressing the very limited rights of African Americans during Presidential Reconstruction was just one revision of the Florida Confederacy that needed to be addressed in the 1865 Constitution; others were economic and political legacies. An important step in abolishing the Confederacy was addressing the war debt, notes, and currency still in circulation. In the fall of 1865, Florida's Treasury Office reported $904,681.99 in total Confederate debt. The Confederate War debt was a national issue because many northern Democrats and Southerners expected the federal government would assume all Confederate and state debt incurred during the war similar to the federal government after the Revolutionary War. But Republicans and northern financiers refused to even consider this because their objective was to get the United States out of debt soon after the war in hopes that it would stimulate the national economy. Foreign bankers and investors who held Confederate bonds lobbied for the United States to assume that debt but to no avail. In the Florida convention, delegates were more concerned for the average person statewide who held on to Confederate or state debt. The Convention Committee on Finance, Accounts, and State Liabilities recommended covering some of the Confederate debt owed to residents who they claimed financed their economic lives in Confederate notes or bonds. The committee noted that the convention should place special exception for state employees during the war who were paid in Confederate funds as payment of salaries. The committee argued that rates of depreciation, especially when calculating original notes or bonds held by residents, would be an insurmountable task to calculate, and without that measure there would not be a fair system to transition funds from wartime monies to postwar monies. As such, the committee recommended that residents with Confederate notes or bonds be paid 10 percent of face value across the board.

Delegates passed an ordinance that provided the future government to pay a rate of ten cents on the dollar for all outstanding treasury notes. In return, residents would be issued bonds that would accrue six cents per year for thirty years. The politics of war debt was hotly debated at the convention and not settled early in the convention. On November 1, 1865, delegates passed an ordinance that required a binding referendum be placed on the first state election for governor where eligible voters could vote to "pay" the war debt or "repudiate" the war debt. In December 1866 the state General Assembly made a single exception in the case of Richard H. Lowndes who in 1861 held $2,000 in state bonds destroyed during the war in South Carolina. Presumably this debt was antebellum debt of a different category from war debt. He was reimbursed at face value for the bonds he once held. Ultimately on November 6, 1865, President Johnson demanded that all former states in rebellion repudiate Confederate war debt, and the delegates complied and did not address the matter or place the issue on the first state election ballot. The 1865 Constitution provided a blanket commitment to recognize all bonds issued by the state government before 1861 and after.[20]

Unwinding the clock on the Confederacy was not just a question of economics. It was also a question of the politics of secession and its legacy. Governor Marvin recommended that the convention declare the Secession Ordinances of 1861 "null and void." On the third day, James A. Wiggins of Marion County presented an ordinance to annul the ordinance of secession. The ordinance was referred to the Committee on the Judicial Department where the language was edited down to "whereas, the people of the State of Florida are desirous in good faith to restore the State to her former peaceful relations with the United States; therefore." The ordinance to annul the ordinances of secession was passed on October 28, 1865. The *New York Times* reporter embedded in Tallahassee believed this debate was more than just semantics. He believed Marvin supported language that would have "repudiated" the secession ordinances. Ultimately, delegates decided to instead "recognize the right of secession." Under President Abraham Lincoln's Ten Percent Plan, white men who lived under rebellion could take an oath to the loyalty of the United States and accept the abolition of slavery and in return enjoy all citizenship rights except property rights to people in bondage. President Johnson continued this practice of loyalty oaths as a precondition for a return to citizenship rights for lower-level participants in the Confederacy. Governor Marvin went even further than Lincoln or

Johnson and demanded that an "amnesty oath" contain a commitment to the "freedom of the former slaves." Amnesty oaths or loyalty oaths did not make it into the final draft of the 1865 Constitution.[21]

The convention addressed the constitutional state of the Civil War and what it meant after the surrender of the Confederacy. Johnson's November 6, 1865, Presidential Proclamation was published in the convention's official record. Like President Lincoln, Johnson did not recognize the Confederate government, nor the state governments in rebellion, as the legitimate civil authority of the people of Florida. Instead, he informed the state that those in rebellion deprived the state of civil government and the "enjoyment of a republican form of government." Governor Marvin, who was a Unionist during the war, saw the Confederate government of the state with more nuance. He recognized there was a government in operation overseen by "civil authorities," but after the fall of the Confederacy that government ceased to exist and the state at that point was without a civil government. Marvin pointed out that the United States was protecting republican government and all civil rights and individual liberties for all residents of Florida until a legitimate government could be formed. Marvin also blamed the rebellion for the poor state of Native people after the war. In a letter to William P. Dole, US commissioner of Indian Affairs, he stated that the Florida Confederate government patronized and offered gifts to the Indigenous societies in Florida in return for their promise to remain neutral and not rise against the state during the war. He further observed that economic activity at these Native trading posts had been almost nonexistent since the end of the war. Marvin called upon Dole because he argued that the Native people of Florida were subjects of the US government and not the state. He expected the US secretary of war to use the troops stationed in Florida to engage the Native societies to guard against a rebellion akin to those suffered during the Seminole Wars. Unlike the West after the Civil War, Southern states like Florida recognized the property rights of Native people, at least the fact that Indigenous people occupied specific land in the state and the role of the federal government in mediating those relations between Native people and the State of Florida. The US commissioner of Indian Affairs later replied that the federal government did not recognize the Native people of Florida as "subject" people, and their conditions and care were the responsibility of the state government. The state General Assembly accepted this interpretation during its first legislative session in January 1866. In the most overt mention of the Confederacy at the convention, delegates passed a resolution on November 4, asking President Johnson to offer release from prison and clemency to former Confederate President Jefferson Davis. At the same time, the delegates passed an additional clemency resolution for Florida officials who were serving time for treason in federal prison. The resolution advocated for the release and clemency of David L. Yulee, Stephen Russell Mallory, and Abraham Kurkindolle Allison who served as governor of Florida after the suicide of John Milton in the last days of the war.[22]

The antebellum and Confederate war debt were not the only economic issues that the 1865 Constitutional Convention had to address. The regulation of banks, corporations, and revenue all had to be adapted to 1865. The language of the "Banks and Other Corporations" article did not change much. Some sections were combined into one from the 1838 Constitution for inclusion in the 1865 Constitution. One article from the antebellum constitution was deleted altogether. In 1838 due to the controversy over state banks, the antebellum convention drafted an article that gave the power of the General Assembly to directly, "regulate, restrain and control, all associations claiming to exercise corporate privileges in the State, so as to guard, protect, and secure the interests of the people of the State, not violating vested rights, or impairing the obligation of contracts." The closest the convention delegates got to that antebellum language was a motion to include as an article one that would prohibit the state, counties, cities, or towns from directly or indirectly assisting any corporation or private organization financially or otherwise. The motion was defeated on its second reading. Anti-bank sentiment divided both political parties in the 1830s broadly in a landed planters versus yeomen farmers division. The 1838 document was a compromise of anti-bank and pro-bank factions, which is why the constitution prohibited the state from investing in banks and gave the power to the General Assembly to regulate banks and other corporations. This power was probably granted because in 1841 the state defaulted on bond interest payments that originated with the Pensacola Bank; some of the holders of these bonds were overseas. By 1865 these divisions over economic self-interest and out-of-state companies had receded and would not return to state politics—at least not in the same way—until the 1880s with the rise of the Independents, Labor, and Populists factions. No article was more similar between the antebellum constitution and the 1865 Constitution than the "Taxation and Revenue" article. The 1865 draft included a new section that gave the power to the General Assembly to levy a capitation tax if they wished. The 1866 General Assembly passed legislation to impose a capitation tax on employers based on the number of workers they hired.[23]

The "Declaration of Rights" from the 1838 Constitution could not exist in its entirety since it preserved the institution of slavery as previously mentioned. Under article I, section 1, in the antebellum Constitution, the delegates at the convention used the term "freemen" to denote white men as citizens in a slave territory where the inheritors of the rights prescribed in that section of the document. In 1865 the delegates still used the word "Freemen" for the same article and same section. The 1838 passage reads, "That all freemen, when they form a social compact, are equal." When drafted for the 1865 Constitution, it instead read, "That all freemen when they form a government." Although the status of statehood in the intervening years would explain the use of social contract versus form of government, the word "equal" was also stripped from the earlier language as well to denote that in the absence of slavery all freemen are not indeed equal. Additionally, section 4 was revised to eliminate the words "That all elections shall be free and equal" from the 1865 Constitution. What remined in whole word for word in both documents was the statement that political power is inherent with the people, and with that authority the people have an "inalienable and indefeasible right to alter or abolish their form of government in such manner as they may deem expedient." This antebellum language seemed to contrast with the spirit of abolishing the Confederacy and slavery, which could be pointed to for a future ordinance of secession. One article eliminated from the antebellum constitution was the state language that paralleled the Second Amendment to the Constitution. The 1838 Constitution noted that "the free white men of this State shall have the right to keep and to bear arms, for their common defense." Why this was eliminated is not known as it did not come up in the convention proceedings. Chief Justice Salmon P. Chase in August 1865 not only publicly told a New Orleans organization of Black men that they are citizens of the United States but also the right to bear arms applied to them now. Antebellum laws in Florida and elsewhere in the South restricted gun ownership from Black people, and the right to form militias applied exclusively to white people. In 1865, African Americans in Mississippi and Charleston, South Carolina, formed armed militias for self-protection, and the state government in both Mississippi and South Carolina passed legislation to disarm them. This outraged many in the Northern press who advocated that Black people in the South were free and enjoyed the protection of the Second Amendment to the Constitution. Delegates probably wanted to make a statement about the rights of Black people and their access to guns and forming militias for self-defense.[24]

Aside from the brief experiments in constitutions during the era of breakaway republics before 1821, the Florida Constitution of 1865 was the shortest-lived government in the state's history. At the end of November, the state held an election to pass the constitution and elect its government officials. The government stood for a little over a year. The state elected David S. Walker as governor along with a new General Assembly in December 1865. Outgoing provisional Governor Marvin addressed the General Assembly on December 20, 1865, preceding Governor Walker's inauguration. In Marvin's address to the legislature, he pointed to the spirit of the Guarantee Clause in defending his tenure by stating:

> The Constitution of the United States guarantees to each State in the Union a republican form of government, and the chief object contemplated by the President in appointing for the State a Provisional Governor, under the circumstances of the case, was, that the latter might make such rules and regulations as were necessary to enable the people of the State to assemble in Convention, and, accepting the results of the war, adopt such measures as were necessary to reestablish a State government, republican in form, and restore the natural and normal relations of the State with the general government.[25]

Governor Walker was a constitutional Unionist in 1861 and unlike Marvin ultimately supported the Confederacy. He advised the General Assembly to create a government that united all the various political factions of the state that appeared five years earlier. The political positions he described as such were the Constitutional Secessionists, the Unionists, and the "Revolutionists." In his inauguration speech Walker defended the Confederacy's right to leave the union but promised a government that "shall know no distinction between citizens on account of past political differences." He imagined a different government for Black people in Florida. He claimed that African Americans while in bondage were "loyal" and "faithful" to the white men of the state. He did acknowledge their freedom but said of Blacks in post-slavery Florida,

> They are no longer our contented and happy slaves, with an abundant supply of food and clothing for themselves and families, and the intelligence of a superior race to look ahead and make all necessary arrangements for their comfort. They are now a discontented and unhappy people, many of them houseless and homeless, roaming about in gangs over the land, not knowing one day where the supplies for the next are to come from—exposed to the ravages of disease and famine—exposed to the temptations of theft and rob-

bery, by which they are too often overcome—without the intelligence to provide for themselves when well, or to care for themselves when sick, and doomed to untold sufferings and ultimate extinction, unless we intervene for their protection and preservation.[26]

Unfortunately, it was Walker's description of Black people as unworthy of equal citizenship that would be the philosophical grounding of state government throughout the Jim Crow years in Florida.

The 1865 Constitutional Convention did not go unnoticed nationally, especially by federal lawmakers who campaigned and supported citizenship rights for African Americans. The newly elected state General Assembly voted to appoint Marvin to the US Senate in December 1865. On January 19, 1866, Senator James Rood Doolittle Sr., from Wisconsin, tried to recognize former Governor Marvin as the newly appointed Senator from Florida from the Senate floor. Charles Sumner, the Massachusetts senator, targeted the state convention in his response to Doolittle and Marvin's nomination. Attacking the convention, he referred to the body as a "pretend convention." Sumner rejected the right of the 1866 Florida state government, as well as Marvin, to represent the people of Florida, when Black citizens of the state could not fully enjoy the rights and protections of their state government. He said, "The question in this body, that no State among these States where the governments have lapsed can be recognized as republican in form which disfranchises any considerable portion of the citizens."[27]

At the end of the convention on November 7, 1865, Governor Marvin gave a speech and advised the incoming General Assembly to allow African Americans to travel unmolested around the state for the holidays but after that to treat Blacks who were in his words "idle and dissolute" criminally as vagrants. This final statement from the convention would set the tone of the new state government to emerge. When Erasmus Darwin Tracy of Nassau County was elected president of the convention, the *New York Times* reported "he hoped that a better more magnificent government [than] the old one would be built up through the action of the convention." The Dunning School historian, William Watson Davis, remarked that the 1865 Constitution "historically considered it *was* liberal." To devotees of the lost cause, indeed it might have been "liberal," but the 1865 Constitution was not much better than its 1838 predecessor in terms of a true republican form of government. The state government that followed the 1865 convention was one that oversaw extreme, state-sanctioned racial inequality. Most famous of which was a series of laws known as "black codes" that targeted

African Americans. Unlike their descendants, the Jim Crow laws, the legislature passed black codes as legislation that specifically and explicitly targeted African Americans. One of the first orders of business for the General Assembly when it convened in December 1865 was to outline the revisions to current statutes and how they might apply differently between the races. The report delivered to the legislature pointed to the Dred Scott decision as sound legal precedent and proof that African Americans were not citizens of the United States still, in what was a pre–Fourteenth Amendment Florida. The report went further to state that according to the Dred Scott decision the US Congress had no authority to grant citizenship rights to Black people, so enshrining racial discrimination in legal code would suffer no consequence. The authors of the report, Florida Chief Justice Charles H. DuPont and A. J. Peeler, pointed to Connecticut and Wisconsin voters who recently rejected granting suffrage to Black men as evidence that only a minority of voices in the North supported equal political rights for African Americans. DuPont and Peeler imagined laws that would restrict the owning of guns based on race, vagrancy laws targeting African Americans, and the prohibition of the intermarriage between the races as the centerpiece of these black codes. The authors made their rationale clear, "We have a duty to perform—the protection of our wives and children from threatened danger, and the prevention of scenes which may cost the extinction of an entire race." When the US Congress pushed through the Fourteenth Amendment, this overruled the black codes in the South and settled the Black citizenship question once and for all. When Republicans in Congress took over Reconstruction from the president, they passed a law stating that the government of Florida created from the 1865 Constitution no longer existed and Florida was placed under military rule so that a new government could be formed, one that would include African American men in suffrage and participation in a future constitutional convention.[28]

The 1865 Florida Constitution was an experiment in Presidential Reconstruction and its politics. Eric Foner described wartime Reconstruction as a first draft of Reconstruction, one that President Abraham Lincoln oversaw, and which was ultimately unsuccessful in any meaningful way. Military leaders and Union governors in the South enacted divergent policies toward the civilian populations. The governments reconstructed before the end of the war in Virginia, Tennessee, Arkansas, and Louisiana were never recognized by Congress during this time and did not have popular support in those states. Presidential Reconstruction overseen by President Johnson would be a second draft of Reconstruction, and, if possible, more unsuccessful than wartime Reconstruction. If Florida can be a case study, what the 1865 Constitution reflects is government formed just inches away from the antebellum conditions of the state under slavery, what Jerrell H. Shofner characterized as fulfilling "the minimum conditions for readmission." Alexander J. Bowen suggests that the Florida 1865 Constitution, and other Southern state constitutions like it, provoked Congressional Reconstruction, the Civil Rights Acts, and the Reconstruction amendments, which ultimately "fought for racial equality, suffrage for Black Floridians, and Republican control of state government." Aside from the revision to make the branches of state government work in parallel ways to the federal government, the greatest concern for the 1865 delegates was to create a status for African Americans that was "free" yet legally unfree. What delegates grappled with in very public ways were legal language and arguments that on paper lawmakers would describe as "freedom" and civil rights "protections" for African Americans, yet that literally prescribed a second-class status to Black people in Florida. After Reconstruction, Florida legislation would evolve. White Democratic Party lawmakers found an ability to draft racially "color neutral" laws that would impose a second-class citizenship on Black people for generations, and courts would uphold these laws in the wake of *Plessy v. Ferguson* (1896). Although this episode was the second draft of Reconstruction in Florida, it was the first draft of a much longer and disgraceful legal history we would come to know as Jim Crow Florida. Although the 1865 Constitution was the state's shortest governing document, it cast a long shadow over the sunshine state.[29]

Notes

1 John Wallace, *Carpet Bag Rule in Florida: The Inside Workings of the Reconstruction of Civil Government in Florida after the Close of the Civil War*, (Jacksonville, FL: De Costa Publishing, 1888), 8–9; Columbus, *Daily Ohio Statesman*, October 23, 1865; *New York Times*, November 10, 1865.

2 Eric Foner, *Reconstruction: America's Unfinished Revolution, 1863–1877* (New York: Harper & Row, 1988), 35–36, 48–50, 179–81.

3 Ryan A. Swanson, "Andrew Johnson and His Governors: An Examination of Failed Reconstruction Leadership." *Tennessee Historical Quarterly* 71, no. 1 (2012): 16–45; Foner, 180–81, Jerrell H. Shofner, *Nor Is It Over Yet: Florida in the Era of Reconstruction, 1863–1877*, (Gainesville: University Presses of Florida, 1974), 13, 39.

4 *Journal of Proceedings of the Convention of Florida* (Tallahassee: Dyke and Sparhawk, 1865) 23, 29.

5 Fla. Const. of 1838, art. XII, § 1, Fla. Const. of 1865, art. XII, § 1.

The 1865 Convention and Constitution · 131

6 *Journal of Proceedings of the Convention of Florida* (1865) 52–56; Fla. Const. of 1838, art. V, § 5, 11, 13, 16; Fla. Const. of 1865, art. V, § 4, 10, 14, 15, 18; *Journal of the Proceedings of the Senate of the General Assembly of the State of Florida, 2nd Session of the Fourteenth General Assembly* (Tallahassee: Office of the Sentinel, 1866), 16–18, 57, 60.
7 Fla. Const. of 1838, art. III, § 2, 3, 16, 18, 19, 21; Fla. Const. of 1865, art. II, § 2, 4, 5, 17, 19, 20, 21; *Journal of Proceedings of the Convention of Florida* (1865) 42–46.
8 Fla. Const. of 1838, art. IV, § 3, 4, 5, 6; Fla. Const. of 1865, art. IV, § 3, 4, 5, 17, 18, 20, 22; *Journal of Proceedings of the Convention of Florida* (1865) 38–42.
9 Fla. Const. of 1838, art. VI, § 1, 4, I, § 4; Fla. Const. of 1865, art. VI, § 1, 2, 9, art. I § 4; *Journal of Proceedings of the Convention of Florida* (1865) 30–35, 42–43, 60.
10 Fla. Const. of 1838, art. VI, § 8, 10, art. IX, § 5; Fla. Const. of 1865, art. VI, § 14, art. IX, § 5; *Acts of the General Assembly of the State of Florida* (Tallahassee: W & C. Bartlett, 1845), 36–37; *Acts and Resolutions of the General Assembly of the State of Florida* (Tallahassee: S. S. Sibley, 1845), 77–79.
11 Houston *Tri-Weekly Telegraph,* August 21, 1865; Philadelphia, *Daily Age,* September 26, 1865; *New Orleans Times,* October 14, 1865; *Journal of Proceedings of the Convention of Florida* (1865) 9; Philadelphia, *Daily Age,* November 9, 1865.
12 Fla. Const. of 1865, art. XVI, § 1.
13 *Journal of Proceedings of the Convention of Florida* (1865) 12, 56, 74.
14 Alabama Const. of 1865, art. I, § 34; *Official Journal of the Proceedings of the Convention for the Revision and Amendment of the Constitution of the State of Louisiana* (New Orleans, W. R. Fish, 1864), 74; Arkansas Const. of 1864, art. V, § 1; *Acts and Resolutions, State of Florida 1845* (Tallahassee, FL: S.S. Sibley, 1845), 78; Fla. Const. of 1868, art. 1, § 18.
15 *Journal of Proceedings of the Convention of Florida* (1865), 9.
16 Eric Foner, *Reconstruction,* 180, 184, and 239; William M. Wiecek, *The Guarantee Clause of the U.S. Constitution,* (Ithaca: Cornell University Press: 1972), 193–94; Laura F. Edwards, *A Legal History of the Civil War and Reconstruction: A Nation of Rights* (New York: Cambridge University Press: 2015), 99, 102.
17 Silas L. Niblack in 1870 challenged Josiah Walls, an African American who was appointed and ran to keep his seat to represent Florida in the US House of Representatives. Walls went on to win that election. Peter D. Klingman, *Josiah Walls: Florida's Black Congressman of Reconstruction* (Gainesville: University Presses of Florida, 1976), 39–40.
18 *Journal of Proceedings of the Convention of Florida* (1865) 9–10, 14, 22, 41, 56, 80–81; Fla. Const. of 1865, art. IX, § 1; See *Acts and Resolutions 2nd Session of the Fourteenth General Assembly of the State of Florida (1866)* (Tallahassee, FL: Dyke and Sparhawk, 1867). A proposed bill to limit the immigration of people of color to Florida was never recorded as a debate in the Florida House or Senate in 1866. The Senate on January 9, 1866, considered a report encouraging the government of Florida to actively boost working-class immigration from Europe, but the body did not record any prohibition to the migration of people of color to the state. *Journal of the Proceedings of the Senate of the General Assembly of the State of Florida, 2nd*

Session of the Fourteenth General Assembly (Tallahassee, FL: Office of the Sentinel, 1866), 183.
19 *Journal of Proceedings of the Convention of Florida* (1865) 71–72, 102, 114, 167; *Acts and Resolutions (1866),* 22; Fla. Const. of 1865, art. XVI, § 2, Washington, DC, *Evening Union,* November 9, 1865; *New York Times,* November 10, 1865.
20 David K. Thomson, *Bonds of War: How Civil War Financial Agents Sold the World the Union,* (Chapel Hill: University of North Carolina Press, 2022), 164–65; *Journal of Proceedings of the Convention of Florida* (1865) 57–60, 77; *Acts and Resolutions (1866),* 88; Fla. Const. of 1865, art. XVII, § 3; Jerrell H. Shofner noted that the total debt in bonds was $1,857,269.99, which would have included antebellum debt. Shofner, *Nor Is It Over Yet,* 41; Edwards, *A Legal History of the Civil War and Reconstruction,* 97.
21 *Journal of Proceedings of the Convention of Florida* (1865) 9, 15, 28, 47, 122, 159; Edwards, *A Legal History of the Civil War and Reconstruction,* 92–93; *New York Times,* November 10, 1865.
22 *Journal of Proceedings of the Convention of Florida* (1865) 121, 124, 134, 165–66; Edwards, *A Legal History of the Civil War and Reconstruction,* 113; Florida, *Senate Journal 2nd Session of the Fourteenth Session* (1866) (Tallahassee, FL: Office of the Sentinel, 1866), 241; Florida, *House Journal 2nd Session of the Fourteenth Session* (1866) (Tallahassee, FL: Office of the Sentinel, 1866), 193–94, 198, 201.
23 Fla. Const. of 1838, art. XIII, § 14; Fla. Const. of 1865, art. XIII, § 10, art. VIII, § 5; *Journal of Proceedings of the Convention of Florida* (1865) 49, 66; *Acts and Resolutions (1866),* 32–33; Edward E. Baptist, *Creating an Old South: Middle Florida's Plantation Frontier before the Civil War* (Chapel Hill: University of North Carolina Press, 2002), 166–67; Sidney Walter Martin, *Florida During the Territorial Days* (Athens: University of Georgia Press, 1944), 270–71; New York, *Albany Argus,* July 20, 1841; Thomson, *Bonds of War,* 17. On the 1880s, see Edward C. Williamson, *Florida Politics in the Gilded Age, 1877–1893* (Gainesville: University Presses of Florida, 1976), 155, 179–85; William Watson Davis, *The Civil War and Reconstruction in Florida* (New York: Longmans, Green & Co., 1913), 28–29.
24 Fla. Const. of 1838, art. I, § 1, 2, 21; Fla. Const. of 1865, art. I, § 1, 2; Boston, *The Liberator,* August 18, 1865; Vermont, *Burlington Daily Times,* December 20, 1865; North Carolina, *Wilmington Herald,* October 25, 1865. There is no record of African Americans in Florida forming militias in 1865, but they did after in places like Jacksonville during Reconstruction. William Watson Davis in his *The Civil War and Reconstruction in Florida* reported that chapters of the Union League and organizations known as Lincoln Brotherhoods started in mid-summer 1865 to organize northerners and African American men throughout the state. They are described as secret armed political societies that were antagonistic to white Floridians. There is no evidence either of these organizations started as early as 1865; other historians have located their origins in 1867 when Congressional Reconstruction was underway. Additionally, historians have treated these organizations as political clubs and not armed militias as Davis originally characterized. See Davis, *The Civil War and*

Reconstruction in Florida, 375, and Jerrell H. Shofner, "Political Reconstruction in Florida," *The Florida Historical Quarterly* 45, no. 2 (1966): 147.

25 Florida, *Journal of the Proceedings of the House of Representatives Fourteenth Session* (1865) (Tallahassee, FL: Dyke and Sparhawk, 1865), 18.

26 Florida, *Journal of the House Fourteenth Session* (1865), 31–35; Davis, *The Civil War and Reconstruction in Florida*, 366–67.

27 Georgia, *Macon Telegraph*, January 27, 1866; Florida, *Senate Journal 1st Session of the Fourteenth Session* (1865) (Tallahassee, FL: Office of the Sentinel, 1866), 87; US Senate, Thirty-Ninth Congress, First Session, *Congressional Globe* (February 19, 1865): Part 1, 313; Davis, *The Civil War and Reconstruction in Florida*, 365.

28 Columbus, *Daily Ohio Statesmen*, November 27, 1865; *New York Times*, November 10, 1865; Davis, *The Civil War and Reconstruction in Florida*, 365; Florida, *Journal of the House Fourteenth Session* (1865), 58–64; Joe M. Richardson, "Florida Black Codes," *The Florida Historical Quarterly* 47, no. 4 (1969): 368; Jerrell H. Shofner, "The Constitution of 1868," *The Florida Historical Quarterly* 41, no. 4 (1963): 356, Alexander J. Bowen, "'Made and Executed by the White Race': Florida's Constitution of 1865 and 'Black Codes,'" *The Florida Historical Quarterly* 101, no. 1 (Summer 2022): 15–19.

29 Shofner, *Nor Is It Over Yet*, 44; Bowen, 21.

6

In Pursuit of a More Perfect Union

The Drafting and Crafting of the 1868 Florida Constitution

Andrea L. Oliver

> We the people of the State of Florida, grateful to Almighty God for our freedom, in order to secure its blessings and form a more perfect government, insuring domestic tranquility, maintaining public order, perpetuating liberty and guaranteeing equal civil and political rights to all, do establish this Constitution.
>
> The Florida Constitution of 1868

By the winter of 1868, Florida was facing the daunting task of writing its fourth state constitution in thirty years.[1] After the Civil War, a conservative-dominated legislature quickly drafted and imposed a state constitution that, among other things, limited the franchise to white men over the age of twenty-one. While this proved an acceptable tenet during the presidential phase of Reconstruction, this measure failed to pass constitutional muster at the federal level. In 1867, a Republican-dominated Congress invalidated Florida's 1865 Constitution declaring that the state had no legitimate government and mandated that it drafted a new instrument that would envelop the newly ratified Thirteenth and Fourteenth Amendments within its framework.[2] As it happened, the year 1868 in Florida, and across the South more broadly, proved to be a revolutionary year, at least as far as Black political power was concerned. As historian Lerone Bennett noted, 1868 was the "glory year" of Reconstruction. He pointed to the passing of the Fourteenth Amendment and reflected that it was the year that "almost all things were made new."[3]

Certainly, 1868 presented a radical departure from Reconstruction's early years. Formerly enslaved Southerners scarcely had time to celebrate their new status before they became the principal targets of an embittered white populace intent on exacting revenge. Making matters worse for them was the cruel reality that they did not have a reliable ally in the White House in President Andrew Johnson. Assuming the presidency in the wake of Lincoln's assassination, Johnson pardoned former slave owners, returned land to them that had been confiscated and redistributed to the formerly enslaved, and extended extremely lenient conditions to Southern states to rejoin the Union. These conditions relegated the freedmen to second-class standing reinforced by the passage of laws that imposed a state of quasi-enslavement on Black people. White planters engaged in terror campaigns to intimidate Black people into accepting submission. Mississippi demanded that freed people carry proof they had entered into labor contracts or they could be imprisoned. Other states passed so-called vagrancy laws, which were as vague in definition as they were arbitrary in their enforcement. The early Reconstruction government of South Carolina mandated that Black people accept no other work than farm work or be subjected to an onerous tax of $10 to $100. This provision placed considerable strain on Black artisans, some of whom had managed to amass modest amounts of wealth and a modicum of independence from the white power structure. White society everywhere conspired to reinforce the narrative that shared political power would lead to social equality, an unfathomable situation.[4]

An 1868 *New York Times* editorial doubted that Black people were capable of maintaining their existence in the South or even in the country as it noted were "the most favorable possible conditions and opportunities."[5] During the presidential phase of Reconstruction, it was painfully evident that white Southerners were not only unwilling to accept the new realities of Black freedom but were willing to resort to violence if necessary to reestablish what in their eyes was the good and proper order of society: white supremacist rule. But 1868 would be a year where a convergence of several events would conspire to test the notion of citizenship and shared power dynamics. The story of the Florida Constitutional Convention of 1868 is a story of political intrigue placing the struggle to become a more inclusive, and therefore more "perfect," society at the state level. The balance of this chapter will endeavor to tell that story.

The story of Florida's 1868 Constitutional Convention begins with the 1866 Republican takeover of Congress. Displeased with President Johnson's general antipathy toward the advancement of Black civil and political rights, further underscored by his general lenience toward those who many considered traitorous enemies of the republic, which included high-ranking

Confederate military and political figures, congressional Republicans set out to impose their will on the Reconstruction process resolute to cement the promise of full citizenship on the nearly four million recently emancipated men, women, and children of the former Confederacy. On April 9, 1866, the Republican-controlled Congress took the unprecedented step of overriding President Andrew Johnson's veto of the Civil Rights Bill of 1866. Additionally, the law marked the first time that Congress took legislative action on civil rights. Chairman of the Senate Judiciary Committee, Lyman Trumbull of Illinois, mandated that the bill declare "all persons born in the United States.... citizens...," that would have the "full and equal benefit of all laws and proceedings for the security of person and property." Curiously, the bill did not extend citizenship to Native people, though it was clear that formerly enslaved African Americans were the intended beneficiaries of this sweeping piece of legislation. Upon the insistence of Republican Ohio Congressman John Bingham, subsequent legislative processes saw the removal of this key provision from its bill:

> There shall be no discrimination in civil rights or immunities among the inhabitants of any State or Territory of the United States on account of race, color, or previous condition of servitude.[6]

Bingham worried that the inclusion of protections targeting racial or ethnic groups might be construed as federal overreach by the courts. Though the architects of this bill acquiesced to the removal of this clause, which would have explicitly clarified the legal standing of the formerly enslaved in no uncertain terms, the law was still regarded as remarkably progressive for its time. In addition, its insistence that the formerly enslaved have their civil rights be recognized and protected at both the federal and state levels, the act barred high-ranking Confederate officials from participation in the political process and granted judicial authority to military courts in legal matters involving civil, criminal, and property rights violations. Perhaps the two most consequential provisions of the First Reconstruction Act were the ones requiring Southern states to ratify the Fourteenth Amendment to be represented in Congress followed by the dictate that Southern states had to enact new state constitutions, which extended the same protections of due process citizenship through the Fourteenth Amendment.[7]

On the heels of the passage of the Civil Rights Act of 1866, the first of what would eventually be four Reconstruction acts, was passed in the spring of 1867 over Johnson's veto. According to this act, the South was to be divided into five military districts. Florida was placed in military district three along with Georgia and Alabama. Now under martial law, states in these military districts were compelled to register all males twenty-one years of age regardless of color and to permit them to vote for delegates to state constitutional conventions, where new state constitutions would be drawn enshrining universal manhood suffrage on a nondiscriminatory basis. Further, the act mandated that these newly elected state legislatures had to ratify the Fourteenth Amendment before their readmission to the Union would be finalized. White state leaders angrily defied the law, refusing to extend the franchise to African Americans. President Johnson was similarly reticent to carry out the will of Congress and patently refused to enforce the law.

In response to this massive level of resistance, Congress passed the Second Reconstruction Act exactly three weeks after the passage of the First Reconstruction Act. In this measure, military district commanders were given directions on holding the state constitutional conventions that would draft these new constitutions. True to ideological form, President Johnson vetoed both measures, only to have both vetoes overridden by the Republican-dominated Congress. The newly empowered Republican majority in the Congress was flexing its muscle, fresh off their convincing electoral wins of the previous fall. They were determined to see serious implementation of this groundbreaking legislation through, despite the vigorous opposition Southern conservatives mounted, which was further amplified by the then current occupant of the Oval Office. No longer leaving it up to state officials to exercise good faith compliance, the electoral power passed into the hands of military commanders. Now, in both a literal and figurative sense, Southern states were being held at gunpoint to create new governments that were closer to the more perfect union ideal.[8]

Those who had been situated in the leadership apparatus in this new governance arrangement included men who had served in the Union Army, or who had extensive involvement in the civilian bureaucratic network dedicated to helping the formerly enslaved transition into their new lives. Thomas Osborn was one such figure. A former Union lieutenant who had seen action at the First Battle of Bull Run, Osborn was appointed assistant Florida commissioner for the Bureau of Refugees, Freedmen, and Abandoned Lands, more commonly known as the Freedmen's Bureau.[9] According to historian Gordon C. Bond, Osborn was one of the first to recognize the full potential of Black people in the political process as he was one of the first to attempt to organize them politically. After resigning his position with the Freedmen's Bureau, he convinced local Black leaders in Tallahassee to protect their newly gained freedom and political rights by organizing a political fraternity known as the Lincoln Brotherhood. A competing organization with aims like that of the Lincoln Brotherhood was the Union League of America. Daniel Richards, an Illinois carpetbagger; Daniel Saunders, an African American barber from Baltimore; and Liberty Billings, a white chaplain from New Hampshire, were the cofounders of the Union League's Florida chapter. More radical in its views than the Lincoln Brotherhood, the Union League sometimes resorted to subterfuge to swell their ranks. For instance, some freedmen were told membership in the Union League was a corequisite to membership in the Republican Party. As it happens, use of such tactics was wholly unnecessary. The Reconstruction-era Black electorate was more favorably disposed to the party of Abraham Lincoln, and their allegiance was made more certain by the hostility of Florida's Democratic Party, the nineteenth-century political party of choice for the conservative status quo.[10]

Pursuant to the Second Reconstruction Act, an election was held to select delegates for the state constitutional convention, which would be tasked with writing a new constitution that Congress would approve. Throughout the fall of 1867, Republicans were well organized and blanketed the state to register the freedmen. Judging from the data, the freedmen seemed anxious to participate in the electoral process. Final registration lists showed that of the 28,003 names, nearly 54 percent of them belonged to Black men. The 1867 election convened over a three-day period from November 14 through 16, to allow voters the opportunity to travel to the polling places in their respective county seats. Voters were confronted with two matters on the ballot: whether to convene a constitutional convention and who would serve as delegates if such a convention were held. White conservatives boycotted the election hoping that an insufficient number of electoral participants would render the elections invalid. Their strategy backfired. Voter turnout was north of 50 percent, and those voters were near unanimous in their support of a convention (14,300 in favor out of 14,503 ballots cast). Forty-six delegates, all but three of whom were Republicans, were elected to meet in a convention in Tallahassee on January 20, 1868. In a level of representation that was certainly not seen before and has not been seen since, 42 percent, eighteen in total number, of the constitutional convention delegates were Black people. Thus, the stage was set for the real work of developing a more perfect union in the state of Florida through a new, more equity-based constitution.[11]

Notwithstanding strong voter engagement as indicated by the high turnout, the elections used to identify participating delegates had their share of intrigue. Conservative whites, united in their opposition to drawing up a new constitution that fully recognized Black Floridians' new status as freed people marched lockstep with the Democratic Party's boycott of the election, despite the ultimate failure of this approach to sabotaging the impending convention. The Republican Party, on the other hand, was not as cohesive. Florida's Reconstruction-era Republican Party was comprised of various constituencies that all had a stake in the development of a revised constitution. Predictably, each one had varying agendas with differing limitations and devices they leveraged in service to those agendas. There were Northern transplants in the state who were serving in either military or civilian capacities. Some of these men had designs on gaining a foothold in the state politically or economically. There was a smattering of native whites who joined the Republican Party, not on ideological grounds, but out of pragmatic concerns. There was the recently emancipated who, dislodged from their old identities, were rapidly descending into quasi-states of enslavement scarcely resembling their former lives. Aside from justifiably being preoccupied with the cares of day-to-day survival, the freedmen, who were largely illiterate and novices in matters of the state, relied on the advice of others to help them negotiate the foreign terrain of public affairs. Their political ignorance was exploited by unprincipled political players who saw in their inexperience a chance to promote their own concerns.[12]

From the morass of competing groups, two elements emerged the most dominant for control of Florida's Republican Party: those who believed that they had momentum on their side in the wake of the radical Republican takeover of Congress and those who believed that radical support in Congress mattered very little in the political calculus of day-to-day life of the freedmen who were the intended beneficiaries of a new constitution. Those of the latter persuasion were known as moderates, because they believed moderating their views on the extent of Black-white social and civic interactions would offer the best chances for the long-term viability that would satisfy Congress and the hardline conservative base in the state. Those who believed Florida's new constitution should be as progressive as possible for the era were similarly known as radicals, just as they were named on the federal level. The former of the two constituencies were willing to broker compromise with conservatives who were intent on retaining white dominance while the former wanted to revolutionize government to create a truly biracial political system. In the two groups' attempts to impose their respective wills on the course of the impending convention, presaged certain events were yet to take place during the convention itself.[13]

In his comprehensive look at the 1868 Florida Constitution, historian Jerrell Shofner asserted that the document resulting from the work of the 1868 convention was not a radical instrument imposed on a "helpless white population by 'carpetbaggers' and Negroes." In advancing his claim, Shofner rejected what he referred to as the standard convention of the time—the one that held that the 1868 Constitution represented the excesses of corruption and incompetence characteristic of what white Southerners derisively referred to as "Negro rule." When Shofner's article appeared in 1963, the Dunning School interpretation of the Reconstruction era had enthralled both the academy and popular sentiment alike. Named for early-twentieth-century Columbia University scholar William Dunning, this interpretation held that white Southerners were sincere in their desire to rejoin national culture and in extending the emancipated freedmen their rights and equal opportunities. Radical Republicans in Congress, inspired by their inherent animus toward the South, forced an unprepared and unqualified Black electorate onto the South using overreach and bullying to achieve these ends. These Reconstruction-era governments were riddled with corruption and incompetence at the hands of Northern carpetbaggers, Southern scalawags, and illiterate freedmen who plunged the South into depression and confusion until the white South banded together to "redeem" their culture and thus restore society to its rightful order. In Dunning's Reconstruction, Black politicians were profligate and an embarrassment to democracy. They were easily manipulated, which made them susceptible to the devious schemes of the white politicians who debased themselves to work with them at the expense of the public good. According to Dunning's narrative, Black politicians, and the constituency they served, lacked the agency that later scholarship confirmed they possessed. Moreover, they leveraged that agency in ways that indicated they were more politically astute than they were previously given credit for. Dunning, and the scores of scholars he either directly or indirectly influenced, had a profound impact on the way Americans viewed the Reconstruction era. For example, in his early-twentieth-century tome dedicated to Reconstruction in Florida, William Watson Davis's classic work on Reconstruction in Florida was completed under the direction of Dunning himself. Davis concluded that the delegates who attended the 1868 convention, pejoratively referred to by critics as Florida's "Black and Tan" convention,[14] were men with little ability who comprised a "rather motley assemblage," marked by "crass ignorance, aggressiveness, [and] vulgarity . . ."¹⁵ As some have observed, while the argument the Dunning School developed was incredibly flawed and heavily influenced by contemporaneous prejudices, it did offer a coherent argument during a time when firsthand remembrances were receding from the forefront of American consciousness. The synthesis of the political, social, and economic aspects of the era provided fodder for subsequent historians to frame their studies, whether those studies sought to ratify Dunning's conclusions or refute them.¹⁶

In 1935, African American intellectual W. E. B. Du Bois produced the first major challenge to the Dunning interpretation of Reconstruction. His *Black Reconstruction in America* issued a stinging rebuke of Dunning and those influenced by him for their systematic sleights of the population at the center of the Reconstruction epic: the freedmen themselves. Du Bois conjectured why the disregard or distortion of the freedman's role in Reconstruction was so prevalent at that time. In Du Bois's estimation, those who studied and wrote American history could not "conceive of Negroes as men." Du Bois's allegations heralded a wave of mid-century scholarship that sought to correct the narrative Dunning crafted, and the research of historians like Jerrell Shofner and Joe M. Richardson who were a part of that movement, which some have referred to as the Revisionist School. The central differentiating feature of Revisionist interpretations of Reconstruction and the Dunning perspectives that preceded it was the focus on freedmen and their being placed at the center of scholarly inquiry. Scholars like Shofner and Richardson made impactful contributions to the canon of Reconstruction scholarship by not only acknowledging the agency of the freedmen but giving that agency favorable appraisals on how their actions positively affected Reconstruction-era policies. Thus, their work rehabilitated the reputations of Black statesmen badly damaged by the near century assault their legacies had withstood at the hands of Dunning School scholars.¹⁷

With the delegates in place and the convention set to start on January 20, 1868, in the state's capital of Tallahassee, work was poised to begin on framing a governing instrument in keeping with congressional dictates that such would make a more earnest effort at incorporating the freedmen into the state's body politic. At first blush, it would appear the only thing at stake was the passage of a state constitution that would be acceptable to Congress so Florida could become an official part of the United States again. Further consideration revealed that something more substantial was at stake. In his study on Southern state constitutional conventions through secession, Reconstruction, and eventual restoration of home rule, Paul Herron took note of the expanding imposition of federal authority on the internal affairs of Southern states during Reconstruction's early years. Herron wrote, "Lincoln and Johnson implicitly required that the South abolish slavery, reject ordinances of secession, and repudiate the war." By way of 1867's Reconstruction Act, Congress explicitly mandated readmission requirements that insisted on universal manhood suffrage and ratification of the Fourteenth Amendment. In the presidential and congressional phases of Reconstruction, state officials and voters were compelled to swear loyalty oaths to the federal government. Indeed, what was to come out of Southern constitutional conventions, including the one convening in Florida during the winter of 1868, would have enduring ramifications on Tenth Amendment state-federal government relationships, namely the furtherance of a trend toward stronger interventions into state-level government affairs.[18]

When the convention opened on January 20, 1868, it was apparent that the radical faction of the Republican Party outnumbered their moderate counterparts by a considerable margin. Union League leaders William Saunders, Liberty Billings, and Daniel Richards arrived in Tallahassee and rented a large rooming house and a wagon. They were greeted with great fanfare at their rooming house and came into the convention in a strong position well organized and with the support of all but three of the eighteen Black delegates. On its first day, convention delegates went about the ordinarily mundane tasks of establishing procedures to conduct the work that lay ahead. Roll call, committee formation, and committee appointments made up the bulk of the first day's business. In that afternoon's proceedings, Daniel Richards was elected president of the convention over the objections of the moderates, led by Thomas Osborn, former leader of the Lincoln Brotherhood. In the acceptance speech he delivered after his election had been secured, Richards made clear his intention to steer the convention toward the formation of a constitution that was more racially inclusive and a radical departure from the most recent document. He reminded convention delegates that the constitution they were being tasked to create was intended to control all the functions of government. He averred, "The great questions of liberty, justice and equal rights to all are committed to us, and may we heed the voice of humanity, and may a merciful Providence aid us in our counsels and direct us in our conclusions."[19]

As Bond noted in his 1975 study of the Black delegates who participated in the proceedings, contention between the moderate delegation and the radicals was apparent from the beginning. The two camps differed on several issues; the real rift occurred over the question of delegate eligibility. Statutes decreed that to be an eligible delegate to the convention, one had to have lived in Florida for at least a year. The eligibility of several radicals, including that of their leader, Liberty Billings, was called into question. Billings was purportedly a citizen of New Hampshire, while William Saunders, one of Billings's chief lieutenants, was a native of Maryland who was not even registered to vote in Florida. Even the newly elected president of the convention, Daniel Richards, was not immune to these ineligibility claims. Not only was Richards not a registered voter, but he was not an inhabitant of the district that elected him.[20]

For the next two weeks, convention business was confined to procedural matters, most significantly committee formation. Secure in his position as president, Richards oversaw the creation of consequential committees headed by chairmen who were closely aligned with the radical leadership triad of Richards, Billings, and Saunders. Unsurprisingly, moderates felt underrepresented and excluded from meaningful participation and mounted procedural roadblocks to thwart these developments. The most substantial of these efforts involved an attempt to unseat radical committee members, known as "mule teamers," from committees with a view toward reconstituting them and starting a new assembly. Led by Representative W. J. Purnam, this tactic only had the effect of delaying the work of the committee by several days. The question of delegate eligibility was settled with the radicals retaining control of the process by a razor-thin margin, and as the convention moved into its second week in early February, seemed poised to get down to the business of drafting the long-awaited state constitution.[21]

But alas, the main objective of the convention was to be stymied yet again. Frustrated over what they perceived was the unevenness with which their views were being represented, moderate delegates staged a boycott of the convention, unbeknownst to their radical counterparts. The absence of fourteen delegates caused the lack of the necessary quorum needed to legitimately conduct the convention's business. Perturbed but undaunted by this unexpected course of events, the twenty-two members of the radical faction simply moved the goalpost in declaring that there was indeed a quorum if the basis of that count was rooted in the presence of the forty-one delegates in attendance on the previous day of business. They used this as a justification for framing their version of a new state constitution, which they hastily sent to General George Meade, commander of the Third Military District.[22]

The boycotting delegation was not idle in the face of these apparent radical advances. Its members, having decamped to the neighboring community of Monticello, conducted a shadow convention of sorts. During the clandestine Monticello conference, more supporting delegates joined the original group of absconders, and a renewed moderate faction returned to Tallahassee in the middle of the night on February 10. Newly emboldened by larger numbers, the Monticello contingent deposed Richards as president of the convention and replaced him with one of their own. They made quick work of the committees and their accompanying leadership, which had enjoyed a three-week period of dominance and likewise had them replaced by more moderate members, thus beginning a days-long stretch of competing conventions, with both sides claiming to be the lawful convention. The Richards-Billings group convened their meetings in a local Black church or in the public square, while the moderate faction, led by Thomas Osborn and Richards's replacement Horatio Jenkins Jr., held court in an assembly hall of the capitol. Over the next several weeks, the dueling delegations wrote and revised their own separate constitutions, during which time General Meade was called in to intervene. Arriving on February 17, he asked for and received the resignations of Jenkins and Richards as presidents of their respective groups. In a letter dated February 18, Richards was overt in his displeasure of having to resign under duress. In his short notice, he wrote: "In compliance with the request of Major General Meade, Commanding Third Military District, and wishing to restore harmony among the friends of reconstruction [sic] in our State, I hereby resign under protest the office of President of the Constitutional Convention of Florida."[23] Meade went on to preside over a newly organized convention where a new constitution was summarily adopted and passed by a majority of the newly convened delegates, a body now in the firm control of the moderates.

Though not actively participating in the official convention proceedings, the state's Democratic apparatus was not impervious to the political happenings in Tallahassee. The state's media outlets were decidedly conservative, and most were vociferously opposed to any modicum of power sharing with the recently emancipated among them. The state's newspaper editors made no secret of their disdain of what had been happening ever since the radical Republican takeover of Congress led to the precipitating events then occurring in Tallahassee. The musings of an editorial from *The East Florida Examiner* published in Ocala offered a representative viewpoint. In describing the convention in Tallahassee, the paper referred to the assembly as "a composition of negroes, mean white . . . deserters, and repudiators of honest debts." The editorial advised its readers that this motley group as it was described was not there to draft a federally mandated state constitution, but they were there instead seeking to, "control [the] intelligence and virtue of Florida." It went on to lampoon the convention as "a caricature . . ." that would in its view, ". . . excite the sensibilities of the serene and thoughtful." The *Florida Union,* located in Jacksonville, decried the devolution of the convention that brought the existence of two delegations to pass at all. "The condition of affairs in Tallahassee, according to our latest published dispatches, certainly presents a singular spectacle," an unnamed reporter wrote. While acknowledging the existence of the two organized bodies each drafting their own constitutional vision for governing Florida, the paper clearly had its favorite. The writer surmised that there was but one convention and proclaimed the minority Billings-Sanders-Richards faction as illegitimate since it did not represent the majority.[24]

The musings of disgruntled editorialists failed to account for the eminent qualifications of convention delegates, especially some of its Black members. While it is true that several were illiterate with very few having formal education—something true of several white delegates as well—there were several who distinguished themselves with certain capabilities and level of influence. William Saunders was an eloquent speaker, a quality he shared with fellow Black delegates Joe Oats and Charles Pearce, better known as Bishop Pearce due to his leadership role in the local African Methodist Episcopal (AME) church. The most notable African American member of the radical contingent was Robert Meacham, who represented Jefferson County. Of mixed-race heritage, he formed the first AME church in the capital city—Bethel AME. Though well respected by both races, he was not immune to attacks from the Ku Klux Klan. He remained active in state politics throughout the Reconstruction era.[25]

Setting aside the legalities of whether the delegates were eligible to serve as delegates in the constitutional convention, there was still the matter of what a newly drafted constitution—and one that would pass congressional muster—would address. This was, after all, what the proceedings were supposed to have been about in the first place. If one could only surmise based on the ideological leanings of the two principal groups at the center of every debate that had so far occurred, it would not have been difficult to predict that the radical faction would put forth a document that would look to give African Americans more substantive freedoms, while the moderate faction would have produced a document that would have only produced the barest of minimum standards necessary to rejoin the Union. While a comparison of the two documents confirms this assertion, suggesting that

Florida's Reconstruction-era Republican Party perfectly mirrored national leadership's druthers is inaccurate also. In his 1960s study on political Reconstruction in Florida, Jerrell Shofner stated that the state's Republican Reconstruction agenda was not formulated starting in 1868 at the outset of Congressional Reconstruction by men who were ideologically aligned with Charles Sumner and Thaddeus Stevens. As both he and earlier junctures of this chapter have already pointed out, the radicals were more in tune with the Stevenses and the Sumners of the political spectrum. They lost the battle over control of the process and the document that it produced to men who Shofner described as "business-oriented . . . who recognized that the state needed to be developed if the problems created by the Civil War were to be permanently solved." In this regard, Republicans of this ilk were not unlike Republicans in other parts of the country, and some conservative Democrats for that matter whom, as early as 1868, were already starting to experience compassion fatigue from the constant drumbeat of the woes of the freedmen that to these groups seemed to always take center stage in the current event discussions of the day. Republican interest in drafting a new constitution was only as intense as their desire to bring about an end to the kind of political and economic instability that the state's uncertain position relative to the rest of the Union was creating.[26]

The differences between the two documents seem apparent from the very beginning. Note the preamble to the constitution that was drafted before the convention was disrupted by the crew of the Monticello delegate contingent:

> We, the people of the State of Florida, by our delegates in convention assembled, in order to secure to ourselves and our posterity the enjoyment of all the rights of life, liberty, and property, and the pursuit of happiness, do mutually agree, each with the other, to form the following constitution and form of government, in and for the said State.[27]

Compare this to the preamble that was drafted after the convention, reformulated with the more conservative moderates in control of the process:

> We, the people of the State of Florida, grateful to Almighty God for our freedom, in order to secure its blessings and form a more prefect government, insuring domestic tranquility, *maintaining public order* (emphasis added), perpetuating liberty, and *guaranteeing equal civil*

and political rights to all (emphasis added), do establish this constitution.[28]

Nothing has been written about the changed language in the two preambles, though it seems curious that the more radical delegation would not include explicit language guaranteeing equal civil and political rights stated up front in its opening words; especially given the scrutiny the framers of this document knew it would undergo.

Notwithstanding this glaring variance between the two versions of the competing constitutions, the more progressive provisions in the constitution framed by the radicals were more reflective of the progressive agenda for Reconstruction in its first article. For example, of the twenty-eight sections outlined in the twenty-eight articles of the radical constitution, eighteen of them guaranteed protections of the civil and property rights of Floridians. Though no explicit prohibitions against race discriminatory policies were contained, given the inspection its framers knew it would undergo, such prohibitions were unmistakable. The more moderate version of the constitution differed in the rights it emphasized, especially when the inclusion of one individual right is considered that was left out of the radical's constitution: the right to bear arms. Moderates included it in their constitution (art. I, § 22); radicals omitted it. Both versions guaranteed due process rights and prohibited chattel slavery.[29]

While both versions of the constitution called for the establishment of a publicly supported system of education to be placed under the jurisdiction of a superintendent of public instruction of the governor's choosing, the two differed in the length of service and scope of responsibilities. In the radicals' constitution, no term limits were set for the office, nor was the method of selection specified. Radicals empowered this officer to not only supervise the educational system, but also gave the office dominion over the state's historical, natural, and mineral resources. In the moderates' constitution, duties were constricted to purely educational matters, and a definitive term of four years was set.[30]

Perhaps the most significant differences between the two constitutions rested in how the two documents dealt with legislative apportionment at the state level. The radical-led convention was more generous with legislative apportionment, especially in Florida's Black Belt, so named because it contained the counties with the highest population of African Americans. Under their plan, there appeared to be no cap on the number of representatives a given county could have.[31] The counties with the highest number of representatives were Leon, which was awarded seven representatives; Marion and Jefferson Counties were to each have five; and Jackson, Gadsden, Liberty, Madison, Levy, and Alachua counties were to have four each. The remaining counties were given one or two representatives each. This apportionment scheme privileged areas where political support for radical Republicans was at its strongest. It is also no coincidence that the radical apportionment plan was similarly generous in appropriating Senate seats. While apportionment assignments were lower per county for the state's upper legislative chamber, a comparable pattern is evident with areas with large numbers of African Americans receiving more representation over those with smaller numbers of African Americans. Further, the radical convention retained the nineteen districts Florida's thirty-nine counties had been divided into, which had been created by military decree in the spring of 1867. The moderate-dominated convention did away with those districts and added five more, giving more sparsely populated counties with larger white majorities greater representation in the legislature.[32]

The issue of apportionment was not the only representation matter where the two documents bore the ideological impressions of their framers. While the moderates' final draft included language that extended the franchise to "all male persons" over twenty-one, instead of "white persons" as stated in the 1865 constitution, it did something that infuriated their radical colleagues: it permitted ex-Confederates to hold state office, did not require a loyalty oath to the United States, and provided for most of the state offices to be appointed by the governor, giving the executive branch extensive power in the state.[33]

Ultimately, there could be only one constitution that could go before Florida voters for ratification. Spokesmen representing both delegations were selected to make the case for their respective documents before a congressional committee. After presenting their arguments, it was left to the congressional committee, which featured a particularly impassioned presentation by Daniel Richards for the radical constitution, the committee chose the moderate draft of the Monticello delegation, which carried with it, General Meade's endorsement. In the May election for ratification, the majority approved by a convincing margin. Along with ratifying a constitution, the state's voters selected a new governor, Harrison Reed, who, like the newly ratified constitution, was ideologically moderate. Though the process was marred by corruption, upheaval, discord, and the ever-present threat of violence, for those wanting to meet the federal threshold for acceptance,

Table 6.1. Apportionment Plan before the Convention Disruption—Proposal for the Florida House

County	Representatives
Escambia	2
Santa Rosa	1
Walton	1
Washington	1
Holmes	1
Jackson*	4
Calhoun	1
Franklin	1
Suwannee	1
Baker	1
Nassau	1
St. Johns	2
Marion*	5
Alachua*	4
Sumter	1
Volusia	1
Dade	1
Polk	1
Monroe	1
Gadsden*	4
Liberty*	4
Wakulla	1
Leon*	7
Jefferson*	5
Madison*	4
Taylor	1
Lafayette	1
Columbia	2
Bradford	1
Duval	2
Putnam	2
Hernando	1
Levy*	4
Orange	1
Brevard	1
Hillsborough	1
Manatee	1
Hamilton	1

Note: * Denotes a Florida Black Belt county.
Source: Journal of the Proceedings of the Constitutional Convention of the State of Florida: Begun and Held at the Capitol, at Tallahassee, on Monday, January 20, 1868, 16–17.

Table 6.2. Apportionment Plan before the Convention Disruption—Proposal for the Florida Senate

County/Senate Districts (Unenumerated)	No. of Senators
Escambia	1
Santa Rosa, Walton, and Holmes	1
Jackson, Calhoun, and Washington	2
Gadsden, Liberty, and Franklin	2
Leon and Wakulla	4
Jefferson and Taylor	3
Madison and Hamilton	3
Suwannee and Columbia	1
Baker and Nassau	1
Duval	1
Clay, St. Johns, and Putnam	1
Bradford, Alachua, and Lafayette	2
Marion and Levy	2
Hernando, Sumter, Orange, Volusia, Brevard, and Dade	1
Hillsborough, Polk, Manatee, and Monroe	1

Source: *Journal of the Proceedings of the Constitutional Convention of the State of Florida: Begun and Held at the Capitol, at Tallahassee, on Monday, January 20, 1868*, 43–44.

the constitution's ratification was all the confirmation needed to support the maxim that in politics, the end justifies the means. The constitution was given the federal stamp of approval on July 4, 1868, which is the date given for the state's official readmittance to the United States. Florida had consummated its reunification with the nation.[34]

Period media observers viewed Florida's convention process with contempt for what they saw were the underhand tactics and subterfuge. The Black press was understandably more critical of additional measured approaches to representation, especially when Black representation was negatively impacted the way the moderate constitution had done. *The Christian Recorder,* a Philadelphia-based African American paper, astutely observed the problematic nature of the badly splintered convention right from the start, calling the proceedings "a house divided against itself." The paper went on to list the various tactics employed to neuter the Black delegation's effectiveness on the convention's meetings, alluding to the use of liquor and money to wield loyalty to certain factions that seemed to only serve their own self-interests. Referring to the moderate convention disrupters as "bolters," the paper referred to the constitution they produced as a "swin-

Table 6.3. Apportionment Plan after the Convention Disruption—Proposal for the Florida House

County	Representatives
Escambia	2
Walton	1
Washington	1
Calhoun	1
Gadsden	2
Wakulla	1
Jefferson	3
Taylor	1
Suwannee	1
Alachua	2
Baker	1
Nassau	1
Clay	1
Putnam	1
Levy	1
Orange	1
Dade	1
Sumter	1
Manatee	1
Santa Rosa	1
Holmes	1
Jackson	3
Franklin	1
Liberty	1
Leon	4
Madison	2
Hamilton	1
Lafayette	1
Columbia	2
Bradford	1
Duval	2
St. Johns	1
Marion	2
Volusia	1
Brevard	1
Hillsborough	1
Polk	1
Monroe	1

Source: *Journal of the Proceedings of the Constitutional Convention of the State of Florida: Begun and Held at the Capitol, at Tallahassee, on Monday, January 20, 1868*, 43–44.

Table 6.4. Apportionment Plan after the Convention Disruption—Proposal for the Florida Senate

District	Counties
District 1	Escambia
District 2	Santa Rosa and Walton
District 3	Jackson
District 4	Volusia and Washington
District 5	Calhoun and Franklin
District 6	Gadsden
District 7	Liberty and Wakulla
District 8	Leon
District 9	Jefferson
District 10	Madison
District 11	Hamilton and Suwannee
District 12	Lafayette and Taylor
District 13	Alachua and Levy
District 14	Columbia
District 15	Bradford and Clay
District 16	Baker and Nassau
District 17	St. Johns and Putnam
District 18	Duval
District 19	Marion
District 20	Volusia and Orange
District 21	Dade and Brevard
District 22	Hillsborough and Hernando
District 23	Sumter and Polk
District 24	Manatee and Monroe

Source: *Journal of the Proceedings of the Constitutional Convention of the State of Florida: Begun and Held at the Capitol, at Tallahassee, on Monday, January 20, 1868*, 43–44.

dle." The editors derided the moderates' constitution for depriving Florida's Black citizens of adequate representation, even as it purported to stand for equal rights and privileges. The paper ruefully expressed its desire to see the constitution of the radicals affirmed by Florida's electorate, but alas, this wish would go unfulfilled as the results of the ratification vote two weeks after the publication of this article would later reveal.[35]

Historians have given the 1868 Constitution mixed reviews. Shofner asserted that the constitution was remarkably progressive for its time and despite the questionable circumstances that led to its adoption, was a "good Constitution." Rights were extended to all men—at this point, quite literally—a public system of education was established on a nondiscriminatory, nonsegregated basis, and in a lesser-mentioned provision, provided for the establishment of state-supported institutions for the physically and mentally impaired.[36]

In line with more current sensibilities, historians look to the 1868 Constitution as setting the stage for the reactionary revolt that was to come in the 1870s. The use of federal troops to protect the interests of the convention's moderate usurpers instead of holding them in contempt for willfully disrupting an official government proceeding duly mandated by Congress was a sign of things to come. The insistence on striking conciliatory notes to appease the state's conservative, anti-reform forces to the exclusion of ensuring adequate legislative representation for freedmen was another enduring flaw of the moderates' constitution. Perhaps the most egregious of all the deficiencies during this time was the allowance made for ex-Confederates to hold state offices. This condition was the very one that led to the implementation of the Black codes in the years before the 1868 Constitution and would most certainly play a role in the reinstitution of Black codes, reformulated as Jim Crow policies of the 1870s and 1880s.[37]

For all its shortcomings, Florida's 1868 Constitution was significant in how it provided an expanded definition of "rights" and who was qualified to access them. In the 1865 Constitution, there was a phrase stating, "That all freemen, when they form a government, have certain inherent and indefeasible rights. . . ." The 1868's Constitution was amended to read, "All men are by nature free and equal . . ." While to some, this may seem like a distinction without a difference, the unqualified tone struck in the amended statement speaks to the incorporation of the Fourteenth Amendment's most consequential demand. For better or worse, Black people were now American citizens, and as such, were entitled to enjoy the presumption of freedom, which could no longer be confined to those who by custom or by law had the wherewithal to form a government. Freedom was enshrined in Florida's governing document as an inalienable right available to all its citizens. This principle is at the heart of a union that is more complete, more inclusive, more perfect. Regrettably, as later events will demonstrate, it was not to last.[38]

Notes

1 Epigraph source, *The Constitution of the State of Florida, 1868,* https://www.floridamemory.com/items/show/1890095.

2 *U.S. Statutes at Large, Volume 14 (1865–1867), 39th Congress,* 1865, 428–29; Jerrell H. Shofner, "The Constitution of 1868," *The Florida Historical Quarterly* 41, no. 4 (1963): 356–74.
3 Lerone Bennett, *Black Power USA: The Human Side of Reconstruction 1867–1877,* (Chicago: Johnson Publishing Company, 1967) 80. Bennett devotes an entire chapter to 1868 titled "The Glory Year."
4 Foner, *Reconstruction: America's Unfinished Revolution, 1863–1877,* 116, 183–84, 199–200, 208–9, 247.
5 *New York Times,* August 22, 1868.
6 Kurt T. Lash, "John Bingham and the Second Draft of the Fourteenth Amendment," *Georgetown Law Journal* 99, no. 2 (2011): 394. Gale Academic OneFile, accessed July 2, 2024.
7 William Watson Davis, *The Civil War and Reconstruction in Florida* (Gainesville, a facsimile reproduction of the 1913 edition by the University of Florida Press, 1964), 469.
8 Foner, 271–91; Hanes Walton Jr. et al., "Chapter 13: African American Voter Registration and Turnout in 1867 Southern State Elections: The First, Second, Third, and Fourth Military Reconstruction Acts," *The African American Electorate: A Statistical History* (Washington, DC: CQ Press, 2012/), 234–35.
9 US Congress, "Thomas W. Osborn," *Biographical Dictionary of the United States Congress,* https://bioguide.congress.gov/search/bio/0000109, accessed March 15, 2022; Joe M. Richardson, "An Evaluation of the Freedmen's Bureau in Florida," *The Florida Historical Quarterly* 41, no. 3 (1963): 223.
10 Gordon C. Bond, "The First Negro Politicians of Florida: The Black Delegates to the Constitutional Convention of 1868," *Negro History Bulletin* 38, no. 8 (1975): 486–89.
11 Bond, 486.
12 Shofner, "The Constitution of 1868," 355–58.
13 Shofner, "The Constitution of 1868," 355–58.
14 Richard Hume noted that the ten state constitutional conventions (including Florida's) convened during 1867–1868 were often branded as "Black and Tan" conventions by white conservative opponents of Congressional Reconstruction. Richard L. Hume, "Membership of the Florida Constitutional Convention of 1868: A Case Study of Republican Factionalism in the Reconstruction South," *The Florida Historical Quarterly* 51, no. 1 (1972): 1–21.
15 Davis, *The Civil War and Reconstruction in Florida,* 497.
16 On Davis see Paul Ortiz, "The Not-So-Strange Career of William Watson Davis's *The Civil War and Reconstruction in Florida,*" in *The Dunning School: Historians, Race, and the Meaning of Reconstruction,* John David Smith and J. Vincent Lowery, eds. (Lexington: The University Press of Kentucky, 2013), 255–79.
17 The 1950s and 1960s were pivotal decades in American Reconstruction-era scholarship. Against the backdrop of the mid-twentieth-century civil rights movement, the academy was diversifying, both in terms of scholarship and in terms of the scholars behind them. The period witnessed a flurry of scholarship focused on various as-

pects of the Reconstruction era from the period's economic dynamics to its social practices, to most consequentially, its political developments. Jerrell Shofner and Joe Richardson were two of the pioneering scholars of the era whose area of emphasis was on Reconstruction in Florida. To read more treatments about Reconstruction in Florida, which were groundbreaking at the time of their publications, see Joe M. Richardson, "The Freedmen's Bureau and Negro Education in Florida," *The Journal of Negro Education* 31, no. 4 (1962): 460–67; Joe M. Richardson, "Jonathan C. Gibbs: Florida's Only Negro Cabinet Member," *The Florida Historical Quarterly* 42, no. 4 (1964): 363–68; Joe Martin Richardson, *The Negro in the Reconstruction of Florida, 1865–1877*, (Tallahassee: Florida State University, 1965); Jerrell H. Shofner, *Nor Is It Over Yet: Florida in the Era of Reconstruction, 1863–1877* (Gainesville: University Presses of Florida, 1974); Jerrell Shofner. "Militant Negro Laborers in Reconstruction Florida," *The Journal of Southern History* 39 no. 3 (August 1973): 397–408; W. E. B. Du Bois, *Black Reconstruction in America 1860–1880* (New York: Harcourt, Brace and Co., 1935).

18 Shofner, *Nor Is It Over Yet*, 178; Paul Emerson Herron, "State Constitutional Development in the American South, 1860–1902," Order No. 3637215, Brandeis University, 2014, 132–34.

19 Shofner, "The Constitution of 1868," 361, *Journal of the Proceedings of the Constitutional Convention of the State of Florida, Begun and Held at the Capitol, at Tallahassee, on Monday, January 20th, 1868.* (Tallahassee, 1868), 3–4.

20 Bond, 487; see also John Wallace, *Carpetbag Rule in Florida: The Inside Workings of the Reconstruction of Civil Government in Florida after Close of the Civil War*, 6.

21 Hume, 4–5.

22 Hume, 4–5.

23 *Journal of the Proceedings of the Constitutional Convention of the State of Florida, Begun and Held at the Capitol, at Tallahassee, on Monday, January 20th, 1868* (Tallahassee, 1868), 34. On that same page, Jenkins's resignation letter struck a more conciliatory tone and was published on the same page. Almost as soon as Jenkins's resignation had been recorded, he was nominated to recapture the presidency, in a motion that won majority support from the reconvened delegation.

24 Reprinted in the *New York Daily Tribune*, February 5, 1868; *Jacksonville Florida-Union*, February 8, 1868.

25 Bond, 486–89.

26 Jerrell H. Shofner, "Political Reconstruction in Florida," *The Florida Historical Quarterly* 45, no. 2 (1966): 145–70.

27 Wallace, *Carpetbag Rule*, 347.

28 *Journal of the Proceedings of the Constitutional Convention of the State of Florida, Begun and Held at the Capitol, at Tallahassee, on Monday, January 20th, 1868* (Tallahassee, 1868), 41–42.

29 *Journal of the Proceedings of the Constitutional Convention of the State of Florida, Begun and Held at the Capitol, at Tallahassee, on Monday, January 20th, 1868* (Tallahassee, 1868), 27, Wallace, *Carpetbag Rule*, 437–38.

30 *Journal of the Proceedings of the Constitutional Convention of the State of Florida, Begun and Held at the Capitol, at Tallahassee, on Monday, January 20th, 1868* (Tallahassee, 1868), 16–17, 35–36.

31 The "Black Belt" is a reference to regions in the South where the African American populations were most heavily concentrated. In Florida, it refers to the state's wealthiest areas during the antebellum period. It included Leon, Gadsden, Jefferson, Liberty, and Jackson Counties. Eventually, cotton cultivation expanded into north-central Florida to include Alachua and Marion Counties. Larry Eugene Rivers, "Florida's Culture of Slavery Forced Labor and Oppression Made the System Run." *The Forum* 34, mo. 01 (Spring 2010): 21–24.

32 *Journal of the Proceedings of the Constitutional Convention of the State of Florida, Begun and Held at the Capitol, at Tallahassee, on Monday, January 20th, 1868* (Tallahassee, 1868), 16, 43–44

33 Shofner, "The Constitution of 1868," 368, 373; Shofner, *Nor Is It Over Yet*, 185–88; see also Thomas V. DiBacco, "Sordid Saga: Drafting Florida's 1868 Constitution," *Orlando Sentinel*, January 14, 2018.

34 Shofner, "The Constitution of 1868," 369; Shofner, *Nor Is It Over Yet*, 185–88.

35 Shofner, *Nor Is It Over Yet*, 185; Philadelphia, *The Christian Recorder*, April 25, 1868.

36 Shofner, "The Constitution of 1868," 369–70.

37 Shofner, "The Constitution of 1868," 371–74; Shofner, "Political Reconstruction in Florida," 145–70; Joe M. Richardson, "Florida Black Codes." *The Florida Historical Quarterly* 47, no. 4 (1969): 365–79.

38 *Constitution or Form of Government for the People of Florida: As Revised, Amended and Agreed Upon at a Convention of the People, Begun and Holden at the City of Tallahassee, on the 25th Day of October A.D. 1865, with the Ordinances Adopted by Said Convention* (Tallahassee: Office of the Floridian, 1865); *Constitution of the State of Florida: Framed at a Convention of the People, Begun and Held at the City of Tallahassee, on the 20th Day of January, A.D., 1868: Together with the Ordinances Adopted by Said Convention* (Jacksonville: Office of the Florida Union, 1868).

7

The 1885 Constitution

CHRISTOPHER DAY

On a cloudy January day in 1885, Governor Edward Alysworth Perry, an ex-Confederate brigadier general, gave his inauguration speech to a crowd of supporters in Tallahassee, Florida. In his message, Perry attempted to assure African Americans that their constitutional rights were not going to be infringed upon during his administration and forthcoming constitution. He expressed his hopes that political tensions would subside in the coming months.[1] His inauguration ceremony did not reflect that sentiment. Tallahassee newspaper *Land of Flowers* reported that a woman refused to wear a sash of a county that had a Republican majority because she argued that they were radical.[2] Political divisiveness expressed itself through rhetoric that equated Reconstruction, federal tyranny, and state debt with the Republican Party. This hostility was an attribute of the redemption process in Florida that bridged the gap between Reconstruction and Jim Crowism. Historian Edward Williamson characterized the time period as the "Redeemer Revolution." He argued, accurately, that it ended with the ratification of Florida's 1885 Constitution, because it required Bourbon Democrats to remove "Republican rule" from all facets of Florida's government and limit African American civil rights. This strategy could not begin until Democrats held the governor's mansion and federal intervention was nothing more than an ethereal threat. That political development ushered in a new constitution that paved the way for Jim Crow Florida and unchallenged home rule by Southern conservatives.

Democrats' political rhetoric sought to "redeem" Florida by villainizing Republicans and criticizing every aspect of Reconstruction associated with African Americans and the federal government. Although Florida was never dominated by Republicans in the same way that other Southern states had experienced, Democrats still equated Republican rule with tyrannical federal authority.[3] Democrats saw the 1868 Constitution as an abuse of federal authority and a Republican failure and wanted it replaced, regardless of its functionality. Democratic publications accused Republicans of being corrupt and manipulative of the African American vote and published accounts of voter fraud laced with racial epithets. Bourbon Democrat Don McLeod's newspaper *Land of Flowers* was a perfect representation of that type of discourse. It reported that during the 1884 state election "Only 1,556 out of 2,500 registered voters of Pensacola voted in the recent municipal election. That accounts for her being controlled by the very worst element of her population. While the kid glove, silk hat, high tone gent sits in his office deploring the situation, the deadbeat, bummer, and n***** is voting early and often."[4] That style of political rhetoric, along with Bourbon Democrats' call for fiscal conservatism and localism, influenced the support for a new state constitution.

The 1885 Constitution was the culmination of resistance to Republican and federal rule under Reconstruction. It was designed not only to remove the last vestiges of the 1868 Constitution but to return Florida to conservative political and racial hegemony. This was created by Bourbon Democrats winning elections, reducing Republican office holding, African American disfranchisement, and reduced federal oversight. The 1885 Constitution created a framework for Bourbon Democrats to hold the reins of power and segregate society well into the twentieth century, but it was not an enterprise of immediacy. This was the result of a calculated and cunning strategy employed by Florida conservatives after the election of George Franklin Drew as the governor of Florida in 1876. It was an integral step toward Jim Crow and the solidification of white hegemony in Florida.

Governor Drew called for a statewide review of the voter rolls to determine the validity of Florida's electorate. In 1877, the state legislature passed a law granting the county boards of commissioners the right to draw the election districts in their counties as well as determine who qualified to be on the voter registration lists.[5] The law does not specifically reference African Americans, but it had a significant impact on their ability to vote in Florida. Historian Thomas Graham states, "Florida politics were in a fluid, transitional stage between the two more clearly defined periods of Reconstruction and the Populist-Progressive era."[6] That Woodwardian description is nothing more than a polite academic response to an increasingly hostile political scene in Florida.[7] For white politicians this soft transition, hence the liquidity, may seem accurate, but for African Americans this period was a siege on their civil rights led by Bourbon Democrats with the quiet complicity of white Republicans. African Americans were not passive in their response to these political challenges during the Redeemer period. Historian Paul Ortiz concludes, "Black Floridians sacrificed tremendously for the principles of representative democracy."[8] Their sacrifice was seen in Florida's State Supreme Court as they fought the onslaught against their right of suffrage.

African Americans fought against the legitimacy of the county commissioners' process for purging voter rolls. The boards removed individuals they believed had left the district or were deceased without verification. They were not required to notify citizens directly of their disqualification, and the law required those who were improperly removed to petition said county board to be reinstated after taking an oath and providing two witnesses who were qualified voters to verify that they were citizens in good standing. Once these tasks were completed at a board meeting, a certificate was to be given to that person who then took it to the clerk of the county court to have their name returned to the voter rolls. These requirements had to be completed at least ten days before the election.[9] Unfortunately, the disqualified voter typically did not find out until said person tried to vote on election day, which was beyond the ten-day qualification period. County boards did not normally hold multiple meetings leading up to the election to deal with these cases. The issue was more apparent in Black Belt Jefferson County. This problem, and the African American response to it, was highlighted in the 1880 Florida Supreme Court case, *The State of Florida, Ex Rel. Charles Scott v. The Board of County Commissioners of Jefferson County*.[10]

Charles Scott was not a novice voter when he challenged the Jefferson County Board of Commissioners about his right to vote in 1878. He along with six other African Americans testified before the US Senate panel about what they witnessed during the canvassing in Jefferson County.[11] He claimed that his name along with several other African Americans was improperly removed from the voter rolls. The Jefferson County Board of Commissioners was set to review its voter rolls during their regular meeting in September 1877. At the meeting, commissioners were supposed to purge the rolls of anyone who was deceased, no longer permanently resided in the county, or had been disqualified from voting. Scott argued that the county commissioners needed to hold public meetings more frequently so that he and others had the opportunity to have their names placed back on the voter rolls in a timely manner. He sought a judicial writ of mandamus ordering the county commissioners to meet more frequently to insure that voters whose names were mistakenly stricken from the rolls could be reinstated as voters in the county.[12]

The case ultimately went before the Florida Supreme Court in 1880. The Board of County Commissioners was represented by T. L. Clarke and Pasco & Palmer, a law firm owned by Samuel Pasco. Chief Justice Edwin M. Randall delivered the court's opinion in favor of the Board of County Commissioners. Randall said, "A few mistakes may be inevitable, and the duty of the board is to give sufficient opportunity to correct them."[13] He appeared to be confident with the procedure the county had in place to return the names to the voter rolls. Randall further stated, "We find in this alternative writ no allegation that any of the persons included in the writ, or described therein, have not had opportunity to apply to the board, or that any of them have applied and been refused anything demanded."[14] He did not believe the board was responsible and did not have the power to merely restore a person to the voter registration beyond what was given to them by statute and the constitution.

The significance of this decision cannot be overstated. Jefferson County was a Republican stronghold during Reconstruction. The decision had the potential of disfranchising numerous African American voters, which would not only diminish the Republican presence in Florida, but the political voice of African Americans in general. The case also shows how the creation of a complicated and unevenly applied system can lead to disfranchisement. Bourbon Democrats equated Republican power to the African American vote, so reducing its impact would allow for the removal of Republican officeholders. It was a significant step in the process of redeeming Florida because Bourbons could solidify their political position in the state by diminishing their opponent's power.

The redaction of African American voters was not limited to Florida's numerous county boards of commissioners; there were other avenues. Conviction in a court of law also threatened the ability to vote as seen during Reconstruction. Ortiz notes that "Conservatives eliminated thousands of African Americans from Florida's voting rolls for minor criminal offenses including petty larceny, and poll observers in the 1880 election swore before a congressional committee that, 'they [white Democrats] challenged men who they said were convicted who they knew were not convicted.'"[15] The 1881 Florida State Supreme Court case *The State of Florida Ex Rel. Richard Jordan v. T.E. Buckman, Respondent* reflects Ortiz's conclusion because it dealt with an African American citizen trying to reestablish his right to vote in Duval County.

Richard Jordan was a member of the Second US Colored Infantry, Company G, and resident of Duval County.[16] He had been politically active in past elections and was involved with Horatio Bisbee's contest against Jesse J. Finley for the US House of Representatives from Florida in 1876. Jordan filed a writ of mandamus in the Florida Supreme Court to force former Confederate soldier and clerk of the Fourth Circuit Court, T. E. Buckman, to place him back on the county voter rolls. Jordan had been removed for a larceny conviction. Bisbee represented Jordan and asserted that petty larceny was a minor grade offense, "conviction for which shall disfranchise, deprive the citizen of being a juror and a witness, and reduce him to a condition of 'civiliter mortuus' to which death itself is preferable."[17] The Florida State Supreme Court did not agree with Bisbee's characterization and did not allow Jordan's suffrage rights to be restored, and recourse from the federal government was becoming limited.

Federal protection of African American rights decreased due to several key US Supreme Court decisions such as *Slaughterhouse, Cruikshank,* and *Reese*. These cases made a clear delineation between state citizenship and national citizenship that reduced the federal government's authority to protect individual rights of African American citizens. The court concluded that the US Constitution only regulated the action of state governments and not individuals because the states were the guarantors of rights. This antebellum-style ruling made it challenging for federal authorities to continue to protect African American civil rights. In the early 1880s, the Enforcement Acts could still be used to punish those who sought to infringe on the civil rights of African American citizens, but it was difficult. The final thread of federal enforcement was removed with the US Supreme Court decision in the *Civil Rights Cases of 1883*. The court stated that the federal government could not enforce laws on individual citizens and that individual citizens could not take away a person's rights; only the government had the power to strip away a person's rights. This meant that as long as the state government did not enact laws that clearly violated the US Constitution, the federal government did not have jurisdiction and could not intervene. That ruling, along with division within the Democratic Party, provided the political environment necessary for Bourbon Democrats to move closer to Jim Crowism.

The call for a new constitution reflected the removal of federal authority. During the 1884 gubernatorial race, Richard Call Long argued that the new constitution needed to restrict African American suffrage. Long states, "We are going to have a Constitutional Convention in less than eight months; that convention will be controlled by white men; no one but white men will be allowed a vote there; the angel Gabriel himself will not be allowed a vote; and don't forget that the status of the n***** as a factor in the politics of this State will then be fixed."[18] It was clear that Democrats sought to eradicate the Republican Party in Florida by restricting African American suffrage thusly reducing the party's ability to hold government offices in the state. Conservatives' political rhetoric focused on issues such as white supremacy. They referred to African American political opponents using racial epithets and attempted to discredit dissident whites by referring to them as "white outcasts" and the "Great Unwashed."[19] Ortiz argues that conservatives sought to end the Black franchise because if they participate in politics, they will not accept their inferior status.[20] African Americans were aware of the threat and sought different avenues to protect their suffrage rights, which led them to disaffected Democrats.

This part of the redemption process was aided by lily-white Republicans who were not always attentive toward their African American constituents. Many were forced to partner with disaffected Democrats to form the Independent Party as a response to the changing political climate. The party was anti-Bourbon and called for better schools, fairer election laws, and full voting rights regardless of race. Independents were also critical of Bourbon small government, unregulated railroads, and land deals that benefited out-of-state interests. Coalition parties such as the Independent Party hastened conservative actions to disfranchise African Americans. That coupled with reduced federal oversight was a disastrous combination for African American political activism. By 1885, advocates of localism had little to fear from lily-white Republicans and African American Republicans. Democrats continued to solidify Redemption as the focal point of their political power in the state at the expense of Republicans and African Americans.

Conservative attacks on Reconstruction continued into the constitutional convention. Former Confederate senator and temporary chairman of the convention from Escambia County, Augustus Emmet Maxwell, noted in his opening speech that the duty of the convention was to protect the rights and property of the citizens of Florida. In that purpose it was the convention's goal to "establish such government as will relieve them from the evils of the present system."[21] This system was created by Florida's 1868 Constitution. As much as some delegates demonized the document, they were not against borrowing from it liberally. The Declaration of Rights provides evidence of the 1885 Constitution's derivative nature. The 1868 Constitution version of the Declaration states, "All men are by nature free and equal." The 1885 Constitution states, "All men are equal before the law." The president of the convention, ex-Confederate Samuel Pasco of Jefferson County said, "In 1865, under the plan of reconstruction inaugurated by President Johnson, another Convention was held 'to amend, alter or change the Constitution.' But though the work of that body was in harmony with the President's plan and met with his approval, it was subsequently overthrown by the action of Congress, and the State remained under military control till 1868."[22] He further argued, "The present is an auspicious time for entering upon the work of revision. The passions engendered by the late war have cooled; the Union is firmly restored and permanently established; the people have become accustomed to their new political relations."[23]

With Pasco's party in firm control of the convention, he stated that he did not want the constitution to be framed in the view of political advantage. There were 108 delegates elected to the convention. There were thirty-five Democrats, twenty-three Republicans (seven of whom were African American), and three Independents.[24] A Bourbon Democrat headed all major committees except the Suffrage and Eligibility Committee, which was chaired by Austin Shuey Mann, a citrus farmer from Hernando County. Bourbons also required that any proposed part of the constitution had to be voted on by the majority of all the convention delegates and not just a quorum. Once the convention began, Democrats started to shape Florida's constitution in their image and they laid the groundwork for this endeavor in the preceding decades as outlined by the Florida State Supreme Court cases discussed earlier in this chapter. The erosion of African American rights was not the result of a singular moment or event; it occurred through purposeful shifts and legislative mandates. The convention's debate over suffrage furthered that strategy.

The focal point of the discourse was on whether a poll tax should be mandated by the state constitution. Mann, as well as the African American delegates, fought valiantly to stop the implementation of a poll tax in the constitution. Mann believed it would be disastrous for the state. The Suffrage and Equality Committee formally stated that it "would be a dangerous clause to insert in the body" of the constitution.[25] Historian Charles D. Farris echoes this sentiment when he states that "whites used disfranchising techniques that were 'informal'—intimidation, violence, and fraud—as well as 'constitutional' and 'legal' . . . poll tax requirements, elaborate and confusing registration schemes, and devious complications of the balloting process."[26] Within the context of the redemption process, this conclusion proves to be accurate as seen through the legal challenges posed by African Americans when their suffrage rights were threatened. Democrats continued their efforts to limit suffrage rights during the convention, but it proved difficult to achieved due to some delegates' resistance to the tax. Mann tried to compromise and allow for a poll tax ordinance to be voted on in various communities, but the motion was denied.

The composition of the committee made their resistance to disfranchisement possible, which angered Bourbon Democrats. The committee's membership was a diverse group of regional delegates from the Panhandle and peninsula, and a lone African American. The delegates from "poorer piney-woods counties" did not unite with Cotton Belt Bourbons.[27] Democrats recognized the need to appeal to peninsula voters. Governor "Perry accepted a young Leesburg lawyer, ... Milton Harvey Mabry, as his ticketmate for lieutenant governor."[28] The majority of the white committee members were from counties in Florida's peninsula, not the Panhandle. As a result of internal and external migration, the peninsula counties saw an increase in not only their white population, but African Americans as well.[29] The connection between the stalwart Cotton Belt power structure and the new up-and-coming peninsular influence minimized the impact Bourbons had on pushing the poll tax through the convention. The ire of the Bourbons tended to focus on Mann himself when the report on the poll tax was filed. Williamson states that they dismissed this advice on race relations from the "young Yankee upstart."[30] The committee's single African American member was a Republican from Jacksonville and the son of Reconstruction political figure Jonathan Clarkson Gibbs, attorney Thomas Van Renssalaer Gibbs. He actively resisted having any power to grant a poll tax placed into the constitution. He did not want it to be a rule of government and did not want the state legislature to have that authority either. In his minority report, Gibbs outlines that "he does not concur in the recommendation of the Ordinance imposing a poll tax as a pre-requisite to the right to vote, and would respectfully recommend that it do not pass."[31]

While the debate over the poll tax clearly had a racial component to it, it also had class implications as well. In Jacksonville, the Florida Mechanic's and Workingmen's Association held a meeting in Livingston Hall about the poll tax. The resulting message was given to the Suffrage and Equality Committee by former State Supreme Court Justice and fellow convention delegate Edwin M. Randall. The association concluded that the poll tax would harm poor whites and create an aristocracy in a "reputed free country."[32]

The association had African American members, but the tone of their message focused on class. They argued that it contradicted American values to pay for the privilege to vote and resembled despotism. They referenced a similar law in Georgia and how those who could pay the tax without effort controlled the reins of government at the expense of those who could not afford it. The convention ultimately did not place a poll tax into the constitution but did give the legislature the power to enact it later, which it did in 1887. The law mandated that the monies collected from said tax were to be deposited into the state's school fund.[33]

Similar to the poll tax, education policy was also a contested issue at the convention. Historian Paul Emerson Herron states, "Redeemers often first looked to weaken rights and institutions associated with Republican rule. This reactive constitutionalism even endangered popular features, like public education."[34] The first part of Herron's conclusion is evident with the debate over the poll tax at the convention. The second part of Herron's statement is accurate because Bourbon Democrats sought to weaken public education and segregate it as a result of the 1885 Constitution. Education was tied to Congressional Reconstruction and the 1868 Constitution, which was heavily influenced by the federal government and the Republican Party. It was deemed a burden on the state budget and under the auspices of fiscal conservatism the convention looked to other funding alternatives such as the poll tax. Historian Samuel Proctor furthers this contention by noting that fiscal conservatism hit education budgets the hardest. He notes that "the literacy rate in Florida was one of the lowest in the South."[35]

Austerity and segregation were significant issues facing the formulation of the public school system at the convention. Williams Sheats from Alachua County fought to maintain the free public school system devised under the 1868 Constitution. The delegates wanted to cut millage rates for school funding and allow counties to determine how much of their property tax dollars would go to schools. Some delegates proposed a provision that required only those with children would pay into the school fund; it did not pass. The failed constitutional provision for a poll tax stipulated that said dollars would be placed into the state's education budget. Even with these new proposals, the new system set up under the 1885 Constitution borrowed heavily from the 1868 Constitution when it came to revenue streams. A significant departure was that the governor had more control over how those dollars were spent as the president of the State Board of Education. The most significant departure from 1868 was the segregation of instruction in Florida public schools; in the entirety of the document this was the only place where the word "colored" was used.[36] African American delegates such as Thomas Gibbs and Henry Wilkins Chandler advocated to give the state the power to allow for the creation of no more than two normal schools in the state. The education institutions were now separated by race due to its vilification as a remnant of federal rule and now looked to reduce Republican authority reimagining the executive branch of Florida's government.

Limited government was a tenet of Bourbonism, and one area they focused on was the governor's office. The 1868 Constitution gave the executive branch substantial power through appointment of political offices. The 1885 Constitution decentralized the governor's authority by making several local offices electable along with cabinet positions. Bourbon Democrats wanted to decentralize this power while independents and county officials wanted more local autonomy. They wished to elect local officials and weaken the authority of the state government. Walton County delegate Daniel Campbell proposed, "The present Constitution of Florida deprives the people of Florida of the privilege of electing the officers of the State and the different county officers, except their Chief Magistrate, the Governor, and in this respect is undemocratic, and contrary to the spirit of republican government."[37] All county officials were elected locally except five county commissioners who the governor appointed, which allowed the executive to control the election process throughout the state. The constitution also dissolved the office of lieutenant governor and prohibited governors from running for a second consecutive term. These changes allowed Bourbon Democrats to maintain control over Florida's government, and Republicans could do little to change it.

Fiscal austerity was another goal of Bourbon Democrats. Florida had accrued significant debt, which was exacerbated by the Panic of 1873. These issues were blamed on Republican administrations and the 1868 Constitution. Williamson concluded, "Alexander McCaskill, chairman of the committee on taxation and finance, not only cut expenses to the bone but inserted a prohibition against state-supported railroad construction."[38] This did not help with the support for economic investment, but the convention managed to stymie the creation of a railroad commission that would regulate those conveyances. There were also cuts in education, mileage rates for representatives, and government salaries. The constitution also maintained the convict-leasing system so that the state did not have to pay for food and shelter for Florida's imprisoned. With these fiscal conservative measures in place, Bourbons achieved their goals of limited government, and the redemption process was on its way to completion when the 1885 Constitution was sent to voters for ratification.

Williamson said, "The 'Redeemer' revolution which began in 1876 was completed on November 2, 1886, when the new constitution was ratified by a vote of 31,803 to 21,243."[39] Democrats managed to craft a framework that kept the control of government in their hands well into the twentieth century. They were able to severely restrict African American suffrage and as a result the legislature enacted segregationist laws with impunity. African Americans continued to fight this civil rights battle in the face of a tremendous setback. The dominance of North Florida over the state government did not last as counties in the peninsula increased their populations, thus Florida had to deal with reapportionment. The decentralized executive persisted into the twentieth century as well. The greatest legacy of the 1885 Constitution was its impact on race relations in Florida as the Redeemer Revolution provided the legal framework that facilitated Jim Crowism in the state's governance; this was evident during the first state legislative session after the ratification of the new state government.

In 1887, lawmakers empowered railroad conductors with police powers to remove African Americans who were found in the "whites only" railroad car.[40] Conductors were allowed to detain the lawbreaker until that individual could be turned over to the local authorities and tried for violation of the Jim Crow law. The statute stated first-class tickets were to be sold at the same rate, but the accommodations provided must be separate and never integrated. The only African Americans allowed to ride in the "white" car were nurses caring for white patients. If an African American refused to comply, the individual faced a $500 fine and a six-month prison sentence.[41] This law infringed upon African Americans' right to navigate public spaces with liberty. The government that empowered the railroads to enforce their laws controlled their movements. Alice Williams, an African American woman, challenged the law in the courts, but her case did not challenge segregation directly. Williams filed a tort case because she was injured when the railroad company sought to enforce the law.

Alice Williams et al., Appellants v Jacksonville, Tampa & Key West Railway Company, Appellee was an appeal from the Fourth Circuit Court of Duval County with Judge James M. Baker presiding. The language in the complaint dealt with the issues of the era. Williams as an African American woman had to define herself as ladylike in all manners of dress and action.

This was used to explain not only that she did not instigate the confrontation, but that she should have been treated as a lady. The other issue at hand was that Williams simply wanted what she paid for, first-class accommodations. According to her complaint on September 20, 1886, Williams and her husband, Daniel B. Williams, were traveling on the railroad between Jacksonville and Palatka. At the Green Cove Springs rail station, the conductor asked her to change cars because of her race. When she refused to change cars, the conductor with the assistance of the brakeman forcibly and violently removed her from the railcar. By way of their lawyer, Joseph Robinson Parrott, the railroad company replied to the declaration stating they were not guilty. They argued, "Alice Williams suffered any injuries at the time set forth in said declaration that said injuries were the result of her own carelessness negligence and wrong-doing."[42] They further argued, "That it or its agents servants or employers never did illegally, wrongfully and willfully order the said Alice as alleged to leave said first-class car."[43] They also alleged they never ordered her into a second-class car, so by default they had not committed assault and battery upon Williams. The company denied any culpability in the physical and mental distress Williams experienced.[44]

The defendant stated they offered "Alice Williams a first-class car and a car equally good with equally good accommodations with every car on the train provided for persons paying the same fare as paid by the plaintiff."[45] The defendants also questioned why Daniel Williams was one of the plaintiffs because he was not injured and therefore had no interest in said case. The railroad company claimed Alice Williams was not a decent lady and was objectionable to the other passengers. They further alleged, "Alice Williams was one of several conspiring on said . . . day . . . to damage and do injury to the said defendant in its business as a common carrier."[46] Williams's counsel, Robert Hilton and John Wallace, tried to have Parrott's pleas set aside because it was not sworn in properly. They also said that each and every one of Parrott's pleas were, "insufficient in law." They argued the pleas did not directly answer their actions and were generally vague and uncertain. Judge Baker responded to the plaintiff's demurrer to the defendant's pleas and sustained their objections to several of the pleas. Hilton and Wallace amended their original plea stating the conductor acknowledged her presence in the first-class car from Jacksonville to Green Cove Springs, about half the distance to Palatka. They argued the conductor permitted and gave Williams sanctuary until Green Cove Springs. Parrott replied to the amended plea stating it was vague and indefinite and if admitted the plaintiffs had no cause of legal action. Judge Baker overruled Parrott's objections.[47]

After all pleas and demurrers were settled, the trial in the Fourth Circuit Court was finally held on May 23, 1888. When the plaintiffs' attorney called Alice Williams to testify, the defense objected to her competency as a witness. They said she could not testify because her husband was a fellow plaintiff in the suit. The court sustained the objection. The plaintiffs' attorney did not have any other witnesses to call and rested their case. The judge ruled the case a nonsuit, and the plaintiffs had fifteen days to draft a Bill of Exceptions in order to appeal the decision. Hilton and Wallace then made a motion for Judge Baker to make a final judgment on the cause in February 5, 1889. The reason this motion was made was because the clerk of the court had failed to file the original judgment on May 23, 1888. Baker officially nonsuited the plaintiffs and made them pay the defendant's court costs. It was officially placed on record, which meant the plaintiffs could now appeal the decision based on their objection to the exclusion of Alice Williams's testimony.[48]

Once they appealed the judgment, the plaintiffs had to agree to pay all court costs with interest if they lost their appeal or it was dismissed. Alice Williams, Daniel B. Williams, and Alonzo R. Jones signed the guaranty. Jones, an African American activist from Jacksonville, served as an election inspector and took an active role in reform movements in municipal governments. He was also a member of the Masons, Odd Fellows, and Knights of Pythias. After an incident between an African American man and a police officer sparked riotous violence, Jones organized groups of armed guards outside of the Jacksonville jail to prevent lynchings. As a result, he was arrested for inciting a riot, but eventually was released and left Jacksonville shortly after. Their appeal bond for $100 was filed on December 25, 1889. The hearing was held on January 14, 1890.[49]

The original appeal had difficulties because of a technicality. After the original trial ruled the case a "nonsuit" the clerk of the court failed to file the dismissal on record, so the Supreme Court refused to hear the case. In response, Hilton filed motions to the court to have the dismissal order vacated and have the case reinstated, because he argued they had the right to appeal due to errors made by the lower court. He said the final judgment was contrary to the evidence proposed. He said the dismissal had been a "mistake of facts the court will now in furtherance of justice vacate the order of dismissal and reinstate the case."[50] The case ultimately appeared on the Supreme Court docket and Chief Justice Raney delivered the court's opinion.

Raney contended that the only error assigned to the original case was the exclusion of Alice Williams's testimony. Raney asked:

> Upon plaintiff's theory of the case she was offered as a witness as to her own interests, in her own behalf, or in behalf of plaintiffs suing in her right, and the question is, did the fact that she was a party to or interested in the suit, or that she was the wife of the other plaintiff, or all such facts, disqualify her from testifying?[51]

Raney stated that Williams could testify in the suit because the act of 1874 allowed her to testify in her own interest regardless of her husband being a fellow plaintiff and ruled that Williams was a competent witness, reversed the judgment, and the case was remanded. It is unclear whether Williams pursued the case any further because there is no record of the case being filed again in the Fourth Circuit Court or the Supreme Court. Regardless of whether she followed up, her actions were clear: challenge the law through direct action within the court system. The railroad company believed it was part of a larger protest, but that claim was not corroborated.[52] The possibility of this type of protest was not unlikely. Homer Adolph Plessy staged a similar type of advocacy in Louisiana by testing the legality of their segregation of public conveyances. This case shows that the bridge to Jim Crow was completed, and the 1885 Constitution was its keystone.

The case of Alice Williams proved that Bourbon Democrats achieved their goal of racial hegemony in Florida. Through dogmatic persistence and a new form of government, Southern conservatives were able to mold Florida's society as they saw fit. The ratification of the 1885 Constitution was the final step in the redemption of the state. It decimated African American civil rights in the state by limiting their ability to vote. Their disfranchisement allowed Bourbon Democrats to take the reins of power by removing Republican officeholders, and rewriting the state constitution that provided the rules needed to maintain authority in the state. It quashed the gains African Americans made in their quest for civil rights as the state once again became the guarantor of rights. As a result, African Americans' activism focused on eradicating all vestiges of segregation through various means such as the use of the court system. The 1885 Constitution and the finality of the redemption process created a legal framework that led to Jim Crow laws, which dominated race relations well into the twentieth century.

Notes

1. *Florida Mirror,* January 10, 1885.
2. *Land of Flowers* (Tallahassee, FL.), January 10, 1885.
3. For further reading, see Ralph L. Peek, "Election of 1870 and the End of Reconstruction in Florida," *The Florida Historical Quarterly* 45, no. 4 (1967): 352–68; Joe M. Richardson, *The Negro in the Reconstruction of Florida, 1865–1877* (Tallahassee: Florida State University Press, 1967); Jerrell H. Shofner, *Nor Is It Over Yet: Florida in the Era of Reconstruction, 1863–1877* (Gainesville: University Presses of Florida, 1974).
4. *Land of Flowers* (Tallahassee, FL.), January 10, 1885.
5. *The Acts and Resolutions Adopted by the Legislature of Florida Ninth Session* (1877), Sec. VII, No. 71, 106.
6. Thomas Graham, "Charles H. Jones: Florida's Gilded Age Editor-Politician." *The Florida Historical Quarterly* 59, no. 1 (July 1980): 2.
7. Woodwardian is a reference to C. Vann Woodward and his thesis on the origins of disfranchisement from Southern Populists' infusion politics. See C. Vann Woodward, *Origins of the New South, 1877–1913* (Baton Rouge: Louisiana State University Press, 1951).
8. Paul Ortiz, *Emancipation Betrayed: The Hidden History of Black Organizing and White Violence in Florida from Reconstruction to the Bloody Election of 1920* (Berkeley: University of California Press, 2005), 27.
9. US Congress, House, *Index to the Reports of Committees of the House of Representatives for the First Session of the Forty-Seventh Congress, 1881–1882* (Washington, DC: Government Printing Office, 1882), 25.
10. For more information about Florida State Supreme Court cases dealing with civil rights, see Chris Day, "Civiliter Mortuus: Florida Supreme Court and the Civil Rights Movement, 1845–1896," 2013. http://purl.flvc.org/fsu/fd/FSU_migr_etd-8699.
11. US Congress, Senate, *Report of Committees of the Senate of the United States for the Second Session of the Forty-Fourth Congress, 1876–77, Vol. II* (Washington, DC: Government Printing Office, 1877), 317. The other African American men were Isaac Williams, A. J. Eston, Willis Young, Nathan Williams, Ed Dallas, and Alex Rains.
12. *Scott v. Jefferson County* (1880). Florida State Archives, Record Group 1100, Series 49, Box #564.
13. P. Raney George, *Cases Argued and Adjudged in the Supreme Court of Florida, During the Years 1878, 1879, 1880, Vol. XVII,* 712.
14. George, *Cases Argued and Adjudged in the Supreme Court of Florida, During the Years 1878, 1879, 1880, Vol. XVII,* 712.
15. Ortiz, *Emancipation Betrayed,* 41.
16. "Muster Roll." 2nd Infantry Regiment United State Colored Troops Living History Association. The 2nd Infantry Regiment United State Colored Troops Living History Association, accessed May 3, 2022. https://www.the2ndusctlha.org/muster-roll.

17 *State of Florida ex rel. Jordan v. Buckman*. Florida State Archives, Record Group 1100, Series 49, Box #580. *Civiliter mortuus* is a Latin phrase referring to the loss of all, or almost all, civil rights by a person due to a conviction for a felony or due to an act by the government of a country that results in the loss of civil rights.
18 Ortiz, *Emancipation Betrayed*, 44.
19 Ortiz, *Emancipation Betrayed*, 43.
20 Ortiz, *Emancipation Betrayed*, 33–34.
21 N. M. Bowen, *Journal of the Proceedings of the Constitutional Convention of the State of Florida, Which Convened at the Capitol, at Tallahassee, on Tuesday June 9, 1885* (Tallahassee, 1885), 4.
22 Bowen, *Journal of the Proceedings of the Constitutional Convention of the State of Florida* , 9.
23 Bowen, *Journal of the Proceedings of the Constitutional Convention of the State of Florida*, 9.
24 Charlton W. Tebeau, *A History of Florida* (Coral Gables, FL: University of Miami Press, 1971), 289.
25 Bowen, *Journal of the Proceedings of the Constitutional Convention of the State of Florida*, 346.
26 Charles D. Farris, "The Re-Enfranchisement of Negroes in Florida," *The Journal of Negro History* 39, no. 4 (October 1954): 259.
27 Edward C. Williamson, "The Constitutional Convention of 1885," *The Florida Historical Quarterly* 41, no. 2 (October 1962): 122.
28 Walter W. Manley II, E. Canter Brown Jr., and Eric W. Rise, eds., *Supreme Court of Florida and Its Predecessor Courts, 1821–1917* (Tallahassee: University Press of Florida, 1997), 266.
29 Manley, Brown, and Rise, 260.
30 Williamson, 122.
31 Bowen, *Journal of the Proceedings of the Constitutional Convention of the State of Florida*, 361–62.
32 Bowen, *Journal of the Proceedings of the Constitutional Convention of the State of Florida*, 403.
33 N. M. Bowen, *The Acts and Resolutions Adopted by the Legislature of Florida, at its First Session, Under the Constitution of A.D. 1885, Together with an Appendix Containing a Statement of Receipts and Expenditures for 1885–6, as Required by the Constitution* (Tallahassee, 1887), 9.
34 Paul Emerson Herron. "State Constitutional Development in the American South, 1860–1902." PhD diss., Brandeis University, 2014, 207.
35 Samuel Proctor, "Prelude to the New Florida, 1877–1919," in *The New History of Florida*, ed. Michael Gannon (Gainesville: University of Florida Press, 1996), 267.
36 A. H. King, *Constitution of the State of Florida Adopted by the Convention of 1885, Together with an Analytical Index* (Jacksonville, FL: Dacosta Printing and Publishing House, 1887), 22–30.
37 Bowen, *Journal of the Proceedings of the Constitutional Convention of the State of Florida*, 33.

38 Williamson, "The Constitutional Convention of 1885," 122.
39 Williamson, "The Constitutional Convention of 1885," 125.
40 Bowen, *The Acts and Resolutions Adopted by the Legislature of Florida* (1887), no. 63, Chapter 3743, (Tallahassee, FL: N. M. Bowen, State Printer: 1887), 116.
41 Pauli Murray, ed., *States' Laws on Race and Color and Appendices: Containing International Documents, Federal Laws and Regulations, Local Ordinances and Charts* (Cincinnati: The Methodist Church Literature Division, 1951), 85–86.
42 *Williams v. Jacksonville, Tampa, & Key West Railway*, Florida State Archives, Record Group 1100, Series 49, Boxes #498 and #685.
43 *Williams v. Jacksonville, Tampa, & Key West Railway*, Florida State Archives, Record Group 1100, Series 49, Boxes #498 and #685.
44 *Williams v. Jacksonville, Tampa, & Key West Railway*, Florida State Archives, Record Group 1100, Series 49, Boxes #498 and #685.
45 *Williams v. Jacksonville, Tampa, & Key West Railway*, Florida State Archives, Record Group 1100, Series 49, Boxes #498 and #685.
46 *Williams v. Jacksonville, Tampa, & Key West Railway*, Florida State Archives, Record Group 1100, Series 49, Boxes #498 and #685.
47 *Williams v. Jacksonville, Tampa, & Key West Railway*, Florida State Archives, Record Group 1100, Series 49, Boxes #498 and #685.
48 *Williams v. Jacksonville, Tampa, & Key West Railway*, Florida State Archives, Record Group 1100, Series 49, Boxes #498 and #685.
49 *Williams v. Jacksonville, Tampa, & Key West Railway*, Florida State Archives, Record Group 1100, Series 49, Boxes #498 and #685.
50 *Williams v. Jacksonville, Tampa, & Key West Railway*, Florida State Archives, Record Group 1100, Series 49, Boxes #498 and #685.
51 William B. Lamar, *Cases Argued and Adjudged in the Supreme Court of Florida During the Year 1890, Vol. XXVI* (Jacksonville, FL: Times-Union Book and Job Office, 1891), 535–36.
52 Lamar, *Cases Argued and Adjudged in the Supreme Court of Florida*, 535–36.

8

Florida's Indigenous Constitutions

Being and Becoming Seminoles and Miccosukee in the Mid-Twentieth Century

Andrew K. Frank

On February 26, 1954, clan leaders from South Florida sent a simple and unified message to President Dwight D. Eisenhower and to the United States. Written on the back of a deer hide and translated into English, these representatives of the General Council expressed their concerns directly to the executive branch. First, on behalf of "the Mikasuki Tribe of the Seminole Nation," they insisted on the tribe's treaty rights to its homelands and demanded that the United States respect their tribal government. Second, the representatives asked the United States and others to stop the "insults to our Nation, chief of which has been the deliberate confusion of our Mikasuki Tribe of Seminole Indians, governed by our General Council, with the Muskogee Tribe of Seminole Indians." Ignoring the distinction between the two "Seminole" tribes—the Mikasuki Tribe and the Muskogee Tribe—in South Florida allowed the United States to "avoid recognition of our tribal government, independence, rights and customs." For the first time in a century, the Mikasuki clan leaders spoke in unison about their rights as an independent people.[1]

The "Buckskin Declaration" did more than express the concerns of Indigenous headmen as they faced the prospects of having their lands and rights stripped from them through the federal policy of termination. The issues expressed on the buckskin reveals several of the core issues that shaped the writing of the two tribal constitutions in the State of Florida—the Constitution of the Seminole Tribe of Florida in 1957 and the Constitution of the Miccosukee Tribe of Indians of Florida in 1962. The Buckskin Declaration defended the sovereignty of South Florida's Indigenous people, insisted on their right to self-determination, and demanded that the United States acknowledge tribal distinctions between Miccosukee and Seminole Indians. In their subsequent constitution, the Florida Seminoles deflected attempts by the United States to eliminate its tribal government, but in doing so it encompassed all Indigenous Floridians under the single tribal banner of Seminole. The Seminole Tribe of Florida, as the federal government insisted, included all the Indigenous people in Florida. Resisting the ambitions of the United States, the constitution's supporters proclaimed, required that Indigenous people unite and centralize in ways that they had not done in the past. At the same time, many Miccosukees, especially those to the south along Tamiami Trail, pushed back. After a campaign designed to convince reluctant state and federal officials that they were a distinctive people, the Miccosukee Tribe of Indians of Florida ratified their own constitution in 1962 and established a separate legal and governmental structure. In doing so, it declared that the Miccosukee right to self-determination should not be superseded by the governments of either the United States or the Seminole Tribe of Florida.[2]

The writing of the Buckskin Declaration was an unusual event for South Florida's Indigenous communities. For several generations, they rarely, if ever, expressed their interests to the public as a unified voice. Instead, the dozens of Miccosukee-speaking and Muskogee-speaking camps privileged localism, with each of the many camps in the region turning to members of their immediate community for guidance. Each camp consisted of an extended matrilineal family (clan), with several clusters of family camps spread across the interior of South Florida. No camp or cluster of camps held power over each other, and several effective local leaders became known as a *miccos* (chiefs) or *harjos* (medicine men). Each cluster of camps also held their own busks or Green Corn Ceremonies, limiting the power of medicine men, with as many as five separate annual busk ceremonies. Some men wielded authority in their communities because they demonstrated wise leadership, had abilities as healers, or could maintain the security and prosperity of the households that surrounded them. These leaders held little in the way of coercive power, instead relying on the actions of women and the communities in general to punish transgressors and otherwise maintain order. Other leaders similarly emerged out of the social context, with elder women holding tremendous authority over the families in their camp. Local clan leaders and others negotiated with itinerant traders and travelers, decided whether to allow missionaries and others to enter their communities, and spoke with Indian agents as they allocated meager resources in Indian country.

Social ties and kin connections, of course, connected the various camps into an unevenly spread web of relationships. Residents of different camps talked, traded, and hunted with one another, and marriages frequently connected the camps as young men typically married women from other camps and clans and moved into the households and camps of their wives and in-laws—sisters, mothers, and maternal aunts. Members of different camps also came together at the annual Green Corn Ceremony to celebrate the harvest, settle disputes, dance, chant, and eat. Marriages only occasionally connected Muskogee- and Miccosukee-speaking families, but networks of clan ties connected the camps through familial ties. In the early twentieth century, members of different camps also met with one another at various tourist sites, at meetings organized to share information on how to best raise cattle, and as field hands on various farms across the region.[3]

Collective political action rarely accompanied these extensive social connections. Instead, in the century that followed the long Seminole War (1815–1858), each camp spoke for itself. The writers of the Buckskin Declaration acknowledged that they were engaged in something new. "Now, and for the first time in over one hundred years," the signers explained, "we are obliged to address ourselves to your government." This is not to say that camp leaders always acted alone. In the century that followed what Seminoles often call the Long Seminole War, Indigenous leaders occasionally discussed issues that lay outside the interests and ability of each of their respective authority. They resolved conflicts during Green Corn Ceremonies and met collectively to share information about cattle herding and job opportunities. Multi-camp meetings or councils, though, seldomly occurred before World War II. More importantly, the councils did not speak as a unified entity to outsiders, whether local, state, or federal officials. In 1954, the writers of the Buckskin Declaration concluded that they needed to direct their attention to the federal government. They had to find a way to combat the government's intentional confusion of the Miccosukee and Muscogee Seminoles, a confusion that has allowed them to "avoid recognition of our [the Miccosukee] tribal government, independence, rights and customs."[4]

As much as South Florida's Indigenous leaders had not collectively addressed the United States since the Long Seminole War, the signers drew on a long tradition of councils speaking as a single entity on behalf of the wider community.[5] In this manner, the Buckskin Declaration was built on a tradition that structured the nineteenth-century letters and protestations in the past. These collective statements have been often described as letters because they were delivered in this format, but they were closer to petitions as statements of councils because they were jointly written and often across clans, villages, and bands. "We the General Council, being the governing body, of the Mikasuki Tribe of Seminole Indians in the State of Florida," the Miccosukee signers explained in 1954, "have met in formal council in the Everglades in this time of decision to our Tribe and appeal to you as a great leader of your people to dispense the justice which will preserve our freedom, property rights and independence." Unlike some of the nineteenth-century statements by the council, though, the Buckskin Declaration did not insist that they had sovereignty because Indians had inhabited Florida since time immemorial. Instead, they emphasized to assurances in US laws and treaties, and in in particular they pointed to the unratified McComb Treaty of 1839. "Under the last treaty your Nation made with our Nation we were entitled to all of those lands as shown by the 'Map of the Seat of War in Florida compiled by order of Brig. General Zachary Taylor, principally from the Surveys and Reconnaissance of the Officers of the U.S. Army by Capt. John MacKay and Lt. J. E. Blake' in 1839; as well as the lands due us under various other treaties." This treaty marked all of South Florida as reserved for Indians, and inferred a baseline for their sovereignty and self-governance.[6]

The general council that met to create the Buckskin Declaration met as a result to respond to the threat posed by the federal government's policy of termination and other postwar changes in the US Indian policy. The termination policy promised to eliminate the reservations in South Florida, disband its governments, and otherwise cut off South Florida's Indigenous communities from federal assistance. As much as the council followed the pattern of several earlier meetings of clan elders and band leaders, the issues that the camps faced in 1953, though, made this council different. Rather than settling internal disputes among the independent Miccosukee camps, the council worked to create a shared voice for the outside world. The nine men who signed the Buckskin Declaration—Sam Jones Micco, Ingraham Billie, Jimmie Billie, Oscar Hoe, Frank Charlie, Jimmie Henry, Willie Jim, George Osceola, and Jack Clay—put aside their personal differences and priviliging of local autonomy in order to speak as a single "General Council." They came from different clusters of camps and different matrilineal clans, and not all camps had representation at the council. Nonetheless, the men all shared a belief that the autonomy and sovereignty of Miccosukee leaders were being threatened.[7]

The premise of termination was as simple as it was sinister. In the early 1950s, President Dwight D. Eisenhower and the Republican Congress sought to strip away protections that Native Americans had recently received during the New Deal. Terminated Native Americans would lose access to federal services, their tribal governments would be disbanded, and their reservations would be dissolved. This policy threatened Indigenous communities across the country. In exchange, Native Americans from these communities received parcels of land that they owned privately and were "free" to enjoy all the rights and privileges of being US citizens. Seminoles and Miccosukees in South Florida had three distinctive reservations and also lived and traveled freely off the reservation through the wetlands of the Big Cypress and Everglades in the south-central part of the Florida peninsula. The Bureau of Indian Affairs (BIA) did not have a large presence in the region, and its meager budget only allowed it to provide some basic services that included health care at a clinic on the Dania (Hollywood) Reservation, a few episodic job training programs, and technical assistance for its relatively nascent cattle industry. The threat of termination went much deeper than removing the BIA. It threatened the independence and self-determination of Seminoles and Miccosukees. It was a threat as great as anything they had experienced in the century since the Long Seminole War.[8]

Indigenous Floridians had declared their sovereignty long before the creation of the Buckskin Declaration. Indigenous communities in the sixteenth and seventeenth century repeatedly proclaimed the validity of their polities and insisted that Spanish and British authorities recognize that they held the power in colonial Florida and they were not dependent on the newcomers. Throughout the nineteenth century, especially as the United States waged a genocidal war against the Seminoles and sought to remove them from their homelands at any cost, various Seminole leaders proclaimed that they had a sacred right to their Florida homelands. Micanopy, one of the most vocal and powerful leaders during the Long Seminole War, insisted that he was not a recent arrival to Florida and thus had sovereign rights to his lands. In doing so he pointed to the tradition of Native Southerners to bury their umbilical cords and ritually marking their homelands. "Here our navel strings were first cut and blood from them sunk into the earth, and made the country dear to us," he insisted.[9] Chief Halleck, one of Micanopy's contemporaries, made similar claims on his sacred right to his Florida homelands. "I had always lived here, and when a boy traveled over the country with my bow and arrow: here my father was buried, and

I thought I might as well die here as to go to another country and die."[10] Coacoochee (Wild Cat) similarly declared, "My father, King Phillip, told me I was made of the sands of Florida, and that when I was placed in the ground, the Seminoles would dance and sign around my grave."[11] Micanopy, Chief Halleck, and Coacoochee all made these declarations knowing the stakes at hand. They were not debating the past for accuracy's sake; these powerful leaders were defending their rights to their homelands. As Micanopy explained, "If suddenly we tear our hearts from the homes round which they are twined, our heart-strings will snap. By time, we may unbind the chords of affection—we cannot pluck them off, and they not break."[12] These words echoed those of Chief Charley Emathla: "When a man has a country in which he was born, and has there his house and home, where his children have always played 15 about his yard, it becomes sacred to his heart, and it is hard to leave it."[13] Seminoles also declared their right to self-determination, an important statement that scholars often overlook in the name of emphasizing the treacherous ways that the United States both negotiated and then failed to live up to the obligations of the treaties.

The twentieth-century Buckskin Declaration repeated many of the ideas that the nineteenth-century leaders had expressed. Once again, South Florida's Indigenous communities insisted on the right to speak for themselves and the rights of self-governance. "We have expressed our wishes, our customs and our view as a Tribe through our General Council which governs us to your government officials," the writers of the declaration explained to President Eisenhower. Unfortunately, they "have been ignored, given little courtesy and much insult, had your local Indian Agent interfering in our internal affairs and had your Secretary of the Interior tell us to change the form of government under which we have lived for centuries." The solution in the twentieth century was the same as in the nineteenth. Whereas the earlier warriors wanted the right to remain on their ancestral lands, the modern clan leaders insisted that "on the preservation of the lands to which we are entitled under all past treaties, under the law of nations, and under justice; and the recognition of our tribal government, the General Council, so that we and you may live together in this land which was all once our land."[14]

The Miccosukee clan leaders wrote the Buckskin Declaration at a moment of crisis, one that was largely about termination but also rooted in social and cultural changes in South Florida's Indigenous communities. The middle of the twentieth century represented a transformative era for South Florida's Indigenous communities. In earlier generations, their connection to outsiders was largely controlled and limited. Indigenous Floridians often worked as agricultural laborers and at various tourist camps where they performed cultural acts for non-Native audiences. Even as they collected cash for their work, they rarely engaged in sustained conversations or lived alongside non-Seminoles. They listened to radios, often learned some English, shopped from white merchants, and otherwise engaged in the marketplace of ideas and commerce. These experiences and access to the marketplace, of course, introduced many Seminoles to outsiders and their norms. Yet for most of the early twentieth century, Indigenous people kept at a social distance.[15]

This social isolation from settler society slowly dissipated in the first half of the twentieth century. The draining of the Everglades and creation of modern water management policies necessarily changed the ways that Indigenous people lived. Canals and drainage made traveling between some camps easier to predict while other paths became only passable by automobile, a luxury that only a handful of Seminoles could afford. At the same time, automobiles brought some outsiders, especially missionaries, teachers, and BIA officials, into Indigenous communities. The communities, even if they remained on the same interior island as they had for decades, became closer to settler communities. Seminoles found themselves living on the edges of the growing non-Native communities of Okeechobee, Clewiston, Moore Haven in the interior, and the various coastal communities in greater Fort Lauderdale, Miami, and Naples. Within a generation, Seminoles had the opportunity to use newly created hospitals, public schools, and dry goods stores. A handful attended boarding schools, more listened to radios, and most Indigenous families hesitatingly participated in the postwar consumer culture. In the end, some Seminoles increasingly began to attend Christian churches and speak English. South Florida's Indigenous communities debated the costs of these changes, and a general apprehension about the changes was widespread.[16]

Termination and the end of social isolationism threatened Muskogee and Miccosukee speakers alike, but the responses to termination created and exacerbated divisions within these communities and revealed and magnified a geopolitical divide within the Indigenous community. Muskogee speakers and Miccosukee speakers similarly protested the threats of the United States, but the communities to the north mobilized in a manner that ultimately gave them leverage to preserve and, in some ways, extend their sovereignty in relation to the United States. These communities consisted of nearly all of the Muskogee speakers on the Brighton Reservation as well as some of the Miccosukee speakers, especially those around the Big Cypress Reservation and on the Dania/Hollywood Reservation.

The Miccosukee speakers to the south, often called Trail Indians on account of their living along US 27 (commonly known as Tamiami Trail), pursued a different path. They insisted that they deserved to be left alone and not to be represented by the Muskogee speakers and other "Seminoles." The heart of this dissenting community lived along the Tamiami Trail, but they also included those to the north on the Big Cypress Reservation and other camps that were closer to Lake Okeechobee. Despite their distance and independence from one another, the residents of these camps spoke the same language (Mikasuki) and shared a cultural and historic heritage that defined them as a people. The Miccosukee traced their heritage to an Indigenous town that once bore the Miccosukee name near modern-day Tallahassee, to other Hitchiti-speaking migrants, as well as to the Calusa and other Indigenous people who lived in South Florida for centuries prior to the arrival of the Spanish. Most camps contained a few dozen residents who lived in chickees that clustered around extended maternal kinship networks. Although Seminoles and Miccosukees shared a long history and were often lumped together as a single people, the Miccosukees were more than a simple ethnic group in the region. Most Indigenous Floridians were Miccosukee speakers and their political and social networks were often distinctive and separate from the better-known Muskogee speakers. In short, the Miccosukee camps were distinctive from the Cow Creeks on the Brighton Reservation even if outsiders lumped them all together as Seminoles.[17]

The Buckskin Declaration's impassioned statement about Indigenous self-governance did not shift federal policy toward Florida's Indigenous communities. It made the news and then was largely forgotten or ignored by the United States.[18] Even the document itself could not be found in the government records for several decades before being rediscovered in 2015.[19] As part of its plans to terminate the Seminoles (who were believed to include all Native people in South Florida), the United States held hearings in South Florida and Washington, DC. Representatives of the Seminoles, both Mikasuki and Muskogee speakers, went to the nation's capital to fight for their rights. As part of these protests, Bill Osceola, Billy Osceola, Betty Mae Jumper, Laura Mae Osceola, and others approached Glenn Emmons, the commissioner of Indian Affairs for the US Department of the Interior, about the possibility of self-determination. Emmons agreed, and Reginald "Rex" Quinn (a Sioux Indian and employee of the BIA) to help them draft the constitution.[20]

A separate contingent of Mikasuki speakers also went to DC to prevent the Seminoles (and the United States) from usurping their rights. Buffalo Tiger, who had translated the Buckskin Declaration, again represented the wishes of clan leaders in his community. Tiger's statement was once again clear: "We were not telling the government what we wanted; we didn't want anything from them. That was my job . . . The medicine men who selected me to speak for them were so particular about not taking anything from the white man, not even ten cents, and not accepting anything from them." These words echoed the words that he had spoken when he presented the Buckskin Declaration. It had proclaimed that they wanted an end to the "interference" from the United States and the Indian agents. They wanted to be left alone to continue living as they had lived for generations. "We do say that we are not White Men but Indians, do not wish to become White Men but wish to remain Indians, and have an outlook on all of these things different from the outlook of the White Man."[21]

To the shock of many, the Seminoles protested. As much as the conservative federal government worked to reduce their obligations to Native American communities across the country, it decided to grant a path toward the federal government recognizing a Seminole government and polity. At the same time, the federal government continued to treat Buffalo Tiger and the Trail Indians and other Miccosukees as Seminoles. In exchange for being taken off the termination list and receiving federal recognition, the Seminoles agreed to write and ratify a constitution that met the approval of officials from the BIA. In essence, they had to engage the colonial structure of the United States and alter their governance to be acceptable to US norms. For many Seminoles, this was an easy choice because the alternative was too risky.

Seven Seminoles formed the constitutional committee. Bill Osceola served as chairman, Mike Osceola was secretary, and Laura Mae Osceola was interpreter. They were joined by Billy Osceola and John Henry Gopher, both from the Brighton Reservation, Frank Billie from the Big Cypress Reservation, and Jackie Willy from Dania/Hollywood. They met on the Dania/Hollywood Reservation under a large and majestic oak tree, which has since been placed on the National Registrar of Historic Places. The committee took the lead, with Quinn offering advice about federal expectations and the administrative process. Quinn recalled that he "got to the agency at 2 in the afternoon, and the Indians were there from all the reservations, and we met under the old oak tree." There, the committee did all of its work. "The Seminoles were there in native dress. It was a natural meeting. There were no chairs or anything. There was a small table and a couple of chairs for me and the superintendent to sit on. The rest of them were either standing or sitting on the ground. Bill and Laura Mae and Billy got up, and they explained to the group what had transpired and that they were now in a position to go ahead with the process of setting up a Tribal government."[22] Quinn, according to many Seminoles, advocated on behalf of the tribe, but it was equally clear that everyone involved recognized that the federal government held tremendous leverage. The costs of failure was high. Without a constitution, the Seminoles faced the likely loss of their reservations and an end to the meager governmental assistance that they received. In addition, Florida and the federal government held on to all outstanding funds that they owed to the Seminoles, holding them in trust until the constitution was passed.[23]

The Seminole Constitution was pretty simple in design but represented a radical reconsideration of how the tribe would be structured and what authority it wielded. The constitution established a tribal council to serve as the focus of governance and a tribal board to run the corporate charter of the Seminole Tribe of Florida, Inc. in order to promote the "economic development of the Seminole Tribe of Florida." They both had elected representatives from the three reservation communities. The chairman of the council would serve on the board; the president of the board would serve on the council. Otherwise, the rest of the elected officials would be distinctive. The constitution also introduced a new notion of authority. In the past, local leaders obtained and kept power because of their ability to solve problems. Leaders were those to whom the people listened, and community members could change who they sought council from with relative ease. Even medicine men had to prove their worth through their healing and guidance. This changed with the regular election of leaders who, once they had won election by convincing citizens to vote for them, maintained power under the next elected regardless of the efficacy of their decisions. Individual clan leaders ceded power to a council with representative from each reservation. Leaders of individual camps, medicine men in particular, would maintain local ad hoc authority but would have to be elected to wield official power. As one newspaper explained, the constitution called for a "consolidation of tribal governments."[24]

The new constitution also used the Western concept of race to define who was, and who was not, a Seminole. In the past, clan membership determined who had a place in a Seminole camp or village. Those without a clan could live in their wives' or mothers' homes, but husbands would be evicted if they divorced and children needed to leave the camp when they married. In place of clan, the United States insisted on the concept of blood quantum—or the verifiable percentage one was "Seminole." The constitution, at first, used the concept of blood but not percentages. Instead, it stated that citizenship extended to "any person of Seminole Indian blood whose name appears on the census roll of the Seminole Agency of January 1, 1957 . . . regardless of blood quantum." They would shortly after amend the constitution to require citizens to be at least one quarter Seminole. For the first time, Seminoles could not fully determine for themselves who was and who was not a member of their community.[25]

The radical nature of the constitution meant that its writers and proponents had to work with other leaders to convince the skeptics of the virtues of a new form of government. It was important, as Quinn stated, to "explain it to the people so they understood it" and then for them to "have a chance to vote on it." The drafters recognized that it was essential that the wider community collectively buy into the benefits of the change. They held public and private meetings, attempting to convince others that a centralized polity was the appropriate means by which to move forward. Official meetings were held at Big Cypress, Brighton, and Dania to discuss the drafting and importance of the constitution. Entire families often attended the meetings, while other families refused to attend the meetings in protest. Some, especially Miccosukee speakers and especially Miccosukee speakers who lived along Tamiami Trail, insisted that becoming a single "Seminole Tribe" was too much. Mike Osceola, himself a Trail Indian, attended the meetings and shaped the discussion. But not all of South Florida's Indigenous people felt represented. Despite Osceola's presence at the drafting of the constitution, consultations were not held at all along Tamiami Trail where the hostility to the constitution were pronounced. Mike Osceola, though, was widely "considered a representative of the off-reservation Indians" and in particular the Trail Indians, but even Quinn recognized that no one on the committee represented "the people living in Immokalee, or over on the west coast or in Fort Pierce."[26]

Nonetheless, on August 21, 1957, the Florida Seminoles overwhelmingly voted to ratify their constitution. By a vote of 241 to 5, the voters officially formed the Seminole Tribe of Florida and separately ratified a corporate charter to form the Seminole Tribe of Florida, Inc. to oversee their economic development. They elected Billy Osceola its first chairman, Bill Osceola its president, and Laura Mae Osceola as its secretary-treasurer. Voters also elected eight tribal members to its first tribal council, with a representative from each of the Hollywood, Brighton, and Big Cypress Reservations as well as members at large. The historic documents were all signed, on long tables, beneath the spreading branches of the stately Council Oak. The vote was momentous. As much as Seminoles had long allowed constituents to voice their concerns, the constitution referendum brought Seminoles to Western-style polls for the first time. Outsiders overstated the transformations toward "independence" and modernity.[27]

Not surprisingly, many Miccosukees did not consider the election to be a success or legitimate. Some of the same issues that they voiced in the Buckskin Declaration remained. Although roughly half of the eligible voters participated in the Seminole's first election, the turnout, though, was more than uneven. All but twenty-two of the voters lived on the Brighton, Big Cypress, and Dania Reservations. The Miccosukee-speakers along the Tamiami Trail largely sat the election out in protest. "The Trail group, the Miccosukees, were hostile to the Big Cypress and Dania and the Brighton group. They expressed this hostility very frequently, in lots of different ways"[28] The Trail Indians, though, did not merely sit out the election. Many of them put their efforts toward creating a separate tribe—insisting as they had in the Buckskin Declaration that they were a distinctive "Everglades Miccosukee Tribe of Seminole Indians."[29] Nonetheless, the abstention of the Miccosukees from the formation of the Seminole Tribe of Florida resulted in precisely the opposite situation that the dissenters wished. After publicly declaring that they wanted to be left alone, they found themselves being incorporated into the Seminole Tribe of Florida.[30]

For several years after the signing of the constitution, the Miccosukee Indians along Tamiami Trail continued their protests. Their words typically fell on deaf ears, as the federal government had no interest in making distinctions between the Indigenous Floridians. With the recognition of the Seminole Tribe of Florida, officials with the BIA widely believed that the issue was resolved. Undeterred by their marginalization from the process, a handful of Miccosukee leaders kept up the fight. With the aid of Morton Silver, a South Florida attorney who represented the tribe for most of the 1950s, the Miccosukees eventually formed their own federally recognized tribe. Convincing the federal government, though, was not easy. The Miccosukees launched a legal and public relations campaign, lobbied state and federal officials, considered taking their case to the World Court at The Hague, and sought allies to speak on their behalf. Success, though, only occurred because of a carefully orchestrated piece of political theater. In 1959, a contingent of leaders flew to Havana, Cuba, to meet with and be recognized by Fidel Castro. They presented him with a letter that referenced eighteenth-century agreements between the Spanish Crown and Indigenous Floridians to reinforce the long history of Spanish-Miccosukee relations. Castro, in essence, was in a position to recognize an old and distinctive Miccosukee polity. The stunt worked. Newspapers widely reported on the inequity of the situation, and the federal government opened the door to federal recognition.[31]

Miccosukees wrote their own constitution and obtained federal recognition shortly after. The Constitution of the Miccosukee Tribe of Indians of Florida followed a similar format as that of the Seminole Tribe of Florida. There were some differences. They did not have to share representation among their reservations, as they had no reservation at the time of recognition. They also restricted citizens to one-half blood quantum. The Miccosukees would eventually drop blood quantum requirements in favor of matrilineal inheritance, a rule that reinforced traditional forms of community membership.[32]

The writing and the ratification of the Seminole and then Miccosukee Constitutions was more than part of the rewriting of the relationship between the federal government and tribal governments. The acts also transformed the lives of Indigenous Floridians. As a result, contemporary Seminoles and Miccosukees frequently lionize the leaders that made it happen. Their reasons are plentiful: since 1957 their tribal councils have led their communities through economic and political transformations that may be unparalleled in Indian country. In the 1950s, the Seminoles and Miccosukees lived largely isolated in the wetlands of South Florida besieged by the transformation of South Florida's agribusiness, modern tourist industry, and proliferating bedroom communities. In the decades after recognition, the Seminole and Miccosukee councils made their tribes into economic powerhouses and, especially in the case of the Seminoles, national leaders in the fight for tribal sovereignty.

The two tribal nations have used new and increased revenues from gaming and other economic enterprises to fund a litany of government services. Under this new form of governance, for example, the Seminoles now have their own court system and departments of housing, education, health, public safety, transportation, and others. They provide a litany of public services to their citizens, often exceeding the promises that were made during its ratification. Miccosukees offer a similar array of services to their communities, providing concrete meaning to the idea of self-determination.[33]

Notes

1. "Buckskin Declaration," *Seminole Tribune* 39 (November 30, 2015). For a definitive discussion of the political history of the modern Seminoles, see Harry A. Kersey Jr., *An Assumption of Sovereignty* (Lincoln: University of Nebraska Press, 1996). See also Mikaëla M. Adams, *Who Belongs: Race, Resources, and Tribal Citizenship in the Native South* (New York: Oxford University Press, 2016), 169–207.
2. "Buckskin Declaration"; U.S. Congress, *House Concurrent Resolution 108, Expressing the Sense of Congress That Certain Tribes of Indians Should Be Freed from Federal Supervision*, 83d Cong., 1st sess., 1953.
3. Roy Nash, *Survey of the Seminole Indians of Florida* (Washington DC: Government Printing Office, 1931), 3–6; Clay MacCauley, *The Seminole Indians of Florida*, Fifth Annual Report of the Bureau of Ethnology to the Smithsonian (Washington, DC: Government Printing Office, 1887), 469–532; Alexander Spoehr, "Camp, Clan, and Kin among the Cow Creek Seminole of Florida," *Field Museum of Natural History Archaeological Series* 33 (1941): 1–28; Alexander Spoehr, "The Florida Seminole Camp," *Field Museum of Natural History Archaeological Series* 33 (1944): 115–50, esp. 146–48.
4. Buckskin Proclamation.
5. Andrew K. Frank, "Preserving the Path of Peace: White Plumes and Diplomacy during the Frontier Panic of 1849–1850," *Journal of Florida Studies* 1, no. 2 (Spring 2013).
6. Buckskin Proclamation. For a discussion of the 1839 Macomb Treaty, see Buffalo Tiger and Harry A. Kersey Jr. *Buffalo Tiger: A Life in the Everglades* (Lincoln: University of Nebraska Press, 2002), 141; Kersey, *Assumption of Sovereignty*, 168.
7. Donald Lee Fixico, *Termination and Relocation: Federal Indian Policy, 1945–1960* (Lincoln, University of Nebraska Press, 1986), esp. 91–93; Kersey, *Assumption of Sovereignty*, 23–25.
8. Kersey, *Assumption of Sovereignty*, 23–50.
9. Talk by the Delegation of Seminole Indians, May 17, 1826, in Clarence E. Carter, ed., *Territorial Papers of the United States* (Washington, DC, Government Printing Office: 1958), 23: 549.
10. John Titcomb Sprague, *The Origin, Progress, and Conclusion of the Florida War* (New York: D. Appleton and Co., 1848), 463.
11. Sprague, *Origin, Progress, and Conclusion of the Florida War*, 325
12. Talk of the Seminole Chiefs, 1834, in M. M. Cohen, *Notices of Florida and the Campaign* (Charleston, SC: Burges and Honour, 1836), 60.
13. Talk of Seminole Chiefs, 1834, in Cohen, *Notices*, 58.
14. Buckskin Declaration.
15. Nash, *Survey of the Seminoles*, 36–40; Patsy West, *The Enduring Seminoles: From Alligator Wrestling to Ecotourism* (Gainesville: University Press of Florida, 1998); Merwyn S. Garbarino, *Big Cypress: A Changing Seminole Community* (New York: Holt, 1972). For a classic look at the Miccosukee from this time period, see William Sturtevant, "Mikasuki Seminole Medicine Ways." PhD diss., Yale University, 1961.

16. Tiger and Kersey, *Buffalo Tiger*, 53–77; James W. Covington, *The Seminoles of Florida* (Gainesville: University Press of Florida, 1993), 219–23; Willie Johns, personal communication.
17. Nash, *Survey of the Seminole*, esp. 3, 64–72; Dave W. Scheidecker, Maureen Mahoney, and Paul N. Backhouse, "Distrust Thy Neighbor: Seminole Florida Camps from the Aftermath of the Seminole War to the Twentieth Century," in Tsim D. Schneider and Lee M. Panich, eds., *Archaeologies of Indigenous Presence* (Gainesville: University Press of Florida, 2022), 126–50.
18. Clipping of "Image of Jimmy Billie, Buffalo Tiger and Georgia Osceola and Morton Silver with the Buckskin Declaration," *Miami Herald*, August 9, 1954, 2005.1.1972, ATTK.
19. Peter B. Gallagher, "Buckskin Declaration Returns to Florida," *Seminole Tribune* 39 (November 30, 2015).
20. Interview with Buffalo Tiger by Jane Dewey, 1973, Samuel Proctor Oral History Center, P. K. Yonge Library, University of Florida; Kersey, *Assumption of Sovereignty*.
21. Buckskin Declaration; interview with Buffalo Tiger by Jane Dewey, 1973.
22. Rex Quinn, interview, September 27, 1978, Sam Proctor Oral History; Matthew L. M. Fletcher, "The Insidious Colonialism of the Conqueror: The Federal Government in Modern Tribal Affairs," *Journal of Law and Policy* 19 (2005): 273–311; Renée Ann Cramer, *Cash, Color, and Colonialism: The Politics of Tribal Acknowledgment* (Norman: University of Oklahoma Press, 2005).
23. "Cabinet Approves Seminole Plan," *Miami Herald*, April 23, 1957.
24. "Consolidation of Indian Tribes to Be Discussed," undated newspaper clipping, Ah-Tah-Thi-Ki Museum, Big Cypress Reservation, 2005.1.1434.
25. Kersey, *Assumption of Sovereignty*, 65. See also Adams, *Who Belongs*, 197–98, 206–7.
26. Quinn, interview. See also Tiger, interview; Kersey, *Assumption of Sovereignty*.
27. "Seminoles Already Are Independent." Undated newspaper clipping, Ah-Tah-Thi-Ki Museum, 2005.1.1085.
28. Quinn, interview.
29. Constitution of the Everglades Miccosukee Tribe of Seminole Indians, amended 1957, 1958, 1959, 1960, 1961, http://www.miccosukeeseminolenation.com/constitution.htm. The tribe would change its name in 1962 as part of the federal recognition process.
30. The conflation of Indigenous Floridians under the common term "Seminole" has a long history. See Andrew K. Frank, "Creating a Seminole Enemy: Ethnic and Cultural Diversity in the Conquest of Florida," *FIU Law Review* 9 (Spring 2014): 277–93.
31. Harry A. Kersey Jr. "The Havana Connection: Buffalo Tiger, Fidel Castro, and the Origin of Miccosukee Tribal Sovereignty, 1959–1962." *American Indian Quarterly* 25 (Autumn 2001): 491–507; Adams, *Who Belongs*, 201–2.
32. Adams, *Who Belongs*, 202.
33. Kersey, *Assumption of Sovereignty*; Jessica R. Cattelino, *High Stakes: Florida Seminole Gaming and Sovereignty* (Durham: Duke University Press, 2008).

9

Crafting Florida's 1968 Constitution

Mary Adkins

While the 1885 constitution was a product of its time, its time had passed by the middle of the twentieth century. In 1885 the Floridian peninsula was sparsely populated; most of the white and Black residents lived within fifty miles of Georgia or Alabama. The state's population lay between 270,000 and 390,000.[1] It was the least populated state in the former Confederacy as of 1880.[2]

But the population grew sharply. By 1950, Dade County had more people than the state had in 1880.[3] The peninsula, especially its beachy edges, was filling with people, many escaping the long winters of their homes: the east coast filled with Northeasterners, the west coast with Midwesterners. The population had boomed in the 1920s with the South Florida land-speculation bubble. In 1926 that bubble burst; the bottom fell out of the market, and on the heels of that fall, a hurricane aimed directly at Miami. This one-two punch caused Florida, especially Miami, to dive into depression three years before the rest of the nation hit the Great Depression. During World War II, American troops trained in large swaths of Florida; after the war, the soldiers, sailors, and airmen remembered the warm climate and moved their families to Florida.[4] That rapid growth continued through the 1950s, accelerated by the aerospace industry and moon race in Brevard County in the 1960s. By 1960 the population of Florida was nearly five million.[5]

Florida's population growth tested its constitution's ability to function under pressure, and the constitution proved wanting. The pattern of population growth—with South Florida gaining the majority of new residents—meant that the legislative apportionment created in the 1885 Constitution was awry. The legislature was bound to reapportion every ten years, but the constitution straitjacketed the plan from meaningful change.[6] For example, each county received one representative, and no county could have more than three.[7] So a rural county with fewer than 3,000 people was guaranteed to have at least one-third of the number of representatives as did the largest urban county, Dade, with 935,000 in 1960.[8] The effect was that decades after the population center had shifted southward, the legislature remained in control of the rural, mostly northern legislators—who had little interest in addressing the urban needs of newcomers to the state. Meaningful reapportionment was impossible under the 1885 Constitution; to achieve it would require amending the constitution. But the only entity that could propose an amendment to the constitution was the legislature, ensuring no significant apportionment would happen.[9] In the 1950s Governor LeRoy Collins initiated three attempts to rewrite Florida's constitution; the legislature either sabotaged or ignored each.[10]

Florida was not unique in its legislative malapportionment. In 1960 nearly every state legislative chamber in the nation was similarly malapportioned for the same reason: populations shifting to urban areas. This was an ugly point of contention in many states, and litigation was active in numerous states to overcome the malapportionment.

The Florida rural legislators who clung to control despite population shifts in the 1950s and 1960s earned a nickname: the Pork Chop Gang, so called, it was said, for the "pork" they brought to their districts through the legislative process.[11] The Pork Chop Gang used its stranglehold over the government to control the governor, judicial system, and even local governments. The governor had no lieutenant and was limited to one term; legislators had no term limits.[12] The judicial system was nonuniform; a special court specifically for Escambia County was written into the constitution, and the legislature was allowed to create some courts and abolish others.[13] The constitution provided for no local home rule beyond the most basic functions, with two effects.[14] First, local governments had to approach their legislator hat in hand, hoping their request would be approved as a local bill by the legislature, and allowing that legislator to wield immense power over his district. Second, the crush of local bills took a disproportionate amount of the legislature's mere biennial sixty days of session, making statewide legislation difficult to pass.

The aging constitution had social effects, too. Even after *Brown v. Board of Education of Topeka* had been decided, the constitutional provision mandating that Florida children be educated in segregated schools stayed put, along with the ban on mixed-race marriages.[15] This stubborn alignment with segregation could not have been welcoming to businesses from other parts of the country that intended to relocate to Florida. Blacks still were discouraged from voting. Women, too, lacked equal rights under the 1885 constitution, though a few had been elected to the legislature by the early 1960s. Native Americans, like women, were simply not mentioned in the constitution, in contrast to the 1868 Constitution, which guaranteed one seat in each house of the legislature to a member of the Seminole Tribe.[16]

Taken together, the constraints of the old constitution stymied economic growth in Florida. Newly urbanized areas lacked necessary services such as modern roads and hospitals because of underrepresentation in the legislature and no home rule. The crazy-quilt court system promised unevenness in resolution of business disputes. No statewide plan or entity ensured protection of natural resources. State revenues and budgeting were unstable. After World War II the legislature imposed a sales tax of 3 percent. Other than that, state revenue depended on excise taxes (primarily on alcoholic beverages and gasoline) and special taxes, such as the estate tax. Yes, taxes were low, but so were services. And the constitution forbade the legislature to issue debt other than to repel invasion or insurrection.[17]

By the early 1960s the situation was coming to a head in Florida. Two important occurrences catalyzed change: first, the federal government had chosen Cape Canaveral, in Florida, to be the launch center for its space program, racing toward putting a human being on the moon; and second, the US Supreme Court decided *Baker v. Carr*, a Tennessee malapportionment case, in which it held that federal courts could pass judgment on state legislative apportionment schemes.[18] The space program put Florida in the world's spotlight, while *Baker v. Carr* shifted the ground beneath the malapportioned legislature.

The same day that the *Baker v. Carr* decision was released, a Florida apportionment challenge was filed in federal court in Miami; the case would become known as *Swann v. Adams*. Similar lawsuits in several other states were also filed in the wake of *Baker v. Carr*. *Swann v. Adams* would eventually force what one legislator would call "creeping reapportionment" through the first half of the 1960s.[19] Yet the significant shift in apportionment that the population shift demanded remained elusive under the restrictions of the constitution.

The federal trial court found in *Swann v. Adams* (then known as *Sobel v. Adams*) that the Florida legislature's apportionment was unconstitutional.[20] The legislature attempted twice to create new, fairer apportionment plans. The first, a constitutional amendment, was approved by the court but rejected by voters; the second was approved by both the Florida Supreme

Court and the federal trial court. However, the US Supreme Court disapproved that plan when it remanded several cases, including *Swann* and the better-known 1964 decision *Reynolds v. Sims*. In that group of cases the Court demanded state legislatures apportion in tune with the one-person-one-vote standard.[21] By the end of 1964 more than half of the other malapportioned states had voluntarily reapportioned.[22] Not Florida. Indeed, the Pork Chop Gang's farcical reapportionments in the early 1960s had intensified Florida's legislative maldistribution so badly that the state was the worst malapportioned in the nation.

This Supreme Court reversal in Florida's *Swann* case finally motivated the legislature to pass a bill authorizing the creation of a constitution revision commission (CRC). The bill had nineteen sponsors and plenty of outside help; both the immediate past president of the Florida Bar, Chesterfield Smith, and the Florida Bar's president, Robert Ervin, took credit for helping craft the bill.[23] The CRC would consist of the state attorney general and thirty-six members appointed by leaders of the three branches of government and the Florida Bar. The CRC was authorized to examine and revise the entire constitution.

There was just one catch: under the then-present constitution, only the legislature could propose revisions to the constitution, so the CRC's power would end when it had to turn its product over to the legislature. This process had killed earlier attempts to rewrite Florida's constitution. The critical path to freeing constitutional revision, therefore, required changing the malapportioned legislature itself.

The members of the CRC were appointed in the fall of 1965. Governor Haydon Burns appointed Bartow lawyer Chesterfield Smith as chair. At this time, Smith was best known for being immediate past Florida Bar president, and most of his firm's work involved representing the phosphate companies that provided money, employment, and environmental devastation to west-central Florida.

As it happened, several of the appointees to the CRC met at a University of Florida football tailgate party in late fall 1965, and the topic of the CRC came up.[24] After this informal meeting, appointee and appellate judge Tom Barkdull wrote to Smith memorializing some of the features that had been agreed on at the tailgate party.[25] Smith organized the CRC following these tenets.

The group first met in January 1966; Smith assigned each member to a committee. Eight covered substantive areas of the constitution; one covered style and drafting—the actual writing of the proposed constitution—

and one acted as the steering committee.[26] Perhaps not coincidentally, the membership of the steering committee overlapped closely with the attendees of the tailgate party.

The membership of the CRC represented a cross-section of Florida politics and business: young reformers like Richard Pettigrew, Reubin Askew, and (later, replacing a member who died) Lawton Chiles; businessmen like Gordon Vickery, an executive with the upscale department store Jordan Marsh; Charlie Harris, president of the Florida AFL-CIO; entrenched Pork Choppers like former acting governor Charley Johns and George Stallings; liberal Miami newspaper editor Bill Baggs; and established and skillful legislators such as Ralph Turlington. Every member of the group was white; just one was female, Senator Beth Johnson of Orlando.

It was in this CRC that chair Smith began to expand his reformist streak that had begun to emerge during his presidency of the Florida Bar. He urged the commissioners to think deeply and imaginatively about what a constitution could and should be. He set up a system that forced debate on many questions to ensure little was taken for granted. Should the legislature begin meeting every year rather than every second year? Should eighteen-year-olds have the right to vote, as they were being drafted into combat in Vietnam at that age? Should the governor have the ability to succeed himself? Should the cabinet, a group of executive-branch officers elected in statewide contests with no term limits, instead be appointed by the governor? Should local governments have stronger home-rule powers? How, if at all, should financing provisions change?

Smith instructed each substantive committee to submit questions like these; he called them "certified questions." When the CRC met again, in March 1966, he had collected the certified questions and assigned two commissioners for each question: one to argue for, the other to argue against. In this way he ensured that no proposed change would be taken for granted or poorly understood.[27]

After the certified questions had been argued, the committees met to draft their respective parts of the revised constitution. Smith urged the commissioners to think of their work as a new constitution, not as simply a rewrite of the existing one. By late May, each committee had submitted its draft constitutional article to the Style and Drafting Committee. At this point, no committee had seen any part of the other committees' work.[28] Accordingly, the potential for overlap and contradictions was high. The task of making this patchwork into a cohesive fabric fell to the Style and Drafting Committee and, primarily, its chair, Gadsden County circuit judge Hugh

Taylor. Smith later described Taylor as a "brilliant, old, savvy, wise trial judge" and had complete confidence in Taylor's ability.[29]

Taylor would describe his role in writing the new constitution as that of a "mere amanuensis," but in fact his task required that he do more.[30] Where the separate parts of the constitution were incompatible, Taylor had to decide how to reconcile them for the public draft that would be published in every major Florida newspaper on June 30, 1966. The impossibility of honoring each committee's draft while knitting together a cohesive whole was so difficult that Taylor circulated a memo to all CRC members before releasing the draft constitution to the public, explaining the problem and stating, "We sincerely hope that all members of the Commission will recognize the problem that confronted the Drafting Committee and will recognize that we have not tried to substitute our views for theirs, but merely to coordinate the various views that have been expressed by the different committees."[31]

The CRC then held a series of public hearings around the state in July 1966; the hearings occurred in Pensacola, Jacksonville, Orlando, Tampa, and Miami, each for one to three days. The public was invited to attend and contribute opinions, suggestions, and concerns. This was also an opportunity for organized groups, such as the Justice of the Peace and Constables Association and the League of Women Voters, to have their say and contribute their agreed-upon speaking points. Each public hearing was recorded and transcribed, as were some of the CRC meetings.

After the public hearings, each committee met again to make any changes it deemed advisable given the public input. A new draft was stitched together by late September, again with Judge Taylor presiding over the draft. It was this draft that would provide the final template for the CRC to review when it had its last marathon meeting of the full commission between Thanksgiving and Christmas 1966. Until then, the CRC members were free to return to their lives. Their CRC work brought them no pay; its only budget was $100,000 to cover all expenses, including member travel, office supplies, and a staff secretary.[32] Even so, Smith leased a Tallahassee apartment for himself and his wife for the year spent working on the CRC.[33]

The CRC's final meeting lasted three weeks. The group met in Tallahassee and borrowed the Senate chamber in the Capitol building. For the purposes of this last push, the draft constitution was treated as a legislative bill to which any commissioner could propose amendments. More than two hundred were proposed. Just before the final meeting, the substantive committees were dissolved, and the CRC was instead divided into four "general" committees, dubbed Committees A, B, C, and D.[34] The proposed amendments were randomly assigned to one of the four committees, with the intent that no one committee should have, or be perceived to have, control over any one issue.

Whoever proposed an amendment would have the opportunity to argue in its favor and take questions. Each proposal was voted on; if it lost, the proponent could ask once for reconsideration. The plan was to go through the draft three times; the third time only committees, rather than individual commissioners, could propose amendments.[35]

The final sessions of the CRC are transcribed and are revealing. Whether to preserve equal rights for women was a point of contention and was pushed more zealously by the left-leaning male members of the CRC than by its lone woman, Beth Johnson, who reversed her position. At first, Johnson argued that if "race" and "creed" were protected, "sex" should be as well, as "there are more women than there are people of differing races" and creeds.[36] Though the initial vote was in favor of adding sex as a protected quality, the following day the CRC approved a motion to reconsider and a motion to refer the issue to a select committee to report on the legal effects of such protection.

In the meantime, the equal rights debate took on the now-familiar subject of unisex restrooms and protections of pregnant women. The closing debate, however, raised a bugaboo that has persisted even to today: gay marriage. Pork Chopper commissioner George Stallings closed with a one-two punch: first, banning discrimination on the basis of sex would lead to the "deplorable situation [of] homosexual marriages"; and second, it would fly in the face of "Judeo-Christian" protections of women by "trying to throw a sop to the women." His final admonition was to "get this nonsense out of the constitution."[37]

The select committee's report came back anodyne: women could continue to serve on juries and could be drafted into military service; either spouse could receive alimony. Beth Johnson reversed her vote and argued that equal rights could strip women of protective legislation relating to automatic inheritance and spousal support rights.[38] The CRC voted to table the proposal, and the draft did not contain protection from discrimination based on sex.

It went without saying that the new constitution would contain no segregationist language. The ban on mixed-race marriages was never discussed and dropped out of the document, even though *Loving v. Virginia* had yet to be decided and mixed-race marriages were generally not socially accepted.

Similarly, school segregation had no place in the proposed new constitution.

One odd provision was retained from the 1885 Constitution, however: it prohibited "aliens ineligible for citizenship" from buying land in Florida. This provision had been added to Florida's constitution, as well as those of some other states, in the 1920s as a racist prohibition keeping Asian immigrants from buying and farming land in the United States. Forty years later, geopolitics had shifted; still, whether to keep the provision or change "prohibited" to "regulated," as Taylor's draft had done, prompted a sharp rebuke of Taylor by the commissioner—and sitting Florida Supreme Court justice—B. K. Roberts:

> If the head of our foreign enemy to the south of us should come into Polk County and start buying up the citrus industry, or the phosphate industry, I think that the Legislature of Florida should have the right to say, "Mr. Castro, you are an alien, you cannot own any property in Florida."

The commission agreed and voted to restore the prohibitory language.

A provision keeping felons from voting was retained but the language streamlined; the minutes from the Suffrage and Elections Committee revealed that Dick Pettigrew attempted to open voting to everyone not actually incarcerated or institutionalized for mental health issues. His view did not prevail. At the full CRC final meeting, commissioners debated whether Floridians aged eighteen and older should be eligible to vote; the CRC finally compromised and drafted a provision allowing nineteen- and twenty-year-olds to vote.

The CRC readily agreed to provide that the legislature meet annually rather than biannually. However, it also strengthened the office of governor by allowing the governor to serve two terms and to have veto power over the state budget. The CRC, however, did not propose a lieutenant governor, apparently agreeing with Commissioner Reubin Askew's observation that a lieutenant governor's only job would be to wait for the governor "to stop breathing."[39]

There was broad agreement among the CRC—many of whom served in the legislature—that local governments should have the option for greater home-rule powers. Along with this decision, though, came the urge to limit local-government spending. Contributing to this urge may have been, according to Talbot D'Alemberte, the recent shocks of Florida Supreme Court decisions holding that ad valorem taxation should be based on the actual fair market value of land, as the constitution provided, rather than on the undervaluations historically prevalent in the state.[40] When the valuations that were the basis for ad valorem taxes were brought up to fair market value, property owners experienced a shock of higher taxes. This shock may have been on the mind of the CRC members when they placed a millage cap on local ad valorem taxes.

Legislative apportionment was not only a constitution-drafting problem, it was also an ongoing issue in the state at the same time the CRC was meeting. From the time the group was appointed until they adjourned in December 1966, three federal court opinions affecting legislative apportionment were decided, necessitating an extraordinary session of the legislature and a special election in addition to the regular November 1966 election. Accordingly, the CRC realized that much of its legislative apportionment drafting would be subject to decisions of federal courts. Every member of the Legislative Committee except one was either a current or former legislator. And Charley Johns, of Starke, who had become acting governor in 1953 by being Senate president when Governor Dan McCarty died, spoke out in favor of fair apportionment, even though he had benefited more than most from malapportionment. The legislature had had to make unprecedented changes to try to satisfy the federal courts, and Johns admitted that he had voted in favor of a plan that had placed his own district within a twenty-four-county senatorial district he had lost. He had voted for it not because he liked it, but because he did not want "those nine gentlemen in Washington reapportioning the State of Florida."[41]

It was almost certainly for this reason that the CRC's draft called for the Florida Supreme Court to review any apportionment plans the legislature drew up: to keep Florida's business in Florida's state courts. And Florida's state courts were historically conservative. Ultimately, perhaps with the pending US Supreme Court decisions on apportionment in mind, the CRC opted to keep constraints on apportionment minimal, giving the legislature maximum flexibility.

When the CRC debated how the new constitution should provide for future amendments, it plainly reacted to the then-current constitutional constraints. Even though many of the CRC members were legislators, as a group they recognized that the people's constitution needed other options. The CRC members added two ways to the existing two. In addition to legislative proposals and a full-blown constitutional convention, they added a relatively new procedure, the citizens' initiative, whereby ordinary citizens who could gather enough signatures on a petition could get a proposed constitutional amendment on the ballot; and an entirely new method for amending: an automatically recurring appointed Constitutional Revision Commission (CRC). This commission would meet every twenty years, review the entire constitution, decide whether it needed changes, and place its proposed changes, if any, on the ballot. The CRC drafted its proposed CRC to have the heads of each branch of the government appoint twelve CRC members, with the attorney general being a mandatory member.

The judicial article was the most controversial part of the constitution, if one counts by number of proposed changes to the draft during the final CRC sessions. Of the 216 proposed changes, 55 were to the judicial article alone. Perhaps this was inevitable in a CRC dominated by lawyers and containing three levels of sitting judges. Much of the difficulty was that all varieties of judges then existing in the state—and, because of the flexible system, there were many—were vested in keeping their jobs. Another challenge was sorting out the varying courts and jurisdictions in the current nonuniform system.

Nevertheless, under the leadership of Reubin Askew, the committee cobbled together a draft, and that draft survived the changes proposed by the CRC members in the final session. This was the state of the draft constitution when it came before the Florida legislature on January 9, 1967.

That date itself had not been expected. The legislature was supposed to consider the draft constitution during its regular session in April. But 1966 had been an unusual year, one unusual occurrence being the election in November of Florida's first Republican governor since Reconstruction, Claude Roy Kirk Jr. Kirk was a successful businessman with no governmental experience. After his election, he spent three weeks of his transition period in the Senate chamber, at Chairman Chesterfield Smith's elbow, watching the proceedings and asking so many questions it sometimes impeded Smith's ability to preside. Kirk, however, had the fire of constitutional reform lit under him. At his January 3 inaugural speech, Kirk announced he would call a special session just six days thence for the newly elected legislature to consider the new constitution.[42]

The legislature, mostly but not completely reapportioned, already had more new members than in memory. New Speaker of the House Ralph Turlington recalled that his new chamber had more Republicans than he had seen: "It looked like the world was going to wipe out all the Democrats."[43] They arrived on their newly announced opening day, found their seats, and settled in to hear Chesterfield Smith give a speech about the need to pass the new constitution.

But during his speech, the Supreme Court of the United States announced that it had decided *Swann v. Adams,* Florida's malapportionment case, and found the legislature illegally apportioned. The legislature was in effect dissolved and lacked power to pass anything. It had to await the federal district court's own apportionment plan.

One month later, that plan was announced. One month after that, a special election was held based on the new, court-approved plan. One more month, and the new legislature was in session. But it was distracted by the galvanizing news that the Walt Disney Company was building a giant new theme park in Florida and needed significant legislation passed.

The legislature did not make serious progress finalizing the constitution until a special session in the summer of 1968. Finally, legislative leaders like Marshall Harris and Murray Dubbin shepherded the constitution to completion. The final document resembled the one the CRC had sent to the legislature eighteen months before, with a few changes. The governor could still succeed himself, but also had a lieutenant governor; the voting age remained at twenty-one. The recurring, constitutional CRC would still be appointed by the heads of the three branches of government, but with a significant change: instead of twelve appointed by each branch, the legislature decided that it should have eighteen appointments (nine per house), the governor fifteen, and the chief justice only three. The reasoning, according to CRC member and Speaker-Designate Dick Pettigrew on a tape recording of the debate, was that the judicial branch was concerned only with its own matters; the other two branches were concerned with all matters of Florida government.

Perhaps, then, it is not too surprising that the one constitutional area the legislature could not agree on was the judicial branch. Despite Askew's committee's focused work in the CRC, the legislature ultimately did not place a proposal for a new judicial article to the constitution on the ballot.

On July 4, the legislature announced it had agreed on a new constitution, minus a new judicial article. That new constitution appeared on the November 1968 ballot in three parts: the local government article, broken out of the main constitution because home rule was feared to be too controversial; the suffrage and elections article, originally because it would have lowered the voting age, even though it ultimately did not; and the remainder of the proposed constitution. The voters approved all three amendments by similar margins of about 55 percent. The remarkable pattern was in which counties approved it. No North Florida county west of Alachua voted "yes."[44]

The legislature had not given up on the judicial article. Under the leadership of Senate Judiciary Committee chair Dempsey Barron and House Judiciary chair Talbot "Sandy" D'Alemberte, the legislature stuck together a proposal for the 1970 ballot.[45] Partly because organized judicial groups opposed it, and partly—it is said—because it wasn't very good, it failed. In 1972 the legislature tried again. Barron, a conservative, and D'Alemberte, a liberal, managed to draft a proposal for a uniform four-tier judicial system. Actually, it was D'Alemberte's general counsel, a young lawyer named Janet Reno, who did the drafting. It was that proposal that appeared on the 1972 ballot and was adopted by the voters.

Florida's new constitution capped a decade in which state legislatures, none more than Florida's, saw great change. Florida was unlike most states in its breathtaking shift from backward-facing backwater to the home of the space race and the planned Disneyland East. Its new constitution reflected both the aspirations of reformers and the stability of established politicians. On this new foundation, Florida's leaders hoped, its future could flourish.

Notes

1. Florida Census: 1890, https://fcit.usf.edu/florida/docs/c/census/1890.htm; Florida Census: 1980, https://fcit.usf.edu/florida/docs/c/census/1880.htm (last visited June 10, 2021).
2. U.S. Census (1880) vols. 1–7, Table 1: Population of the United States by States and Territories, https://www2.census.gov/library/publications/decennial/1880/vol-01-population/1880_v1-07.pdf.
3. Florida Census: 1950 (usf.edu), https://fcit.usf.edu/florida/docs/c/census/1950.htm (last visited June 10, 2021).
4. Nick Wynne and Richard Moorhead, *Florida in World War II: Floating Fortress* (Charleston, SC: The History Press, 2010), 120; Tracy J. Revels, *Sunshine Paradise: A History of Florida Tourism* (Gainesville: University Press of Florida, 2011), 2.
5. Florida Census: 1960, https://fcit.usf.edu/florida/docs/c/census/1960.htm (last visited June 10, 2021).
6. Fla. Const. art. VII § 3 (1885).
7. Fla. Const. art. VII § 3 (1885).
8. Florida Census: 1960, https://fcit.usf.edu/florida/docs/c/census/1960.htm (last visited June 10, 2021).
9. Fla. Const. art. XVII (1885).
10. Mary E. Adkins, *Making Modern Florida: How the Spirit of Reform Shaped a New State Constitution* (Gainesville: University Press of Florida 2016), 20–27.
11. Stephen Ansolabehere and James M. Snyder Jr., *The End of Inequality: One Person, One Vote and the Transformation of American Politics* (New York: Norton, 2008), 73.
12. Fla. Const. art. IV § 2, art. III, art. VI (1885).

13 Fla. Const. art. V §§ 24, 32, 34 (1885).
14 Fla. Const. art. VIII §§ 5, 6 (1885).
15 *Brown v. Board of Education of Topeka (Brown I)*, 347 U.S. 483 (1954); *Brown v Board of Education of Topeka (Brown II)*, 349 U.S. 294 (1955); Fla. Const. art. XII § 12, art. XVI § 24(1885).
16 Fla. Const. art. XVI § 7 (1868).
17 Fla. Const. art. IX, § 6 (1885).
18 *Baker v. Carr*, 369 U.S. 186 (1962).
19 Ralph Turlington interview with Mary Adkins, June 13, 2014.
20 *Sobel v. Adams*, 208 F. Supp. 316 (S.D. Fla. 1962).
21 *Reynolds v. Sims*, 377 U.S. 533 (1964); *Swann v. Adams*, 378 U.S. 553 (1964).
22 Adkins, *Making Modern Florida*, 51.
23 *Florida Senate Journal*, May 13, 1965, 441; Chesterfield Smith interview by Julian Pleasants, March 9, 2000, 51 (Samuel Proctor Oral History Program); Robert Ervin interview by Denise Stobbie, December 16, 1986, 18 (Samuel Proctor Oral History Program).
24 Thomas Barkdull interview by Sid Johnston, December 16, 1986, 2–3. Samuel Proctor Oral History Project.
25 Thomas Barkdull to Chesterfield Smith, December 2, 1965, box 22, O'Neill, William G., Papers, Lawton Chiles Legal Information Center, University of Florida, Gainesville.
26 CRC Transcript, January 11, 1966, Florida State Archives, RG 1006, series 720, box 1, folder 9.
27 Joseph C. Jacobs and Hugh Taylor interview by Sid Johnston, December 16, 1986, 17. Samuel Proctor Oral History Program.
28 Adkins, *Making Modern Florida*, 107–8.
29 Chesterfield Smith interview by Julian Pleasants, March 9, 2000, 53. Samuel Proctor Oral History Program.
30 Murray Dubbin interview with Mary Adkins, August 1, 2014.
31 Hugh Taylor to CRC members, June 22, 1966, box 182, Circuit Judge Hugh M. Taylor Papers, Florida State University Libraries.
32 Senate Bill 65–977.
33 Mary E. Adkins, *Chesterfield Smith, America's Lawyer* (Gainesville: University Press of Florida 2020), 77.
34 Adkins, *Making Modern Florida*, 120.
35 Thomas Barkdull interview by Sid Johnson, December 1986, 4. Samuel Proctor Oral History Project.
36 1966 CRC transcript, December 13, 1966, Florida State Archives, RG 1006, series 722, box 2, folder 2, vol. 2, p. 272.
37 1966 CRC transcript, December 13, 1966, Florida State Archives, RG 1006, series 722, box 2, folder 2, vol. 2, p. 41–42.
38 1966 CRC transcript, December 13, 1966, Florida State Archives, RG 1006, series 722, box 2, folder 2, vol. 2, p. 113.

39 Reubin Askew interview by Mike Vasilinda, May 9, 2001, Tallahassee: Legislative Research Center and Museum.
40 Talbot D'Alemberte, *The Florida State Constitution: A Reference Guide* (New York: Greenwood Press, 1991), 224, 233–34.
41 1966 CRC transcript, December 16, 1966, Florida State Archives, RG 1006, series 722, box 3, folder 4, vol. 22, 492–96.
42 Florida Memory, "Governor Claude Kirk Inauguration (1967)," https://www.youtube.com/watch?v=7GSip8DSVlY (accessed June 11, 2021).
43 Ralph Turlington interview by Jack Bass and Walter DeVries, May 18, 1974, 19, Chapel Hill: Southern Oral History Program, Southern Historical Collection, Wilson Library, University of North Carolina.
44 Adkins, *Making Modern Florida*, 178–79.
45 Adkins, *Making Modern Florida*, 189.

Conclusion

The Twenty-First Century and a New State Constitution

Robert Cassanello

During the 1919 Florida legislative session, lawmakers in both the House and Senate introduced resolutions calling for a constitutional convention to draft a new constitution. The issue at the heart of this effort was an attempt to address the apportionment of representatives and senators, which had not been changed since 1885. Unlike later in the twentieth century, this demand came from lawmakers in the northern part of the state while lawmakers in the south were successful in thwarting the resolution. This demand for a new constitutional convention might have been limited to just a handful of voices, similar to those a decade later. This legislative session did pass a bill to empanel a legislative committee to recommend a spot to later erect a monument on the site of the 1838 Constitutional Convention. From the legislative debates there is no indication that the desire for a new constitution and the historical reverence for the first state constitution were related or influenced each other. What both moments had in common was a birth in the rapid and haphazard growth in the state. In their 1921 report, "The committee respectfully begs leave to emphasize the historical significance of this spot upon which was enacted one of the most important scenes in the proud history of our great State, and to call attention to the necessity of setting it apart and marking it as a public memorial before it has been desecrated by industrial and agricultural buildings."[1] The growing pains of demographic expansion and economic transformation seem to be a catalyst for the debates over constitutional reform between Florida constitutions as much as political crises like the Civil War or court cases such as *Baker v. Carr*.

Late into the production of this volume, legal scholar William J. Chriss published *Six Constitutions over Texas: Texas' Political Identity, 1830–1900*. Texas and Florida share some historical similarities with each other. Before they were states they were colonies of the Spanish Empire and thus people of different ethnic origins inhabited the lands throughout that time. They share a history of settler colonialism (and revolt), an antebellum slave economy, along with the emancipation of enslaved people following the Civil War. Chriss documented a constitutional tradition by white lawmakers that expressed a fervent nationalism centered in a spirit of Texas as an exceptional land and people. There does not seem to be an analog or at least to that degree an analog in the Florida experience. What seems to be the case in both examples is the creation of legal documents intended to impose an otherness or *alterité* on certain citizens. In the Texas example lawmakers codified an otherness directed at Tejanos, Mexicans, Indigenous people, and African Americans. Florida lawmakers and constitutional delegates, too, had ambitions to privilege the white native-born population over Indigenous people, immigrants, the enslaved, and African Americans generally. Chriss concluded that a purpose of the nineteenth-century Texas constitution was to cement the "stranger" in legal and constitutional form. According to Chriss the impetus for targeting groups as the other occurs when the political-dominated group feels "threatened with control, infiltration, or subversion by powerful or numerous neighbors to protect their collective identity by morally marginalizing them."[2] At least in the nineteenth century both Texas and Florida share this constitutional history of manufacturing the other as an attempt to maintain order.

This volume encompasses the conception and birth of governments but not the maturation of those constitutions. Although the constitutional conventions may draft a system of government, in some cases it takes years for a new state constitution to come to fruition, maybe decades. Talbot "Sandy" D'Alemberte concluded in *The Florida State Constitution: A Reference Guide*, "Given the willingness of the legislature to propose amendments, the availability of the initiative process to the citizenry, and the frequent review by appointed commissions, it is clear that this history of the Florida Constitution will continue to be written in virtually every election."[3] In the three decades since D'Alemberte made that observation, it still seems to be the case.

More recently researchers have come to the conclusion that voters are less interested in state constitutional reform or overhaul than previous generations.[4] The growth of Florida throughout the first part of the twentieth century was an impetus for some advocates to ditch the 1885 Constitution for good. The germ of that idea probably began soon after the real estate boom of the 1920s, until it caught the imagination of Frank Shutts and the *Miami Herald* in 1930. William C. Havard, writing in 1959, had a pessimistic opinion about whether the forces supporting a new Florida Constitution would eventually be successful. He described a political, legislative, and judicial process that found a way to maintain the status quo in the face of a byzantine effort at reforming the 1885 document. Since the 1885 Constitution, proponents for a constitutional convention faced strong headwinds. Amending the Indigenous Constitutions in Florida are more streamlined. Authority to amend governing documents are typically held with an Indigenous governing council. The Seminole Tribe has amended their constitution over the years.[5]

Legal scholars Mila Versteeg and Emily Zackin noted that Florida's constitutional revision rate is 0.43, which is the twelfth most revised state constitution in the United States. A figure that is comparable to Russia, Zimbabwe, and Bangladesh, which again demonstrates that state constitutions may have more in common with world constitutions than we would imagine.[6] As we are reminded by this book, it is not unusual to revise a state constitution. The process by which constitutions change can come in a variety of forms. The modern process is mapped out by Albert L. Strum who states:

> Two phases are involved in formal constitutional changes: initiation of proposals and adoption. The organic laws of the fifty states expressly authorize four techniques for initiating proposals for their amendment, revision, and rewriting. These are: (1) proposal by the state lawmaking body, now available in all the states; (2) the constitutional initiative, authorized in seventeen state constitutions; (3) constitutional conventions, which may be used in all states but are not expressly authorized in nine states; and (4) the constitutional commission, specifically authorized only in the 1969 [sic] Florida constitution. The Florida document is the only state constitution that provides expressly for the use of all four methods.[7]

With the adoption of the 1968 Constitution, the popular will to overhaul the Florida Constitution declined. Florida leads other states as the only state that allows a periodic constitutional commission to send revisions and amendments directly to voters. However, the use of a constitutional commission has been popular with states since the 1960s. In the Florida CRC's first attempt at revising the state constitution in 1978, their efforts were rejected by the voters. However, two years later voters rejected a proposed amendment to abolish the CRC thus showing that Florida voters wanted to preserve the various ways they can easily revise their constitution. The reluctance of states to revise their constitutions in the twenty-first century has not stopped politicians from advocating for a new constitution. State Representative Spencer Roach told a group of people from the Real Estate Investment Society in Lee County in 2023 that it was time for Florida to adopt a new constitution. His rationale was that "the Florida Constitution has been amended 144 times in 55 years—that's an average of five amendments every election cycle. Contrast that with the U.S. Constitution, which has only been amended 27 times in 235 years. To me, that indicates a deeply flawed document that has served its purpose but is in desperate need of revision." What Roach does not seem to appreciate is that to most voters the ease at which the constitution can be amended might be the actual appeal to voters.[8]

The conditions governing amending the constitution seem to be changing in Florida. Beginning in the twenty-first century, Florida lawmakers started to pull back the means for the public to easily amend the state's constitution. An editorial in the *Orlando Sentinel* criticized the recent effort by the state legislature to punish organizations that gather voter signatures for referendums. In 2020 the law cut the time in half to collect signatures. During the 2020 legislative session one speaker remarked, "Why, if the Legislature hates citizen-led constitutional amendments so much, it doesn't [sic] just put its own amendment on the ballot asking voters to do away with them." A similar effort in Ohio put to voters in 2023 failed. The measure would have required a 60 percent threshold for passing ballot amendments in the state. It was an attempt to thwart an abortion rights amendment. As recently as the Florida 2023 legislative session, Representative Rick Roth of Palm Beach tried to introduce a bill raising the threshold for passing a state ballot initiative to 67 percent. It failed in the Senate that year, and a similar bill failed to make it out of a House committee in 2024.[9]

Two decades into the twenty-first century are we looking at a period when comprehensive state constitutional revision is rare and a new Florida constitution unlikely? It is impossible to predict the future, but based on recent precedent, Floridians might be under the 1968 Constitution for quite some time. The political incentives for state lawmakers to keep the mechanics of a state constitution status quo incentivizes lawmakers since the 2020s as much as it did in the 1950s. Although ballot amendment initiatives in Florida are more difficult to pass, they are not impossible. Ballot referendums and periodic CRCs might make revising the Florida Constitution too easy, unless the revisions and amendments accumulate to the point that lawmakers and voters throw their hands up into the air and want to start over.

Notes

1 *Miami Herald*, February 20, 1919; *Tampa Daily Times*, May 13, 1919; *Laws of Florida, Vol. 1, Part 2* (1919) "Senate Concurrent Resolution No. 19," 348; *Laws of Florida, Vol. 1, Part 1* (1921), Chapter 8481 (No. 86), 202–3.
2 William J. Chriss, *Six Constitutions over Texas: Texas' Political Identity, 1830–1900* (College Station: Texas A&M University Press, 2024), xiii, 219, 221.
3 D'Alemberte, *The Florida State Constitution*, 16.
4 See Daniel C. Lewis, Jack D. Collens, and Leonard Cutler, "Conventional Wisdom? Analyzing Public Support for a State Constitutional Convention Referendum," *State & Local Government Review* 51, no. 1 (2019): 19–33; William D. Blake and Ian G. Anson, "Risk and Reform: Explaining Support for Constitutional Convention Referendums," *State Politics & Policy Quarterly* 20, no. 3 (2020): 330–55.
5 William C. Havard, "Notes on a Theory of State Constitutional Change: The Florida Experience," *Journal of Politics* 21, no. 1 (February 1959): 80–104; Adkins, *Making Modern Florida*, 20–54; *Miami Herald*, March 31, 1973; US Department of the Interior, Records Bureau of Indian Affairs, "Constitution and Bylaws of the Seminole Tribe of Florida," August 21, 1957; Central Classification Files, 1940–1957, (RG 75, Box 7, P-163); US Department of the Interior, Records Bureau of Indian Affairs, "Constitution and Bylaws of the Seminole Tribe of Florida," August 21, 1957; Central Classification Files, 1940–1957 (RG 75, Box 7, P-163), "Amendment to the Constitution of the Miccosukee Tribe of Indians," Central Classified Files, 1958–1975, Miccosukee (RG 75, Box 1, PI-163).
6 Mila Versteeg and Emily Zackin, "American Constitutional Exceptionalism Revisited," *The University of Chicago Law Review* 81, no. 4 (2014): 1676.
7 Albert L. Sturm, "The Development of American State Constitutions," *Publius* 12, no. 1 (1982): 76.
8 Jacob Ogles, "Spencer Roach Says It's Time the Legislature Write a New Florida Constitution," *Florida Politics*, June 19, 2023, https://floridapolitics.com/archives/619282-spencer-roach-says-its-time-the-legislature-write-a-new-florida-constitution/ (accessed June 19, 2023); Strum, 84.
9 *Orlando Sentinel*, January 19, 2020, November 16, 2016; Noreen Marcus. "State Lawmakers Fight Citizen Initiatives." *U.S. New and World Report*, March 11, 2024, https://www.usnews.com/news/best-states/articles/2020-03-11/lawmakers-fight-citizen-initiatives-in-florida-other-states, accessed 2-13-2024; Mitch Perry. "Ohio Could Match FL for one of the Highest Thresholds to Pass Citizen-Led Constitutional Amendments," *Florida Pheonix*, August 8, 2023.

SELECTED BIBLIOGRAPHY

Primary Sources

Constitution and Bylaws of the Seminole Tribe of Florida (1958). University of Oklahoma College of Law, https://thorpe.law.ou.edu/IRA/flsemcons.html, accessed July 5, 2023.

"Constitution of West Florida" (1810) in Horst Dippel, ed., *Constitutional Documents of the United States of America 1776–1860, Part VII: Vermont-Wisconsin Addendum et Corrigendum*, Germany: K. G. Saur Verlag, 2009, 143–53.

Convention, Florida Constitutional. *Journal of the Proceedings of the Constitutional Convention of the State of Florida: Which Convened at the Capitol, at Tallahassee, on Tuesday, June 9, 1885*. United States: Creative Media Partners, LLC, 2015.

Florida. Constitutional Convention (1838). *Constitution of the State of Florida, 1838*. 1839-01-11. State Archives of Florida, Florida Memory, https://www.floridamemory.com/items/show/189087, accessed July 5, 2023.

Florida. Constitutional Convention (1865). *Constitution of the State of Florida, 1865*. 1865-11-07. State Archives of Florida, Florida Memory, https://www.floridamemory.com/items/show/189093, accessed July 5, 2023.

Florida. Constitutional Convention (1868). *Constitution of the State of Florida, 1868*. 1868-02-25. State Archives of Florida, Florida Memory, https://www.floridamemory.com/items/show/189095, accessed July 5, 2023.

Florida. Constitutional Convention (1885). *Constitution of the State of Florida, 1885*. 1885-08-03. State Archives of Florida, Florida Memory, https://www.floridamemory.com/items/show/189169, accessed July 5, 2023.

Florida Convention of the People. *Ordinance of Secession, 1861*. 1861-01-10. State Archives of Florida, Florida Memory, https://www.floridamemory.com/items/show/339353, accessed July 5, 2023.

Florida Department of State. *1968 Florida Constitution*. https://files.floridados.gov/media/693801/florida-constitution.pdf, accessed July 5, 2023.

Journal of Proceedings of the Convention of Florida: Begun and Held at the Capital of the State, at Tallahassee, Wednesday, October 25th, A.D. 1865. Tallahassee: Office of the Floridian, 1865.

Journal of the Proceedings of a Convention of Delegates to Form a Constitution for the People of Florida: Held at St. Joseph, December 1838. United States: Printed at the Times Office, 1839.

Journal of the Proceedings of the Constitutional Convention of the State of Florida: Begun and Held at the Capitol, at Tallahassee, on Monday, January 20th, 1868. United States: E.M. Cheney, printer, 1868.

Proceedings of the Convention of the People of Florida, at Called Sessions, Begun and Held at the Capitol in Tallahassee, on Tuesday, February 26th, and Thursday, April 18th, 1861.

Republic of East Florida. *"Patriot Constitution" of the Republic of East Florida, 1812.* 1812-07-17. State Archives of Florida, Florida Memory, https://www.floridamemory.com/items/show/264067, accessed July 5, 2023.

Secondary Sources

Adkins, Mary E. *Making Modern Florida: How the Spirit of Reform Shaped a New State Constitution.* Gainesville: University Press of Florida, 2016.

Baptist, Edward E. *Creating an Old South: Middle Florida's Plantation Frontier before the Civil War.* Chapel Hill: University of North Carolina Press, 2002.

Biklé, Henry Wolf. "The Constitutional Power of Congress over the Territory of the United States." *The American Law Register (1898-1907)* 49, no. 8 (1901): 11–120. https://doi.org/10.2307/3306271.

Billias, George Athan. *American Constitutionalism Heard Round the World, 1776–1989.* New York: New York University Press, 2009.

Borrows, John. *Canada's Indigenous Constitution.* Toronto, Canada: University of Toronto Press, 2010.

Brown, Canter, Jr. *Ossian Bingley Hart: Florida's Loyalist Reconstruction Governor.* Baton Rouge: Louisiana State University Press, 1997.

Burdine, J. Alton. "Basic Materials for the Study of State Constitutions and State Constitutional Development." *The American Political Science Review* 48, no. 4 (1954): 1140–52. https://doi.org/10.2307/1951016.

Chriss, William J. *Six Constitutions over Texas: Texas' Political Identity, 1830–1900.* College Station: Texas A&M University Press, 2024.

Currie, David P. "Through the Looking-Glass: The Confederate Constitution in Congress, 1861–1865." *Virginia Law Review* 90, no. 5 (2004): 1257–1399. https://doi.org/10.2307/3202380.

Cusick, James G. *The Other War of 1812: The Patriot War and The American Invasion of Spanish East Florida.* Athens: University of Georgia Press, 2003.

D'Alemberte, Talbot. *The Florida State Constitution: A Reference Guide.* New York: Greenwood Press, 1991.

Denham, James M. *Florida Founder William P. DuVal: Frontier Bon Vivant.* Columbia: University of South Carolina Press, 2015.

DeRosa, Marshall L. *The Confederate Constitution of 1861: An Inquiry into American Constitutionalism.* Columbia: University of Missouri Press, 1991.

Dinan, John J. *The American State Constitutional Tradition.* Lawrence: University Press of Kansas, 2006.

Dippel, Horst. "Modern Constitutionalism: An Introduction to a History in Need of Writing," *Tijdschrift voor Rechtsgeschiedenis/Revue d'histoire du droit (The Legal History Review)* 73, 1–2 (2005): 153–70.
Dodd, Dorothy. *Florida Becomes a State.* Tallahassee: Florida Centennial Commission, 1945.
Doherty, Herbert J., Jr. *The Whigs of Florida,* Gainesville: University of Florida Press, 1959.
Dovell, J. D. *History of Banking in Florida.* Orlando: Florida Bankers Association, 1955.
Edwards, Laura F. *A Legal History of the Civil War and Reconstruction: A Nation of Rights.* New York: Cambridge University Press, 2015.
Fehrenbacher, Don E. *Constitutions and Constitutionalism in the Slaveholding South.* Athens: University of Georgia Press, 1989.
Foner, Eric. *Reconstruction: America's Unfinished Revolution, 1863–1877.* New York: Harper & Row Publishers, 1988.
Gannon, Michael, ed. *The History of Florida.* Gainesville: University Press of Florida, 2013.
Grotke, Kelly L., and Markus J. Prutsch (eds), *Constitutionalism, Legitimacy, and Power: Nineteenth-Century Experiences.* Oxford: Oxford University Press, 2014 (online edition, Oxford Academic, November 20, 2014). https://doi.org/10.1093/acprof:oso/9780198723059.001.0001.
Hall, Kermit L., and James W. Ely Jr., *An Uncertain Tradition: Constitutionalism and the History of the South.* Athens: University of Georgia Press, 1989.
Herron, Paul Emerson. "State Constitutional Development in the American South, 1860–1902." PhD diss., Brandeis University, 2014.
Hershkoff, Helen. "Positive Rights and State Constitutions: The Limits of Federal Rationality Review." *Harvard Law Review* 112, no. 6 (1999): 1131–96. https://doi.org/10.2307/1342383.
Hoskins, F. W. "The St. Joseph Convention: The Making of Florida's First Constitution." *The Florida Historical Quarterly* 16, no. 1 (1937): 33–43.
Jameson, John Alexander. *Constitutional Convention; History, Powers, and Modes of Proceeding,* New York: Charles Scribner and Company, 1867.
Knauss, James Owen. *Territorial Florida Journalism.* Deland: Florida Historical Society, 1926.
Kincaid, John. "State Constitutions in the Federal System." *The Annals of the American Academy of Political and Social Science* 496 (1988): 12–22. http://www.jstor.org/stable/1046314.
Lee, Charles Robert, Jr. *The Confederate Constitutions.* Chapel Hill: University of North Carolina Press, 1963.
Martin, Walter Sidney. *Florida During Territorial Days.* Athens: University of Georgia Press, 1944.
May, Janice C. "Constitutional Amendment and Revision Revisited." *Publius* 17, no. 1 (1987): 153–79. http://www.jstor.org/stable/3330031.
McHugh, James T., *Ex Uno Plura: State Constitutions and Their Political Cultures.* Albany: State University of New York Press, 2003.

Miller, Robert J. "American Indian Constitutions and Their Influence on the United States Constitution." *Proceedings of the American Philosophical Society* 159, no. 1 (2015): 32–56.

Mirow, M.C. "The Age of Constitutions in the Americas." *Law and History Review* 32, no. 2 (2014): 229–35.

Mirow, M.C. "The Patriot Constitution and International Constitution Making," *Texas Review of Law & Politics* 21, no. 3 (September 20, 2017): 477–517.

Moussalli, Stephanie D. "Florida's Frontier Constitution: The Statehood, Banking and Slavery Controversies." *The Florida Historical Quarterly.* 74, no. 4 (1996): 423–39.

Murphree, R. Boyd, and Robert A. Taylor, eds., *The Governors of Florida.* Gainesville: University Press of Florida, 2020.

Patrick, Rembert W. *Florida Fiasco: Rampant Rebels on the Georgia-Florida Border 1810–1815.* Athens: University of Georgia Press, 1954.

Savage, Mark. "Native Americans and the Constitution: The Original Understanding." *American Indian Law Review* 16, no. 1 (1991): 57–118. https://doi.org/10.2307/20068692.

Shofner, Jerrell H. "The Constitution of 1868." *The Florida Historical Quarterly* 41, no. 4 (1963): 356–74.

Shofner, Jerrell. "Militant Negro Laborers in Reconstruction Florida," *The Journal of Southern History* 39 no. 3 (August 1973): 397–408.

Shofner, Jerrell H. *Nor Is It Over Yet: Florida in the Era of Reconstruction, 1863–1877.* Gainesville: University Presses of Florida, 1974.

Sieder, Rachel. "The Challenge of Indigenous Legal Systems: Beyond Paradigms of Recognition." *The Brown Journal of World Affairs* 18, no. 2 (2012): 103–14. http://www.jstor.org/stable/24590866.

Stagg, J.C.A. *Borderlines in Borderlands: James Madison and the Spanish-American Frontier, 1776–1821.* New Haven: Yale University Press, 2009.

Stephenson, Margaret. "Indigenous Lands and Constitutional Reforms in Australia: A Canadian Comparison." *Australian Indigenous Law Review* 15, no. 2 (2011): 87–108. http://www.jstor.org/stable/26423231.

Sturm, Albert L. "The Development of American State Constitutions." *Publius* 12, no. 1 (1982): 57–98. http://www.jstor.org/stable/3329673.

Tarr, G. Alan. *Understanding State Constitutions.* Princeton, NJ: Princeton University Press, 1998.

Thompson, Arthur W. *Jacksonian Democracy on the Florida Frontier.* Gainesville: University of Florida Press, 1961.

Tsai, Robert L. *America's Forgotten Constitutions: Defiant Visions of Power and Community.* Cambridge, MA: Harvard University Press, 2014.

Versteeg, Mila, and Emily Zackin. "American Constitutional Exceptionalism Revisited." *The University of Chicago Law Review* 81, no. 4 (2014): 1641–1707. http://www.jstor.org/stable/43151587.

von Holst, Hermann Eduard. *The Constitutional Law of the United States of America.* Translated by Alfred Bishop Mason. Chicago: Callaghan and Company, 1887.

Wallace, John. *Carpetbag Rule in Florida: The Inside Workings of the Reconstruction of*

Civil Government in Florida after Close of the Civil War. Kennesaw, GA: Continental Bk. Co., 1959.

Weitz, Seth A., and Jonathan C. Sheppard, eds., *A Forgotten Front: Florida During the Civil War Era*. Tuscaloosa: University of Alabama Press, 2018.

White, Thomas Raeburn. "Amendment and Revision of State Constitutions." *University of Pennsylvania Law Review* 100, no. 8 (1952): 1132–52. https://doi.org/10.2307/3310069.

Whitfield, James B. "Florida's First Constitution." *The Florida Historical Quarterly* 17, no. 2 (1938): 73–83.

Williamson, Edward C. "The Constitutional Convention of 1885." *The Florida Historical Quarterly* 41, no. 2 (1962): 116–26.

Wooster, Ralph A. "The Florida Secession Convention." *The Florida Historical Quarterly* 36, no. 4 (1958): 373–85.

CONTRIBUTORS

Mary Adkins, Master Legal Skills Professor, the University of Florida Levin College of Law

Robert Cassanello, Associate Professor of History, University of Central Florida

Christopher Day, History Instructor at Maclay School, Tallahassee, Florida

James M. Denham, Professor of History and Director of the Lawton M. Chiles Jr. Center for Florida History at Florida Southern College

Andrew K. Frank, Allen Morris Professor of History, Florida State University

Samuel C. Hyde, Director of the Center for Southeast Louisiana Studies; Professor of History, Leon Ford Endowed Chair in Regional Studies, Southeastern Louisiana University

M.C. Mirow, Professor of Law, Florida International University, College of Law

R. Boyd Murphree, Project Manager, Florida Family and Community History, Digital Services and Shared Collections, University of Florida, George A. Smathers Libraries

Andrea L. Oliver, Assistant Professor of History at Tallahassee State College

INDEX

Abolition, 79, 88, 89, 112, 113, 118, 123; abolitionists, 72, 73, 76, 78, 85n68, 92
Adams-Onis Treaty (1821), 62, 81n9
Agriculture, 62, 135, 180, 186, 196, 203
Alachua District, 38
Alice Williams v Jacksonville, Tampa & Key West Railway Company, Appellee, 167
Allen, Richard C., 61, 65, 66, 72
Alterité, 204
Amelia Island, 36, 92
Amending. *See* Revisions (to Constitutions)
American Revolution, 10, 16, 88, 122
Annexation, 24, 33–34, 41, 65, 51n8
Apportionment, 2, 6, 7, 12, 22, 43, 117, 121, 147–52, 189, 190–91, 197, 199, 203
Askew, Reubin, 193, 198
Attorney General (Florida), 115, 192, 198
Attorney General (US), 65

Baker, James M., 167–69
Baker v. Carr, 7, 191, 203
Banking, 60, 63, 67–69, 71, 74–77, 79, 117–18; bankers, 122; banks, 5, 24, 36, 63, 66–70, 74–78, 82n24, 83n48, 96, 118, 125
Bartlett, Cosam Emir, 60, 67, 68
Baton Rouge, 16–20, 21, 28
Bellamy, Abram, 66, 68, 72, 74
Bellamy, Samuel, 66, 70, 72
Bennett, Lerone, 134
Big Cypress Reservation, 178, 181–82, 184–85
Billings, Liberty, 138, 142, 143, 144, 145
Bisbee, Horatio, 161
Black codes, 129, 153
Blood quantum, 184, 186
Bonds, 63, 67, 74, 75, 78, 122–23, 125, 132n20
Boundaries, 4, 114

Bowen, Alexander J., 130,
Brighton Reservation, 180, 181, 182, 184, 185
British (Great Britain), 16, 17, 20, 21, 22, 24, 29, 37, 39, 48, 178; loyalists, 17, 22, 24
British colonies, 10, 24, 64–65
Brown, Thomas, 66, 68, 88, 96
Buckman, T. E., 161
Buckskin Declaration, 174–78, 179, 181–82, 185
Burdine, J. Alton, 6, 9
Bureaucracy, 7, 8, 137, 182
Bureau of Indian Affairs (BIA), 178, 180, 182, 185, 184
Burns, Haydon, 192

Cádiz Constitution, 10, 38, 49
Calhoun, John C., 79, 87, 94, 105
Call, Richard Keith, 61, 62, 161
Carpetbaggers, 140
Castillo de San Marcos, 37
Castro, Fidel, 186, 196
Chase, Salmon P., 126
Chriss, William J., 204
Citizenship, 5, 8, 11, 12, 16, 17, 18, 44, 98–99, 112–13, 119, 120, 123, 128–30, 135–36, 161, 184, 196
Civil rights, 11, 119, 124, 130, 136, 154n17, 158, 159, 161, 167, 170, 172n17
Civil Rights Act of 1866, 120, 136
Civil Rights Cases (1883), 161
Civil War (US), 7, 8, 11, 86, 87, 93, 97, 99, 105, 106n1, 112, 114, 116, 121, 124, 134, 146, 203, 204; Confederate, 11, 86, 90, 93, 94, 96–101, 104–5, 106n3, 113–14, 122–25, 136, 148, 153, 157, 161, 162, 163; Union, 86–93, 97, 99–100, 104, 105, 135, 137, 145

218 · Index

Claiborne, William C. C., 28, 29
Clemency, 125
Collins, LeRoy, 190
Commerce, 4, 17, 45, 47, 48, 49, 61, 93, 180
Commissioner of Indian Affairs, 124, 181
Committee on General Provisions, 72, 73, 121, 122
Confederate Constitution (CSA), 94, 96–98
Constitutional Conventions, 2, 6, 9, 12–13, 94, 97, 137, 142, 144, 154n14, 204, 205
Constitutionalism, 2–6, 8–9, 12–13, 33, 49, 51n3, 57n133, 165
Constitution Revision Commission, 192–99
Convict labor, 119, 167, 172n17
Creeks. *See* Native people
Criminal convictions, 43, 85n68, 117–19, 128, 136, 160–61, 166

D'Alemberte, Talbot "Sandy," 2, 5, 204
Dania Reservation (Dania/Hollywood), 178, 181–82, 184–85
Davis, Jefferson, 94, 100, 125
Davis, William G. M., 90
Davis, William Watson, 106n1, 128, 132n24, 140
Debates, 68, 70–72, 79n2, 83n46, 97, 120, 123, 131n18, 145, 163–65, 193, 195, 199
Debt, 22, 76, 113, 122–23, 125, 132n20, 144, 157, 166, 191
Declarations of Causes, 91–92
Delegates, 2, 3, 5–9, 11–12, 14n7, 204; in 1810, 19, 21, 25; in 1812, 41; in 1838, 60, 61, 65–68, 70–74, 76–78, 79n2, 84n59; in1861, 88–89, 91, 93–95, 97, 99, 101; in 1865, 112, 114–16, 118–26, 130; in 1868, 137–46; in 1885, 162–66
Democratic Party, 63, 68–69, 77, 83n48, 122, 130, 138, 139, 144, 146, 157–67, 170, 198
Dinan, John, 4, 5, 7–8, 9, 13
Diplomacy, 10, 46, 57n137, 57n141
Disfranchisement, 12, 158, 160, 164, 170, 171n7
Dred Scott decision, 129
Drew, George Franklin, 158
Du Bois, W. E. B., 141
Dunning School, 106n1, 128, 140–41

DuPont, Charles H., 83n48, 129
DuVal, William P., 60–62, 66–71, 73–75, 79, 83n48, 84n59

East Florida, 3, 10, 14n7, 33–41, 44, 46–50, 51n4, 51n5, 52n18, 52n20, 52n22, 53n40, 55n106; Eastern District, 61, 62, 64–65, 67–68, 70–71, 77–78, 81n9, 83n48, 85n68. *See also* Patriot Constitution
Economics, 1, 4–7, 8, 11, 26, 28, 34, 36, 47, 60–64, 67, 76, 78–79, 91–92, 105, 118, 122, 124–25, 141, 146, 154–55n17, 168, 183, 184, 186, 191, 203. *See also* Commerce; Trade
Education, 8, 120, 145, 147, 153, 165–66, 186
Eisenhower, Dwight D., 174, 178, 179
Elections, 1, 3, 21, 22, 42, 61, 67, 68, 69, 77, 79, 88, 89, 94, 100, 113, 115–16, 118, 123, 127, 131n17, 138–39, 142, 148, 158–60, 162, 166, 169, 183, 185, 197–99, 204, 206. *See also* Ratification
Emmons, Glenn, 181
Estrada, Juan José de, 36–37
Executive branch, 3, 5, 7–8, 23, 39–41, 42, 49, 72–73, 87, 95–96, 102, 103, 104–5, 106n3, 112, 115–16, 119, 148, 166–67, 175, 194. *See also* Governor
Expansion, 3, 7, 63, 79, 203

Federal government, 4–5, 7, 12–13, 45, 87–92, 112–13, 117, 120, 122, 124, 130, 142, 157, 161, 165, 175, 176, 182–83, 185–86, 191
Felons, 22, 98, 119, 172n17, 196
Fernandina, 10, 14n7, 36, 38
Fifteenth Amendment, 7
Flag, 18, 28, 30n7, 36, 87
Florida Constitution (state), 1; of 1838, 5, 11, 76, 79–80n2, 86, 93–98, 114–15, 117–18, 125–26, 204; of 1861, 95–98, 106n2; of 1865, 11, 112, 114–17, 119, 120, 122–26, 128–30, 134, 148, 153; of 1868, 4, 11, 140, 152–53, 158, 162–63, 165–66, 191; of 1885, 157–58, 163, 165–67, 170, 189–91, 196, 205; of 1968, 3, 4, 204–5, 206, 207
Florida House of Representatives, 88, 114, 131n18, 200, 203, 206
Florida lawmakers, 3, 5, 11, 112, 128, 130, 167, 203–4, 206–7

Florida legislative council (territorial/state government), 37–42, 44, 61, 63–64, 73, 77–79
Florida Mechanic's and Workingmen's Association, 164
Florida Senate, 99, 115–16, 128, 131n18, 148, 150, 194, 197, 198, 200, 203, 206
Foner, Eric, 129
Forbes, John, 48
Fourteenth Amendment, 120, 129, 134, 136–37, 142, 153
France, 16, 19, 20, 24, 25, 27, 34, 49
Freedmen's Bureau, 137
Freedmen and freedwomen, 26, 121, 135, 138, 139, 140–41, 146, 153
French Indian War, 16

Gambling, 8
Georgia, 10, 33, 35–37, 40, 41, 42, 50, 61, 66, 89, 90, 91, 97, 113, 114, 137, 165, 189; Constitutions (of 1789 and of 1798), 9, 40, 41–44
Gibbs, Thomas Van Renssalaer, 164
Goldsborough, Louis, 65–67, 75, 76
Governor, 8, 35, 37, 41, 42, 60–62, 67–69, 73, 79, 83n48, 87–89, 91–94, 96, 100–105, 113, 115–16, 117–20, 122, 123–25, 127–29, 147–48, 157–58, 164–66, 190, 192–93, 196–97, 198–99; colonial governors, 10, 19, 36–37, 88; Patriot Constitution, 39–40, 50; Republic of West Florida, 19, 23, 27–28; veto, 8, 43, 69, 103, 116, 136–37. *See also* Lieutenant Governor
Graham, Thomas, 158
Green Corn Ceremony, 175–76
Guarantee Clause (US), 120, 127
Gulf Coast, 18, 60, 61

Harris, Buckner, 37–38
Havard, William C., 205
Herron, Paul, 142, 165
Hitchiti (language), 181

Impeachment, 39, 43, 115
Independent Party, 162
Indian agents, 176, 182
Indians. *See* Native people

Indigenous people. *See* Native people
Internal Improvements, 63, 88

Jacksonian Democracy, 3, 7, 11, 117
Jim Crow laws, 128–30, 153, 157, 158, 161, 167, 170
Johns, Charley, 193, 197
Johnson, Andrew, 113, 118, 120, 123–24, 129, 135, 137, 142, 163
Johnson, Beth, 193, 195
Johnson, John H., 20
Jordan, Richard, 161
Judicial branch, 3, 5, 7, 39, 40, 64, 95, 96, 114–15, 121, 123, 136, 160, 190, 198–200, 205; Florida supreme court, 115, 159, 160–61, 163, 164, 169–70, 196–97; judicial review, 8; Republic of West Florida, 23
Jury service, 17, 98, 122

Kemper Rebellion, 17–18
Kimball, Frederick, 29,
Kirk, Claude Roy, Jr., 198

Land grants, 17–18, 20, 24; land ownership 5, 24. *See also* Property ownership
Land of Flowers, 157–58
Legislative branch, 3, 5, 7, 10, 23, 25, 37–44, 56n108, 66, 76, 87, 95, 103, 115–16, 124, 136, 147–48, 153, 163, 167, 189–92, 194, 197, 199, 203, 205, 206
Legislature (state), 2, 4, 7, 21–23, 26–27, 43, 73–74, 85n68, 93, 95, 96, 101, 103–4, 115, 116, 127, 129, 134, 148, 158, 164, 165, 167, 189–93, 196–200, 204, 206. *See also* Florida legislative council
Leonard, John W., 20
Lieutenant Governor, 23, 115–16, 164, 166, 190, 196, 199
Lincoln, Abraham, 79, 91, 113, 123–24, 129, 142
Lincoln Brotherhood, 132n24, 138, 142
Loco-focos faction, 63, 66
Louisiana, 9, 22, 25, 28–29, 34, 90, 119, 129, 170
Louisiana Purchase, 18, 20–21
Lowndes, Richard H., 123

Madison, James, 20–21, 34–35, 37–38, 51n5
Marriages, 121, 176, 190, 195
Marvin, William, 67, 68, 72, 74, 113, 118–24, 127, 128
Mathews, George, 33, 35–37, 41, 45–46, 48, 50, 53n40
Maxwell, Augustus Emmet, 162
McComb Treaty of 1839, 177
McGehee, John C., 67, 89, 96, 97, 100, 103, 107n9
McIntosh, John Houston, 33, 35–38, 42, 45, 46–47, 49–50
McLeod, Don, 158
Meade, George, 143–44
Miccosukees, 2, 4, 12, 13, 175, 178, 181, 182, 185–86; Constitution, 4, 10, 186. *See also* Mikasuki Tribe; Native people
Miccosukee Tribe of Indians of Florida, 174–78, 179–82, 184, 186
Mickler, Joseph R., 1
Middle District, 61, 69
Mikasuki (language), 181–82
Mikasuki Tribe, 174, 177
Military, 10, 33–38, 49–50, 87, 92, 95, 99–102, 104, 112, 117, 129, 136–37, 139, 143, 148, 163, 195; army, 17–23, 28, 63, 94, 99–100, 137, 177; militia, 23, 52n22, 56n124, 92, 93, 95, 101, 103–4, 117; navy, 23, 36, 100; Spanish, 10, 37
Miller, Robert J., 4
Miller v. Johnson, 9
Milton, John, 87, 100–104, 125
Mitchell, David Brydie, 37
Model Treaty, 45, 47
Modernization, 11
Monroe, James, 34, 36–38, 45, 46,
Monticello Contingent, 144, 146, 148
Morton, Jackson, 66, 84n59, 94
Moseley, William D., 87–88, 96
Mule teamers, 143
Muskogee, 174–76, 180–81

Native people (Indigenous people), 2, 4, 12, 48, 63, 124, 136, 174–81, 182, 184–86, 191, 204, 206; assimilation, 4; clan, 174–77, 179, 182–84; Creeks, 2, 24, 34, 63, 181; Sioux, 181

Niblack, Silas L., 120, 131n17
Nineteenth Amendment, 7
No Transfer Resolution, 34
Nucleus faction, 62, 76
Nullification, 88, 92

Oaths, 39, 123, 124, 142
Ordinance of Secession (Florida), 86, 89, 90, 92, 93, 95, 99, 104, 105, 123, 126
Ortiz, Paul, 159, 160, 162
Osborn, Thomas, 137, 142, 144
Osceola, 177
Osceola, Bill, 181, 182–83, 184
Osceola, Billy, 181, 182–83, 184
Osceola, Laura Mae, 181, 182–83, 184
Osceola, Mike, 182, 184
Owens, James B., 94

Panic of 1837, 60, 63
Panton, Leslie, and Company, 48
Parkhill, Samuel, 66, 67, 68, 82n24, 84n59
Pasco, Samuel, 160, 163,
Patriot Constitution (East Florida), 3, 10, 33–34, 37, 38, 39–42, 44–47, 49–50, 50n1, 53n29
Patriot Revolt: of 1812, 10; of 1817, 14n7; Articles of Cession, 36, 45–50; Declaration of Independence, 36, 45, 49, 50, 51n3, 53n40; manifesto, 36, 45, 49, 50, 53n40
Peeler, A. J., 129
Perry, Edward Alysworth, 157, 164
Perry, Madison Starke, 88–89, 91, 92–94, 101–2
Pinckney Treaty, 35
Poll tax, 117, 163–65
Popular vote, 9, 97
Pork Chop Gang, 190
President of the Senate (Florida), 23, 115–16
Prohibition of alcohol, 8
Property ownership, 5, 9, 16, 25, 28, 47, 123–24, 136, 147, 177
Purnam, W. J., 143

Quinn, Reginald "Rex," 181, 182–84

Railroads, 74, 104, 162, 167
Randall, Edwin M., 160, 164

Ratification, 94, 96–97, 142, 148, 150, 152, 157, 167, 170, 186
Reconstruction, 4, 11, 105, 113, 118, 129–30, 132n24, 134–36, 138, 139–42, 144, 145–47, 157–58, 160, 162, 164; Acts, 136–38, 142; Congressional, 11, 112, 120, 129, 130, 146, 154n14, 154n17, 165; Presidential, 11, 112–13, 122, 129, 134, 135, 163; Radical, 120, 139–40, 142–48, 152, 157
Redeemers (redemption), 157, 162, 164, 165, 167, 170
Reid, Robert Raymond, 60, 62, 66–69, 71, 72, 77–79, 83n48
Religion, 26, 47, 49; Catholic, 18, 26, 38, 46; Protestant, 18, 26
Republican Party, 89, 91, 138–39, 142, 146, 157, 162, 165
Republic of West Florida, 3, 4, 10, 19, 24, 27, 30n7; Constitution of 1810, 17, 20–29, 31n18; Declaration of Independence, 19, 21, 27, 53n29
Revenue, 92, 125, 165, 191
Revisionist School of History, 141
Revisions (to Constitution), 5, 7, 75, 77, 86–87, 93, 95, 102, 103, 104, 106n1, 115, 120, 129, 163, 184, 192, 205–7
Revolutionary Portfolio, 45, 47, 49
Reynolds v. Sims, 192
Rhea, John, 19, 20
Richards, Daniel, 138, 142–45, 148
Richards-Billings Group, 144
Richardson, Joe M., 141, 156n17
Rights, 5, 8–9, 11, 20, 22, 26, 33–34, 40, 56n109, 62, 72, 76, 79, 81n9, 87–91, 100, 119–20, 122, 123, 126, 128, 140–42, 146, 147, 152–53, 161–63, 165, 170, 174, 176, 178–79, 181–82, 191, 195, 205; Bill of Rights, 26, 51n3; Constitutional, 12, 157; political, 7, 129, 135, 147; Positive Rights, 8–9; property rights, 9, 17, 24, 25, 28, 47, 119, 121, 123, 124–25, 136, 138, 147, 177, states' rights, 87–88, 92, 101, 104, 105, 113. *See also* Civil Rights; Suffrage
Roach, Spencer, 206
Roth, Rick, 206
Rural populations, 7, 190

St. Augustine, 10, 36–38, 61, 63–65, 68, 78, 92
St. Francisville, 10, 16–17, 18–19, 27, 28
St. Joseph, 60–63, 65, 78, 79n2, 82n24, 114
Sanderson, John P., 90
Saunders, Daniel, 138
Saunders, William, 142–43, 145
Scalawags, 140
Scott, Charles, 159
Second Amendment, 126
Second Seminole War, 11, 62, 63, 78–79; long, 176, 178
Segregation, 12, 105, 165, 167, 170, 190, 196
Self-determination, 175, 178–79, 181, 186
Seminoles, 2, 4, 12, 13, 38, 63, 175–76, 178–86; census, 184; Constitution, 174–75, 181–85. *See also* Native people; Second Seminole War
Seminole Tribe of Florida, 4, 174–75, 183–86; Tribal Council, 183, 184
Shaw, John, 28
Sheats, Williams, 165
Shofner, Jerrell H., 130, 132n20, 140, 141, 146, 152, 154n17
Silver, Morton, 185
Slavery, 25, 34, 40, 48, 50, 55n106, 60, 62, 65, 72–73, 75–76, 79, 87–89, 91–92, 94, 98, 112–13, 118–21, 123, 126, 130; abolition, 79, 85n68, 88, 112, 118, 120–21, 123, 127, 134 142, 147; Free Blacks, 62, 98, 126, 153; tribunals, 97–98
Smith, Chesterfield, 192–94, 198
South Carolina, 9, 63, 66, 88, 90, 91, 97, 102, 113, 123, 126, 135
Southern District, 67
Sovereignty, 4, 41, 47, 48, 49, 87–88, 90, 93, 94, 105, 175, 177–78, 180, 186
Spanish Florida, 2, 3, 10; legal system, 17, 40; loyalists, 18–19, 21, 24. *See also* Cádiz Constitution
Speaker of the House (Florida), 116, 198
Stallings, George, 193, 195
Staples v. Gilmer, 9
Statehood, 11, 41, 45, 60, 61, 64–65, 67–70, 72, 77, 78, 79, 126
The State of Florida v. The Board of County Commissioners of Jefferson County (1880), 159

The State of Florida Ex Rel. Richard Jordan v. T.E. Buckman (1881), 159, 160
States' rights. *See* Rights
Suffrage, 3, 5–7, 113, 117, 120, 122, 129–30, 137, 142, 159, 161–64, 167, 196, 199
Sumner, Charles, 120, 128, 146
Supervisor of Elections, 117
Swann v. Adams, 191, 199

Tariffs, 88
Tarr, G. Alan, 2, 4, 6, 13
Taxes, 17, 18, 39, 64, 117, 125, 135, 163–65, 191, 197
Taylor, Hugh, 193–94, 196
Taylor v. Commonwealth, 9
Ten Percent Plan, 113, 123
Tenth Amendment, 142
Termination Policy, 174, 177–80, 182
Terms of Office, 41
Texas, 3, 30n7, 72, 91, 113, 204
Thirteenth Amendment, 120, 121, 134
Thomas, Philemon, 19
Tiger, Buffalo, 182
Trade, 36, 45, 47–49, 64, 92, 93, 100
Trail Indians, 181, 182, 184, 185
Treaty of Amity, Settlement and Limits. *See* Adams-Onis Treaty,
Treaty of San Lorenzo (1795), 35

Unionists, 113, 127
Union League, 132n24, 138, 142
United States Constitution, 2, 4–5, 7–8, 11, 57n137, 57n141, 94, 120, 121, 161, 206
United States House of Representatives, 74, 75, 88, 161
United States Senate, 128, 136, 159
United States Supreme Court, 2, 7, 105, 191–92, 197, 199
Urban, 7, 190

Vagrancy, 128–29, 135
Van Buren, Martin, 69, 79
Versteeg, Mila, 6, 8–9, 205
Virginia, 9, 66, 69, 97, 129, 195

Walker, David S., 127
Westcott, James, D., 66, 68, 69, 72, 73–74, 77, 79
West Florida, 61–62, 65, 71, 78, 84n63, 114; Western District, 66. *See also* Republic of West Florida; Spanish Florida
West Florida Revolt, 19–20, 24, 27
White, Joseph, 61
Williams, Alice, 167–70
Williamson, Edward, 157, 164, 166–67
World Court at the The Hague, 185

Zackin, Emily, 6, 8–9, 205

Government and Politics in the South
Edited by Sharon D. Wright Austin and Angela K. Lewis-Maddox

Writing for the Public Good: Essays from David R. Colburn and Senator Bob Graham, edited by Steven Noll (2022)
"Chambers v. Florida" and the Criminal Justice Revolution, by Richard Brust (2025)
Crafting Constitutions in Florida, 1810–1968, edited by Robert Cassanello (2025)

Printed in the United States
by Baker & Taylor Publisher Services